BIOETHICS

WHAT EVERYONE NEEDS TO KNOW®

BIOETHICS

WHAT EVERYONE NEEDS TO KNOW®

BONNIE STEINBOCK AND
PAUL T. MENZEL

OXFORD
UNIVERSITY PRESS

OXFORD
UNIVERSITY PRESS

Oxford University Press is a department of the University of Oxford. It furthers the University's objective of excellence in research, scholarship, and education by publishing worldwide. Oxford is a registered trade mark of Oxford University Press in the UK and certain other countries.

"What Everyone Needs to Know" is a registered trademark of Oxford University Press.

Published in the United States of America by Oxford University Press 198 Madison Avenue, New York, NY 10016, United States of America.

© Oxford University Press 2023

CIP data is on file at the Library of Congress
ISBN 978–0–19–765796–6 (pbk.)
ISBN 978–0–19–765799–7 (hbk.)

DOI: 10.1093/wentk/9780197657997.001.0001

1 3 5 7 9 8 6 4 2

Paperback printed by Sheridan Books, Inc., United States of America
Hardback printed by Bridgeport National Bindery, Inc., United States of America

To the memory of John D. Arras, beloved friend,
astute philosopher, incomparable wit.

CONTENTS

3 Do Advance Directives Protect Patient Autonomy?   40

4 When Is Experimentation on Human Subjects Unethical?   57

5 How Should Death Be Defined and Determined?   77

6 Is Physician-Assisted Dying an Ethical Choice?   94

PREFACE

Bioethics is an inherently interdisciplinary field, engaging healthcare professionals, lawyers, theologians, philosophers, sociologists, anthropologists, economists, and others. Each discipline has its own take on the field. As philosophers, we approach the various topics through a philosophical lens, critically assessing the arguments on all sides and at times exploring distinctively philosophical issues raised. While we consider the perspectives of other disciplines such as law, medicine, and public health, this book would be very different if written by someone from a discipline other than philosophy.

Within the larger field of applied ethics, bioethics focuses on ethical issues across the whole spectrum of healthcare (medicine, nursing, pharmacy, dentistry, and more), health policy, and biomedical research. Recently, bioethics has expanded to include such issues as the treatment of animals, environmental ethics, and global health policy. A complete treatment of all of these issues is impossible within the scope of a book in this series. What we intend is a solid introduction to the themes and topics that have engaged bioethics since its inception, as well as most of the main issues being discussed and debated today.

The research each of us has engaged in throughout our careers has naturally affected the choice of topics in the book. For Bonnie Steinbock, that includes reproduction, genetics, and end-of-life issues. For Paul Menzel, it includes health policy, healthcare economics, and end-of-life issues. At the same time, together we have eighty-plus years of teaching bioethics—teaching that has also very much informed the content. Virtually every topic that would be included in a standard textbook in bioethics is included in this book. In addition, we include issues not found in most introductory textbooks, such as those raised by COVID and future pandemics. Another topic rarely if ever discussed in introductions to bioethics, covered in Chapter 12, is justified drug pricing, an issue of general importance that warrants as much attention from ethicists as it has attracted from economists, research scientists, and pharmaceutical industry representatives. The topic also comes up in other chapters—Chapter 9 on assisted reproduction and infertility, and Chapter 13 on genetic modification. On new chapter topics that can be found in some other introductions—the genetic modification of humans, for example (our Chapter 13)—we incorporate very new developments in gene therapy, CRISPR technology, and international scientific guidelines for human germline genetic modification.

We begin in Chapter 1 with the philosophical foundations of bioethics. Several important theories in moral philosophy—utilitarianism, Kantian ethics, and Natural Law ethics—have heavily influenced bioethical decision-making. They are presented and critically discussed using specific ethical issues. We do not wish to determine which moral theory is correct, but rather to understand how each emphasizes important elements in moral thought that need to be considered in real moral problem-solving. We also present, along with views from its critics, the influential contemporary "principles approach" that pulls elements from several moral theories to create a framework appealing to many practitioners and other non-philosophers on the front lines of clinical bioethics.

In addition to treating the topics conveyed in the titles of the other chapters, various other themes are treated throughout the book. Race and ethnicity are addressed in various respects in Chapters 2–6, 9, and 11. Gender is discussed in Chapters 4,

7, and 9. Disability is the focus of all of Chapter 8 and arises also, along with chronic illness, in Chapters 4, 5, 6, and 11.

Bioethics has global dimensions, of course, not only the American, British, and European discussions that dominate much of the literature. We do not devote a separate chapter to "global bioethics," but international and global aspects arise explicitly in Chapters 2, 4, 6, 10, and 12.

Ethical issues raised by pandemics and COVID-19 are treated in Chapters 4, 10, 11, 12, and 13. Both of us have been influenced by a public health approach. Steinbock is a co-author of two books on public health ethics, and Menzel has written on system-wide health policy issues for much of his career. In this volume, a public health approach enriches the foundational discussion of autonomy and paternalism early in the book, in Chapter 2, justifying certain coercive restrictions not on the basis of promoting the good of individuals, as in medical paternalism, but as necessary to protect the health and common good of an entire population. Never is this consideration as important as during a global pandemic.

Two prominent topics in bioethics do not have chapters: pediatric bioethics and ethical issues in organ transplantation beyond those involved in the definition of death (Chapter 5) and the allocation of scarce supply (Chapter 11). Bioethics as an entire field is simply too wide to have chapters on all major topics within one concise volume. We do, however, provide some suggested readings on these two topics (Further Readings).

In each chapter, an array of ethical issues are described, along with major different positions on them. We do not, however, limit ourselves to describing the issues and major positions taken on them. On many issues we argue for or against particular positions, making the book a reflection of our own views but in such a way as to encourage readers, we hope, to form their own views on the matter.

It is a truism in biomedical ethics that not everything that can be done should be done. This issue is particularly salient in Chapter 13, as critics of genetically modifying humans have conjured up nightmarish scenarios, alleging, for example, that the autonomy of modified people would be violated, inequality would be exacerbated, and the very nature of humanity would be irrevocably changed for the worse. Are these genuine threats or mere speculation? What limits should be imposed on new technologies, and what criteria should determine those limits? It is our hope that readers of this book will be better equipped to address such questions, both the ones we cover and new ones as they arise.

This book had its genesis in eleven lectures intended as an introduction to bioethics that we gave in the fall of 2015 at the newly opened Centre for Bioethics at the Chinese University of Hong Kong (CUHK). Our audience for the lectures included members of CUHK and other universities, both students and professors, but it also included many community members: healthcare professionals, lawyers, and laypeople interested in the topics. Thus, the lectures were good preparation for this book. As with our lectures, the book is intended to appeal to nonspecialists who want to learn more about the field of bioethics. To the topics we addressed in the original lectures at CUHK we have added two additional chapter topics, on drug pricing and genetic modification. All of the chapters have been extensively updated and revised in expanding the original lectures.

ACKNOWLEDGMENTS

We are grateful to the staff at the Centre for Bioethics at CUHK for their support during our stay. We are particularly grateful to the Centre's supporting founder, Dr. Edgar Cheng, who first encouraged us to turn our lectures into a book, and to Professor Hon-Lam Li, who originally invited us to the Centre and set the project in motion. Without them, this book would not have been written. While both of us have been influenced by too many philosophers and bioethicists to mention, one individual stands out: the late Professor John Arras. In thinking through the topics for the book, as in so much else, we have benefited greatly from his body of work. We are very appreciative of the sage advice and encouragement from our editor, Peter Ohlin at Oxford University Press over nearly two decades, and now again here. We are also indebted to the fine work at the Press of Project Editor Chelsea Hogue, Project Manager Nirenjena Joseph, and copy editor Annie Woyat. We thank Susan Vermazen for finding the cover photo.

1

WHAT ARE
THE PHILOSOPHICAL
FOUNDATIONS OF BIOETHICS?

As we noted in the Preface, bioethics is multidisciplinary and can be approached from the perspective of any of the disciplines that contribute to it. In general, a philosophical perspective is characterized by asking for justifications of our moral claims and beliefs. Thus, in asking "What are the philosophical foundations of bioethics?" we are asking for the ethical principles that guide moral reasoning in bioethics and justify conclusions.

Ethics can be divided into two branches: theoretical and applied. Applied ethics refers to judgments of right or wrong about actual behavior or policy. Some of these are expressed in codes adopted by professional groups, such as lawyers, doctors, or government officials. By contrast, theoretical ethics is concerned with the underlying justification of those judgments, referred to as "normative ethics."

What is "normative ethics"?

All societies regard some actions as right and others as wrong. With many of these judgments, societies have little moral hesitation—for example, lying, stealing, assault, and murder are wrong. This is not surprising, given that a society that did not condemn actions of these sorts would not be sustainable. About other actions, such as premarital sex or abortion, moral judgments are more controversial. *Normative ethics,* the branch of philosophy from which bioethics has emerged, asks what makes a right act right, a wrong act wrong. That is, what are good reasons for making moral judgments?

That is distinctly different from an empirical investigation into what various people and populations *think* is right or wrong. It is even different from exploring how, as a matter of fact, people come to think things are right or wrong. Such empirical investigations, as interesting and as relevant to understanding people as they might be, do not tell us whether people are *correct and justified* in their moral beliefs. Something widely viewed as wrong could be merely a prejudice—consider, for example, how many societies have recently evolved in their treatment of gays and lesbians. Or something that is widely viewed as morally acceptable could be wrong. For example, the current treatment of nonhuman animals as sources of food or clothing, in scientific research, and for the entertainment of human beings is already considered by some to be reprehensible and could in the future be considered to be a mistake like slavery. The important thing is to subject moral views, one's own as well as others', to critical and rational assessment.

Before exploring some of the major contending views in normative ethics, we should notice that moral judgments come in different basic kinds. Some—most, perhaps—are about *actions,* while others are about *persons.* Judgments about actions, in turn, are of different sorts.

1. *Obligations and permissions.* Some actions are obligatory—duties. Others are only morally permissible—permissions. Conceptually, permissions and obligations are a function of each other. To say that I am morally obligated to tell the truth to a dying patient about her fatal illness can also be expressed by saying that it is not morally permissible for me to withhold the truth. And the opposite claim—that it is permissible for me to withhold the truth—is the same as saying that I have no moral duty to reveal it.

2. *Supererogatory actions.* These are especially good actions, commonly expressed by saying that what a person does is "beyond the call of duty" or "going the extra mile." Pursuing a discussion with a patient and family to enable them not only to understand treatment options but also to reflect more deeply on the difficult choice involved, for example, might not be a caregiver's obligation in the process of obtaining the patient's informed consent, but it may be a very good thing to do. People are not morally obligated to act in "supererogatory" ways, but we judge such actions to be very good indeed.

3. *Moral rights.* These are moral liberties, or moral "protections." Asserting such rights is asserting that others should not interfere with certain judgments or actions. They protect individual liberty. If I claim a moral right to do something, I assert that others would be wrong to interfere.

In this book, most of our discussion will be about the first of these kinds of judgment—moral obligations and permissions. In assessing what caregivers, patients, families, the society, and the law ought to do, the concern is typically what they are obligated or permitted to do.

Some discussion, though, will involve assessment not of actions, but of people and their character. One normative moral theory in particular, *virtue theory*, focuses on the habits and intentions that mark good character. In this tradition, associated with the Greek philosopher Aristotle, judgments about what actions are morally justified are not made directly but through asking what a person of good character—a virtuous person—would do. Honesty, for example, is a virtue, as is courage. In the Aristotelian view, moreover, a virtue is a "mean" between extremes. Courage, for example, is the mean between timidity and recklessness; the courageous person will be neither timid nor reckless by foolishly taking too much risk. Similarly, honesty is the mean between deception and revealing too much.[1]

What does a physician have to be to be a good doctor? Among other things, be honest, courageous, and empathetic. Developing the character of being honest, courageous, and empathetic (among other things) is central to being a good physician. In this tradition the focus is not directly on what action in a situation a person is morally obligated or permitted to do, but on what action reflects virtuous character.

In this book we generally focus directly on actions as right or wrong, not on what action a virtuous person would take. One reason is skepticism about virtue theory itself: How do we know what a virtuous person should do? How can one determine, for example, what really is the proper mean between the extremes of timidity and recklessness without assessing what action would be morally justified? The theories we discuss in the ensuing sections assess actions directly.

What are some important moral theories for bioethics?

Various theories of normative ethics provide bioethics its foundation. Three especially influential ones focus respectively on consequences, the inherent nature of an act, and intentions.

Utilitarianism: consequences. What makes an act right or wrong is the good or bad consequences likely to flow from it. Will telling the truth to a patient about his fatal illness create, on balance, a good set of effects or largely harmful ones? In utilitarianism an act is right if it maximizes the aggregate "utility" (subjective well-being) of all those whom the act affects.

Kantian ethics: the inherent nature of the act. The rightness or wrongness of an act is located right within the nature of the act itself. This view was famously articulated by the 18th-century German philosopher Immanuel Kant. Kant thought lying and blatant deception, for example, were inherently wrong because they harbored an internal contradiction. To be fair when one lies and deceives, one must acknowledge that lies and deception are permissible for others, too. Pervasive attempts to deceive, however, would erode the very trust in language that makes it possible for deception to be effective.

A theory of this sort is often referred to as "deontological," meaning an ethic of duties—the duty not to deceive, for example. Rather than using that label, we will typically refer to this kind of reasoning as "Kantian ethics," after Immanuel Kant who provided its well-known principles that are very different from reasoning to achieve the best consequences.

Natural Law ethics: intentions and natural goods. A person's good or bad intentions often make her action right or wrong. In not telling a patient in his last weeks that he is dying, for example, what is a caregiver's intention? If her dominant intention is to avoid the difficult task of informing the patient of the bad news, news that may even be seen as indicating failure on her part, her deception would not be justified. On the other hand, if it were to save the patient needless anguish, it could be. In Natural Law ethics, so-called *natural goods* matter a great deal, too, and the intentional destruction of a natural human good like reproduction or life itself is especially wrong.

Each of these three forms of moral reasoning—utilitarian, Kantian, natural law—will now be articulated in more detail.

How does utilitarian reasoning work?

In utilitarianism, an action is morally justified if, among its plausible options, it maximizes the total net good achieved among all whom the action affects. To use this principle in making moral judgments, some crucial clarifications are needed.

1. Maximize good effects, yes, but *good in what sense?* In most versions of utilitarianism, the "utility" to be maximized is understood as something intrinsically good *to the person* to whom it accrues—that is, something that has *subjective*

value to that person. In the literature of utilitarianism and its popular renditions, "happiness" or "well-being" is often used rather than "utility" for this sense of subjective value.

Utilitarianism at its core thus has a significantly nonpaternalist character: someone else does not get to tell me what experiences of mine have value for me; I make that judgment (see Chapter 2). Of course, people can be confused in remembering what has given them subjective value/utility/happiness or in predicting what will provide it, but in those cases they are factually mistaken still about what has been or will be valuable *to them.*

2. Good effects, but *good for whom*? The effects on all who are affected by the action must be counted. This aggregate is not correctly captured by the phrase "the greatest happiness *of the greatest number*," so commonly used to express the central principle of utilitarianism. For maximum utility the point is not to make the most people happy, but to maximize the amount of happiness. If many people are made just a little bit happy by a policy, while a smaller number are made miserable, the policy may not have maximum utility. Or the reverse: a policy that made most people a little bit unhappy but saved a few people's lives may well have maximum utility.

3. In adding up all the effects, *how do benefits relate to harms*? Utilitarian reasoning is focused on "net benefit" or "net harm." Many choices result in both positive and negative effects. Utilitarianism tells us to choose what will promote the most positive effect in combination with the least negative effect. For example, it may feel good to eat too much because the food is delicious, but the immediate pleasure is likely to be outweighed by subsequent indigestion or unwanted weight gain. In medicine, people make such net benefit assessments when they decide, for example, whether to undergo various treatments for cancer: Will the additional time in life that

the treatments might achieve be worth its side effects and months of difficult treatment?

4. Consequences, yes, but *actual or expected*? If we judge an act right or wrong on the basis of its actual result, all sorts of "bad luck" and intervening events may turn what was a reasonable decision at the time into an awful one. Utilitarianism focuses on the consequences that can be *reasonably expected* at the time of decision. Sometimes, of course, we do not know what consequences to reasonably expect, in which case a utilitarian would say that we just do not know what the right course of action is.

5. *Interpersonal comparisons of utility.* Suppose two people both rate their level of pain in an objectively similar state of recovery from a surgery as 7 (on a 1–10 scale, 10 the worst). How can we know they are talking about the same level of real experienced pain? Perhaps a 7 expressed by one of them is no worse than a 5 by the other. No one can get inside their minds to say. People frequently, however, make interpersonal comparisons in ordinary life. For good practical reasons, we may know enough about the people involved to think that one who behaviorally writhes in pain and another who stoically endures the same anatomical injury are likely not that different in their levels of suffering. To be sure, it is sometimes very difficult to know how different persons' experiences of a similar event compare, but we get by with common-sense estimates nonetheless. Utilitarian reasoning does also.

Clarified in these respects, we can see that utilitarian reasoning is *empirical* and *realistic*. It asks what can reasonably be expected to result from the action being considered, and what actual value those results will likely have on those affected. Only experience and empirical observation can tell us. One should not insist, for example, that a patient ought to pursue chemotherapy and radiation treatment if the treatment is likely to have such negative value to her that any additional life gained comes at the cost of too much suffering. This empirical and realistic character of utilitarian reasoning is one of its great attractions. It looks at real-world effects, on real people.

Despite this fundamental attraction, utilitarian reasoning faces some poignant objections in the form of counter-examples—actions that we firmly believe are wrong but which utilitarianism would seem to permit. We discuss two of these before turning to a third example that reveals how resourceful utilitarian reasoning can be when pursued carefully.

Organ conscription

Human beings have five vital organs of potential use for lifesaving transplant (heart, lungs, two kidneys, and liver). Organs for transplant are stubbornly scarce; medical need greatly exceeds supply, and real lives can be saved by additional organs. If we had a conscription system, using a fair lottery to select donors, and from each donor we took all five vital organs to transplant to five recipients, we would likely save four lives (80% success rates are now realistic). The human cost is one life taken by organ removal; the benefit is four lives saved.

So why do we not conscript organs for transplant? If we should not, *why* not? Each of us, after all, looking at this when we do not know whether we will be one of the conscripted "donors" or one of the recipients whose life is saved, could view such a conscription policy as likely to benefit us. We are four times more likely to be one of the lucky recipients than one of the conscripted "donors."

So utilitarian reasoning would seem to justify such a policy. But we shouldn't sacrifice one person in this way to save four, should we?

Request for a placebo

All plausible treatments have been ineffective in halting a father's advancing lymphoma. His prognosis is terminal. Now at home, the father says, "They've given up on me." A daughter wants the physicians to provide a "placebo" so that her father can believe the doctors are still treating him and thus retain hope. If the placebo would indeed provide such hope and improve the man's remaining days, shouldn't it be provided?

Straightforward utilitarian reasoning would seem to say "Yes, provide the placebo." But even if this is not as objectionable as conscripting organs, how can utilitarian reasoning account for our distinct reservations about deceiving someone in this way? To explain our resistance, there must be more to good ethical reasoning than utilitarian considerations.

Informed consent

The requirement of "informed consent" forbids imposing treatment on a patient who has decision-making capacity without informing her of essential details of the treatment that are relevant to making a reasonable decision (see Chapter 2). Both the provision of such information and full voluntariness of the consent—not coerced, pressured, or manipulated—are essential. Why should we have such a strong informed consent requirement, rather than allow those who may know more about the situation, such as physicians, to sometimes provide treatment without such consent? A strong informed consent requirement would seem to get in the way of maximizing benefit in situations where a physician or influential family member knows better.

Pursued in a more refined way, however, there is a pragmatic justification within utilitarian reasoning for a strong informed consent requirement. In practice, informed consent creates wider trust in medicine, with patients less fearful of being manipulated or misused. With such trust, patients are likely to reveal more about themselves to their caregivers, generally enhancing the quality of their care. When looked at as an ethical requirement in actual practice, therefore, informed consent is likely to create more benefit in the long run than not having such a requirement.

When the wider and long-term effects of a practice are considered, behavior that at first appears not to have utilitarian justification may indeed be justified. Utilitarian reasoning does have something valuable to offer.

What principles are featured in Kantian ethics?

A very different kind of moral reasoning was defended by the German philosopher Immanuel Kant (1724–1804). He proposed two fundamental principles:

> *Universalization*: For an act to be morally permissible, one must be willing for all others to act in the same way.
> *Respect for persons*: Always treat others as dignified individual persons, never merely as means to other people's ends.

The first is a principle of *fairness*: it is not fair for you to regard an action as permissible if you do not accept it as permissible for others. In language closer to Kant's actual statement of this principle: always act so you can will (choose or wish) that the motivating principle of your action be a universal moral law—that is, that when anyone has this motivation for acting in that way, they act that way.

For example, if you cheat on an exam in order to improve your grade, you have to be willing that others who can improve their grades would also cheat on exams. However, this creates a contradiction in what one wills. To even have the opportunity to cheat on an exam, there has to be a system of examinations. But if people routinely cheated on exams in order to do better, the system would implode. It can't exist without a general belief that most students are not cheating. Thus, there's a contradiction within what one wants (in one's will) when one cheats: that exams exist and that they also not exist. The behavior of cheating to get better grades cannot be willed to be universal moral law.

The second principle, respect for persons, is a recognition of every individual person's *autonomy*. Using people as a means to achieve your goals is acceptable if they and you are in a collaborative or contractual arrangement in which they accept your use of them to achieve your goals. This still recognizes them as autonomous persons who consent to the arrangement. But if you do not include them as persons with their own decision-making capacity, you have impermissibly treated them merely as means. People may be treated as means, and, in fact, it is impossible to avoid treating others as means. When we buy groceries, we treat the cashier as a means to making the purchase. What Kant rules out, though, is using people *merely* as means—tools for our own purposes. In our interactions with others, we must also treat persons with respect.

In direct response to utilitarians, Kantians insist that individual persons must be respected and not regarded as "containers" for maximizing utility. This means no organ conscription, no placebos to cover up deception about dying, and no imposition of medical treatment without the patient's informed consent. Even if prohibiting actions of these kinds would lead to better consequences, from a Kantian perspective, that is not the basis for regarding them as wrong.

The value of *patient autonomy* that has played such an important role in biomedical ethics in the past century is a direct reflection of this Kantian respect for persons. The principle that we should never treat persons merely as means is frequently used in bioethics, though it is also sometimes misused. To see how it can be misused, consider the act of creating one child to save another—parents intentionally creating a new child who can then provide the tissue or organ to save the life of one of their existing children.

Actual cases illustrate this. With the use of prenatal genetic diagnosis (PGD), in vitro fertilization (IVF), and embryo implantation, Lisa and Jack Nash became parents of Adam Nash. Adam's umbilical cord blood was then used in effective lifesaving treatment for his older sister Molly's anemia.

Similarly, Abe and Mary Ayala had Abe's vasectomy reversed so that Mary could have another child, Marissa, who became a bone marrow donor for her 17-year-old sister Anissa with leukemia. Both the Nashes and the Ayalas used their new child as a means to saving one of their other children.[2]

Many critics condemned them on the grounds that creating children for the purpose of saving existing siblings treats the new children as means to an end. As we have noted, however, the Kantian principle does not rule out *treating someone as a means*. It only prohibits treating someone *merely* as a means. What would it be to create a child merely as a means? Suppose the Nashes or Ayalas did not love Adam and Marissa, or that they were willing to inflict serious pain or injury on them. That would constitute treating them merely as means to save their siblings. But that was simply not the case. Adam Nash was not affected at all by the use of his umbilical cord blood. Marissa, to be sure, did have to undergo a bone marrow transplant at 14 months, obviously at that age without her consent. While the procedure was painful, her parents did not disregard Marissa's interests, but reasonably judged that the temporary pain of removing her bone marrow was justified by the much greater good to be achieved, even to Marissa, by saving her sister's life. As an adult, Marissa was glad she was able to save her sister. Yes, the motivation for having Adam and Marissa was to save their older children, but the Nashes and Ayalas truly loved their new son and daughter, cherishing them for their own sake and not just as ways to save Molly and Anissa. They were not using their new children merely as means.

Much discussion in bioethics of how to respect patients as persons with dignity employs these resources of Kantian ethics.

What does Natural Law ethics contribute to bioethics?

Another view, too, has been notably influential in bioethics—"Natural Law." Numerous versions come under that term.

Historically, and even now, the most important is arguably
Roman Catholic moral theology, based largely in the writings
of St. Thomas Aquinas. The foundation of the view is that,
for human beings, four things are "natural goods": (1) *life*, for
without that, there would be nothing more to say; (2) *procreation*, for without that, the human species would end; (3) *knowledge and reason*, a high capacity of human beings that flows
from a variety of their other natural characteristics; and (4) *so-
ciability*, their capacity to share things and relate to each other
in communities. The deliberate destruction of any of these natural goods is "naturally bad"—bad on the basis of the most
fundamental characteristics of human life.[3]

Many philosophers have held, against the whole grain of
this view, that an "ought" cannot typically be derived from an
"is." Something that occurs in nature is just that, something
that occurs in nature, and it takes something more to make it
good or bad and provide it moral value. But given human nature, Natural Law ethics claims, these four goods are vital for
any human morality. They are *natural goods*.

When is human behavior that affects those four natural
goods not permitted? In Roman Catholic moral tradition, any
action that directly and intentionally causes their destruction is wrong. The harms in such destruction cannot just be
weighed against the benefits that might come; any intentional,
direct destruction of these goods is simply prohibited. *It is always wrong to intentionally destroy a natural human good.*[4]

What does "intention" cover? On the one hand, a lot. Not
only is one's goal in an action what one intends. One also
intends the means of achieving that goal. For example, by
separating two conjoined twins, parents and surgeon intend
to save one of them. Both would die if not separated, and separation directly causes one of them to die. The parents or surgeon cannot say, "but I intended only to save the one, not to
cause the other's death by separation." Causing the death of
the twin who is not saved *is* the means—here *the only means*—
by which the other can be saved, and if one intends to achieve

something, one intends the necessary means for achieving it. In separating the twins, therefore, one intentionally causes the one twin's death.

What we see here is that, in Natural Law ethics, some things are *absolutely* prohibited. Yet Natural Law ethics also contains a principle that can soften this hard edge. Some results of an action, even when they are clearly anticipated, are not intended. This is expressed in Natural Law ethics by the "doctrine of double effect" (DDE). Action can have "double" effects: those *intended* and those only *foreknown*. Effects that are not intended, but only foreseen, allow an action to still be permissible if certain conditions are met. For example, the prohibition on intentionally destroying the natural good of life does not extend to causing a death that is only a foreknown consequence. The classic example is using certain painkillers (morphine, for example) to relieve suffering at the end of life. The caregiver knows in advance that dosage will have to be increased to maintain the drug's effectiveness and that, ultimately, increasing dosage is likely to retard respiration enough to cause death. Is the use of morphine to relieve intense pain at the end of life then prohibited? It is not. The DDE offers an escape. The caregiver's intention is to alleviate suffering, and, as long as the dosage is only increased as necessary to provide comfort, the patient's eventual death is only foreknown, not intended. Using morphine in this way is morally permissible.

Contrast this justification of the judicious use of such medications with the Roman Catholic moral tradition's opposition to using directly lethal medicine to hasten death (physician-assisted suicide, medical aid-in-dying, or euthanasia—see Chapter 5). Killing by lethal drug is the means of relieving the patient's suffering, and the aim is precisely to end the suffering by using that means. The result (death), though, is not merely foreknown but intended, for one cannot intend the end—relieving suffering—without intending the necessary means—causing death. Thus, the DDE is not applicable in the case of medically assisting dying, and hastening death by lethal prescription is morally prohibited. One cannot escape this conclusion by noting the immense human benefit in the relief of suffering that may be accomplished by deliberately hastening death, for in Natural Law ethics, right and wrong are not a matter of weighing up benefits and harms. The ethic is absolutist: *never intentionally destroy a natural good.*

Whether the DDE can be defended is highly debatable. From a consequentialist, utilitarian perspective, it cannot be: What is wrong with intentionally ending life if that is more beneficial to the patient than lingering in a longer death? And why is causing an intended bad effect (if it is bad) worse than causing a foreknown one? Both, after all, are real effects on human beings, effects that one is aware of when acting.

We do not attempt to resolve this debate about the traditional Roman Catholic version of Natural Law and its DDE. Even if the DDE and its absolute prohibition of intentionally and directly causing the destruction of any natural good are highly questionable, what people intend to do is surely morally relevant. Utilitarianism's sole focus on consequences, not intentions, is deficient. Moreover, an ethic focused on discerning and supporting what is centrally and universally good for people given their human nature has considerable appeal.

What is the "principles approach" to bioethics?

Virtues, intentions, the likely consequences of actions, respect for individual persons, fairness between them, preservation of humans' natural goods—all of these, it would seem, are important in moral assessment. Each moral theory focuses on some aspect of what makes right actions right, and, in doing so, the theories help to illuminate moral dilemmas. In presenting them as we have, our aim has been not to decide which one is correct, since we believe that all of them contribute significantly to the moral discussion. Still less is it our approach, when confronting a moral problem, to just "plug in" one of these theories and let it generate the right answer. The goal of bioethics is to understand the important elements in moral thinking that are represented by major moral viewpoints and then to arrive at reasoned judgments.

In the past four decades a prominent position has developed that explicitly articulates an eclectic approach of this sort: the *principles approach* (or *principlism*) of Tom Beauchamp and James Childress.[5] In this approach, people confronting an issue in bioethics should consult four moral principles: *nonmaleficence, benevolence, autonomy,* and *justice.* Each of the four has roots in one or more of the moral theories we have discussed. Nonmaleficence (do not harm) and beneficence (help people, improve things) are clearly present in utilitarianism. Autonomy and self-determination are rooted in Kantian respect for persons, and the achievement of justice emerges from the fairness theme in Kantian ethics. Natural law can be seen as a basis of the first two principles and perhaps for all four. The principles approach, however, is not intended to be a new foundational moral theory, and, in general, no one principle takes priority over the others.

Such a pragmatic, eclectic approach may be especially attractive to clinicians who want "practical" reasoning without needing to get "philosophical." In confronting an issue or considering an individual case, one sorts out what each of the four principles has to contribute. Sometimes, when two or more of them conflict, one emerges as dominant in the actual context—in risky research, for example, the autonomy-based requirement to obtain a subject's informed consent may nearly always dominate (see Chapter 4). In other cases and issues, no principle may emerge as dominant, in which case the dilemma is likely to be unresolved. That is less than ideal but occasionally unavoidable. Hopefully, considering the basic principles will deepen our understanding of hard cases even when they cannot be resolved.

Bioethicists have debated at length the advantages and weaknesses of such a principles approach.[6] We have briefly described the approach here both because it emerges from reckoning with all of the three major theories in normative ethics we have presented and because it is particularly appropriate for an area of applied ethics like bioethics that so frequently involves hard cases.

A related view that pushes even further the "bottom-up" role of cases over a "top-down" dominance of theory is *casuistry*, or case-based reasoning. Paradigmatic cases are grouped around a rule that evidently applies to them, such as informed consent in research ethics. Their lessons are then applied to more nuanced or complex cases. Casuistry is sometimes associated historically with moral reasoning in Roman Catholic moral philosophy, but it has its own separate identity.[7]

Concluding thoughts

Normative ethical theories attempt to explain what ultimately makes right acts right and wrong acts wrong. Bioethics' foundations lie in such theories but attempting to discern which theory is correct may be left to ethical theorists who regard such attempts as important and attainable; it is not essential to doing bioethics. The theories, with their different emphases, serve to reveal much about the nature of the fundamental values that inevitably surface in issues in medicine, healthcare, and health policy. Patient autonomy, patient well-being, and justice in a healthcare system have their basis in philosophical traditions. When autonomy, well-being, and justice are better understood from having considered certain moral theories, participants are better prepared to dissect and clarify what is ethically at stake in particular clinical cases and issues. The ensuing chapters explore such issues in twelve major topics within bioethics.

2

HOW HAS THE SHIFT FROM PATERNALISM TO AUTONOMY SHAPED BIOETHICS?

In this chapter, we examine two ideas instrumental in the birth of bioethics, specifically, the rejection of medical paternalism and its replacement, for the most part, with respect for patient autonomy. While these concepts do not apply to all of bioethics, they have had a highly formative role. Together with related ideas, such as the doctor–patient relationship, truth-telling, and informed consent, they continue to play a very important role. The chapter ends with a discussion of racism's contribution to health disparities and the significance this has for the doctor–patient relationship.

Before we look specifically at medical paternalism, we need to understand what paternalism in general is. Many of the examples have to do with protecting public health and safety, which is clearly relevant to bioethics. Nevertheless, as we will see, there are important differences between paternalism in general and medical paternalism.

What is paternalism in general?

A crucial feature of paternalistic restrictions of liberty is that they are justified on the ground that they will promote the well-being of those very individuals whose liberty is restricted. This makes paternalistic interventions very different from the usual justifications for restricting liberty intended to protect individuals from harms that others might inflict on them. The primary function of the criminal law, for example, is to prevent harm to others, which is often referred to as "the harm to others" principle or, more simply, "the harm principle." Unquestionably, the state is entitled to use the harm principle to justify restricting liberty since a society cannot exist at all if people are at liberty to inflict harm on others.

By contrast, paternalistic laws restrict individuals' behavior in order to protect them from their own harmful choices and actions. Examples include laws that ban certain recreational drugs, prevent people from buying certain medications unless they have a prescription, require people to wear seat belts in cars or wear helmets while riding a motorcycle, and erect barriers on bridges to prevent people from jumping off. While all these examples are reasonably regarded as falling under paternalism, it should be noted that harm principle justifications can also often be given for them. For example, the rationale for requiring motorcyclists to wear helmets need not be limited to protecting motorcyclists but could also be reducing medical costs borne by taxpayers. The prohibition of certain recreational drugs could be justified by the impact on others, including dependent children or the community at large.

If a law is justified on the basis of the harm principle, it should not be characterized as paternalistic. The claim that COVID vaccine or mask mandates are unjustified paternalistic violations of individual liberty is unwarranted since these mandates can be justified by a harm principle argument. They protect not only the people required to be vaccinated or to wear masks, but they also protect others who cannot be vaccinated, such as young children not yet eligible for the vaccines, people who for medical reasons cannot be vaccinated, and those with compromised immune systems who are not fully protected by vaccination. Insofar as the rationale for these mandates is the protection of others, they fall within the harm principle and are not instances of paternalism.

Whether mandates are justifiable on harm principle grounds depends on a number of relevant considerations. Is there sound evidence that the measures are actually effective in protecting others? Are there no less restrictive measures that could accomplish that? How should the risks and burdens imposed by the policy be measured against the benefits? To say that a law or a policy falls within the purview of the harm principle is not to say that it is justified, but rather that it can be justified on harm principle grounds if certain facts obtain.

A different, though related, objection to vaccine mandates is that they violate the principle of bodily autonomy. Some who object to vaccine mandates have adopted a slogan from the abortion rights movement: "My body, my choice." However, there is no absolute right to make one's own decisions if those decisions inflict harm on others. The failure to get vaccinated can cause others to become sick, including those who are not eligible to be vaccinated and those who are not fully protected by being vaccinated due to autoimmune conditions. To be sure, it may be questioned whether the prevention of harm to others outweighs the harm of mandating vaccination, which deprives individuals of the right to make their own decisions regarding their bodily autonomy. The answer depends on several factors, such as how necessary a mandate is, what the actual risks to others are, and what risks vaccination imposes. If vaccine mandates were an instance of paternalism, those who absolutely reject all paternalistic restrictions on freedom could reject them. But they aren't, and that is why the right to make one's own decisions about vaccination cannot be absolute.

This is reflected in US law. The right of states to mandate vaccination goes back to the 1905, when the Supreme Court ruled in *Jacobson v. Massachusetts* that mandating vaccination against smallpox was not unconstitutional and was reasonably required to protect public health and safety. Since the 1980s, all 50 US states require that children receive certain vaccines in order to attend both public and private schools. Vaccines mandated in all states include polio, chickenpox, measles-mumps-rubella (MMR), and diphtheria-tetanus-pertussis (DTaP). It is an interesting and puzzling fact that these mandated vaccinations have not resulted in anything like the resistance to COVID vaccines.

How do strong and weak paternalism differ?

The main objection to genuinely paternalistic laws is that they give the state the power to make decisions for competent adults who should generally be allowed to make their own decisions about what is in their own interest, even if those decisions are foolish or misguided. Paternalistic laws are particularly offensive when they force individuals to act contrary to their own values. This is often referred to as "strong paternalism." For example, some people not only enjoy, but find meaning in, engaging in challenging activities like mountain climbing or race car driving. A complete ban on such activities, as opposed to regulations to make them safer, would force individuals to regard safety as always trumping challenge that involves risk.

Sometimes, however, restrictions do not force people to go against their own values. This occurs when people acknowledge that something is bad for them, and that they would be better off not doing it, but which they continue to do anyway. An example is smokers who know that smoking is harmful to their health and express a desire to quit, but who continue to smoke either because they are addicted or lack the will power to stop. Measures to help people to stop smoking, such as banning smoking indoors, can be characterized as "weak paternalism." Are such measures an objectionable restriction on liberty?

Banning smoking indoors might be justifiable on the ground that secondhand smoke is harmful to others. If that's the justification, then the ban is not paternalistic but comes under the harm principle. For that to be an adequate justification depends on the facts—for example, whether exposure to indoor smoke is in fact an actual health hazard or merely something unpleasant. In some circumstances, a harm principle justification could be used. Bartenders and waiters exposed to secondhand smoke in restaurants and bars before smoking bans were imposed had a 50 percent higher risk of getting lung cancer than other people. On the other hand, it is unlikely that the harm principle could be used to prohibit people from smoking in their own individual offices since the involuntary exposure of others to smoke would be minimal. Moreover, even if a ban on smoking in individual offices cannot be justified on harm principle grounds, it might be justifiable as an instance of weak paternalism. Many weak-willed smokers regard measures that limit their smoking as welcome, rather than objectionable; it does not go against their own deeply held desires.

So far, we have been discussing whether the state has the right to control behavior that does not harm others, for the individual's own good. A separate issue is whether a prohibition is the most effective way to get people to do what is in their own best interest. It may be possible to influence behavior through less intrusive methods, such as education and public service messages. Another strategy is to use "nudges"—attempts by institutions to steer people's choices in ways that will improve their lives.[1] Nudges make use of social science research that predicts which noncoercive arrangements affect choice. For example, people in a supermarket are more likely to buy food that is close to the entrance. If you want to encourage the purchase of nutritious, healthful foods, put the fresh produce near the entrance and highly processed foods further away. Both education and nudges attempt to get people to make the choices that are in their own best interest while not constraining their choices. You can still buy the potato chips; you just have to walk a little further to get to them.

Medical paternalism is quite different from these examples of paternalistic laws. It seldom involves legal prohibitions. Rather, it involves the relationship between doctors (or other healthcare providers) and patients and their respective roles in medical decision-making.

What is medical paternalism?

At its core, it is the view that physicians should decide what medical treatments are appropriate for their patients. The idea that patients should participate in medical decisions is nowhere to be found in traditional medical ethics, which goes back to ancient Greece and the teachings of the famed physician Hippocrates.

A notable element of Hippocratic ethics is the identification of well-being with physical health. Given this rather narrow conception of individual welfare, it is not surprising that physicians regarded themselves as uniquely qualified to make medical decisions for their patients. After all, physicians are trained to make medical decisions and have a lot of experience in doing that. Lacking such training and experience, it may be thought that patients cannot make such decisions and should simply follow the advice of their physicians.

One aspect of traditional medical ethics reflecting this paternalism is its attitude toward deception: deception is sometimes necessary to protect the patient from anxiety or to achieve compliance. It may take the form of outright lying about the patient's condition or, more subtly, of shading the truth. Far from expecting physicians to be forthcoming with their patients, traditional medical ethics advises them to distract their patients from what they are doing, as revealed in this passage from a Hippocratic text, the "Decorum": "Perform [these duties] calmly and adroitly, concealing most things from the patient while you are attending to him. Give necessary orders with cheerfulness and serenity, turning his attention away from what is being done to him; sometimes reprove sharply and emphatically, and sometimes comfort with solicitude and attention, revealing nothing of the patient's future or present condition."

Although the Hippocratic tradition regarded physicians as the sole decision-makers, it also insisted that treatment decisions be made solely in the interests of patients and not those of physicians. Nor are physicians permitted to weigh the interests of society in general against the interests of patients. The obligation of physicians is first and foremost to their patients. This patient-oriented aspect has remained a central part of contemporary medical ethics, even as the paternalism of the Hippocratic tradition has been rejected.

The move from medical paternalism to respect for autonomy has been based partly on understanding that medical decisions are not purely a matter of science but are value laden. Moreover, physical health is not the only or necessarily highest value. In addition, the values of physicians and patients may differ. For example, a patient may reject a recommended treatment if the suffering the treatment would cause is, in the patient's view, intolerable. Or a patient may reject treatment because, while it would prolong life, that life would be, in the patient's judgment, of such low quality that it would be, for them, a life not worth living. When physicians and patients differ on values, respect for autonomy requires that the values of the patient prevail. Physicians can inform and persuade; they may not force treatment on unwilling patients.

What does autonomy mean in bioethics?

The word "autonomy" can be used in two different ways. It can refer to a *capacity* that individuals have or lack, namely, the capacity to make decisions. Someone who has the capacity to make decisions is autonomous. Here we are not talking about simple choices, such as what to have for breakfast. Even a very young child can make that sort of decision. Rather, to be an autonomous decision-maker in medical matters is to have the ability to make important and complex choices. This requires certain cognitive capacities, including the ability to understand information and appreciate its significance, to reason and weigh options, and to determine which choices best reflect the agent's own values. An important feature of the required capacity is that it is not a global characteristic. That is, we cannot say that a person is or is not competent, full stop. Rather, capacity is decision-relative—that is, relative to the kind of decision to be made. Someone might not be competent to make financial decisions, for example, but perfectly competent to make treatment decisions.

Autonomy can also refer to a *right*: namely, the right to make medical decisions. This right belongs to all and only individuals who have the capacity for autonomous decision-making. Some people, of course, have a greater degree of understanding and reasoning capacity than others, but a right to autonomy does not depend on a high level of these capacities. All that is required is that the individual has the capacities of an adult with relatively normal intelligence. All adults who meet this minimal condition have the right to participate in medical decision-making. By the same token, those who lack the capacity for decision-making, such as minors or severely cognitively impaired adults, are not autonomous and do not have a right to participate in medical decisions.[2]

The right to participate in medical decision-making engenders another right: the right of individuals not to have medical procedures performed on them without their informed consent, referred to simply as "the right of informed consent."

What is informed consent?

The concept of informed consent is central to clinical ethics. Indeed, the philosopher Onora O'Neill[3] argues that autonomy in the medical context amounts to little more than informed consent and that autonomy in this narrow sense is too impoverished a notion to have the moral significance bioethics has accorded it. We think she is wrong about this. The rejection of medical paternalism is based on recognizing the dignity of persons and having respect for them, and these ideals do have great moral significance (see Chapter 1, Kantian ethics). O'Neill may be right in thinking that bioethics has overemphasized patient autonomy to the detriment of other values, such as trust, but she is wrong to discount its moral significance.

The doctrine of informed consent, that doctors may not treat patients without their consent, has two parts. First, consent must be given freely; that is, the patient must not be subject to any coercion or undue influence. Second, the patient's consent must be informed; that is, patients must receive adequate information on which to base their choice. The informed consent requirement does not apply when consent is impossible, as in the case of an unconscious patient who needs emergency treatment. However, once the patient regains consciousness and is able to express a preference regarding treatment, informed consent is again required.

How much information is required to make the patient's consent truly informed? The standard doesn't require informing a patient of all risks, no matter how remote, but rather giving information that a patient would want to have to make a reasonable decision about treatment. Doctors are not permitted to say that they didn't inform a patient about the risks of an operation, because, if they had, the patient would have refused the operation. In the United States, patients have a legal right to refuse any medical treatment, including life-saving treatment, and doctors are legally required to provide them with the information they need to make the decision whether to have the treatment or not (see also Chapter 4).

The doctrine of informed consent has its origin in the law, not in medicine. In 1914, in one of the earliest cases in the United States, *Schloendorff v. Society of New York Hospital*, Justice Cardozo expressed the ideal of self-determination, saying "Every adult human being of adult years and sound mind has a right to determine what shall be done with his own body."

In subsequent cases, judges who were appalled by cases in which doctors lied or withheld information from their patients, ostensibly for their own good, created the doctrine of informed consent.

Although the legal doctrine has been extremely important in protecting patients, the origin of informed consent in judicial decisions has created an unfortunate dynamic. Instead of focusing on the information necessary for patients to participate meaningfully in treatment decisions, doctors have understood the informed consent requirement to be the information they must provide patients in order not to be sued.[4] This focus on their potential liability—the risk of harm to *them*—is contrary to a patient-centered medical ethics.

The way in which a legalistic approach to informed consent distorts the doctor–patient relationship is revealed in the way hospital staff speak about getting a patient's consent. They typically say, "Did you consent that patient?" as if "consent" were a transitive verb and something to be performed on a patient. "Did you consent the patient?" really means, "Did you get the signature?" and not, "Did you have a meaningful conversation with the patient, about the prognosis, the diagnosis, and possible treatment options?" While a lengthy conversation may not be needed for every procedure, it is needed in the case of serious illness and major treatment options.

What was the significance of the Belmont Report?

An especially significant event in the turn from medical paternalism to patient autonomy was the 1976 Belmont Report by the National Commission for the Protection of Human Subjects of Biomedical and Behavioral Research. The Commission, charged by Congress to identify the basic principles that should govern research with human subjects, identified three basic principles: respect for persons; beneficence, which includes both preventing harm to subjects and promoting their well-being; and justice. Although these principles were originally intended specifically for research with human subjects, they became the basic principles of bioethics generally. The principle of respect for persons morphed into respect for autonomy, which soon began to be referred to as just "autonomy."

The wider historical context is also important for under-standing how patient autonomy came to replace traditional medical paternalism.

What historical forces led to the rejection of medical paternalism?

In the United States, the rejection of medical paternalism in medical ethics was fueled in part by social upheaval, including the civil rights movement, the women's movement, and the so-called student movement spurred by the Vietnam War and the draft. While each movement had its own focus, all incor-porated values of autonomy, dignity, and respect for persons, values that came to be included in modern bioethics.

A specific goal of feminism was enabling women to have control of their reproductive lives. An unplanned pregnancy could severely disrupt or even end a woman's education or career. Full equality for women required access to birth con-trol and abortion, access that did not exist in the early 1960s. At that time, it was illegal in many US states to distribute contraceptives or even provide information about birth con-trol, and abortion was illegal in all 50 states. However, gender equality was not the only rationale behind the call for re-productive rights. Equally important was the right to self-determination and, in particular, bodily autonomy.[5] Just as the civil rights movement brought into the national conversation the ideals of justice, equality, autonomy, and respect for per-sons regardless of race, so the women's movement brought to the forefront these same ideals, regardless of gender.

The student movement was somewhat different from the other two movements for social change. It was not primarily aimed at claiming rights for students but rather at ending the War in Vietnam.[6] However, activism against the war resulted in increased social awareness, especially on the part of young people who demanded social change to combat racism and poverty. In addition, college students began to demand that they be treated as adults. They rejected the principle of "loco parentis" under which colleges and universities prevented students living off-campus, imposed curfews on students living in dormitories, and restricted the hours dormitory residents could entertain guests of the opposite sex. Moreover, the demands for increased control were not limited to living conditions. Students also demanded the offering of courses more relevant to their lives. For the first time, universities offered courses in applied ethics, which enabled the emergence of bioethics as a scholarly discipline in its own right.

All of these factors—changes in the law regarding informed consent, the Belmont Report, and social movements—resulted in the rejection of medical paternalism. Some bioethicists, however, have questioned whether the pendulum has not swung too far. In the following sections, we consider several such critiques.

Do the effects of serious illness justify medical paternalism?

One argument in favor of some degree of medical paternalism is that illness itself impairs autonomy. The physician Eric Cassell argues that it is unrealistic to expect a seriously ill person to participate in medical decision-making in the way a healthy person might.[7] Moreover, Cassell argues, patient-centered medicine should focus more on the relief of suffering, not patient autonomy, especially in the case of terminally ill patients.

Yet neither of Cassell's points about impaired autonomy or the importance of relieving suffering justify deception. Physicians can be truthful without burdening patients with more information than they can handle, and the importance of relieving suffering does not preclude respecting the patient's wishes.

Do irrational choices justify medical paternalism?

A more recent defense of paternalism stems from work in decision theory. Does the emphasis on autonomy assume an overly rational view of human choices? Even competent adults can make irrational choices if they are unduly influenced by emotions, such as fear. Patients may also be more susceptible to cognitive fallacies than are trained physicians. They may fall prey to the *hasty generalization fallacy*, as when a patient refuses a recommended treatment because he knew someone who had that treatment and died. Or a smoker may reject the claim that smoking causes cancer because she knew someone who smoked all his life and never got cancer. Moreover, even when choices are not distorted by emotion or cognitive deficits, they sometimes are at odds with the patient's own goals and values. These critics argue that a choice-limiting paternalism that aligns medical decisions with patients' values is preferable to respecting choices that neither benefit patients nor accord with their values.

This sort of weak paternalism is more defensible than a strong paternalism that ignores or rides roughshod over a patient's values. But does the possibility of cognitive errors justify medical paternalism? For one thing, it may be difficult to determine when a choice about treatment reflects the patient's values and should be respected and when it stems from ignorance or cognitive fallacies and should be challenged. Moreover, if a doctor suspects that a decision does not stem from or promote the patient's own values, this should be the impetus for a longer conversation about why the patient is refusing medical advice. It should not be used as an excuse for ignoring the patient's own wishes.

Does respect for cultural differences justify deception?

In some cultures, it is regarded as permissible, or even obligatory, to withhold or shade the truth in order to spare such patients needless anxiety and suffering. In Chapter 1, we encountered the example of a daughter who asked her terminally ill father's doctors to give him a placebo so that he would not think that his doctors had "given up on him." She wanted his doctors to pretend to continue to treat him, to give him hope and a reason to go on living. On this defense of medical paternalism, truth is best seen as a tool in the doctor's little black bag: to be used it if it will help patients, but not if it will harm them.

It's not hard to understand why physicians have resorted to deception to avoid causing anxiety and loss of hope in seriously ill patients. However, deception itself has serious costs. Deceiving patients about their diagnosis or prognosis ignores the fact that many people prefer to know the truth about their condition, even at the cost of increased anxiety, so that they can make plans for the time they have left. Trust, which is essential to the doctor–patient relationship, is eroded when doctors regard themselves as free, or even obligated, to deceive patients out of concern for their well-being. Fortunately, doctors do not have to practice deception to spare their patients anxiety. Instead, they can focus on *how* to deliver bad news.

How should doctors give bad news to patients?

The wrong way to deliver bad news is simply to deliver a blunt and devastating diagnosis and then walk out of the room. It is hard to imagine how any physician could think this is the right way to deliver bad news, but there are abundant anecdotes from patients who have experienced this sort of treatment. In part, this is because, traditionally, medical education has not emphasized communicating with patients and how best to deliver bad news. It also stems from a deficient model of the doctor–patient relationship. Having been instructed about the evils of medical paternalism and the need to deliver even hard truths to patients, too many physicians have conceived their role as simply providing patients with factual information. It is then up to patients to decide what treatment is appropriate based on their own personal values, while the physician's health-related values are regarded as irrelevant. Ezekiel and

Linda Emanuel have called this the "informative model" of the doctor–patient relationship.[8]

The problem with the informative model is that it may give physicians the idea that their obligation to patients is only to provide truthful information about the condition and possible treatment options. Sometimes physicians do not even talk to patients or families themselves, leaving to nurses the task of communicating with patients and families. While the informative model emphasizes nondeception, it is devoid of the trust and caring that is essential to the doctor–patient relationship. Of course, physicians should respect the values and choices of their patients. But that does not mean that they are merely purveyors of technical expertise. A better model of the doctor–patient relationship is the deliberative model offered by Emanuel and Emanuel in which physicians first give information on the patient's clinical situation and then discuss with patients in a real dialogue the health-related values embodied in the various options. Some patients will want to prolong life at all costs. Others will reject the prolongation of life if the quality of life is unacceptable to them. These value judgments are as important in deciding what to do as the diagnosis of a condition and the existing medical options.

Physicians need to remember that even very bad news can be presented with kindness and empathy. They should choose language that patients can understand, which may differ depending on the individual patient, and avoid medical terminology that may be precise but unfamiliar. They need to ask if patients have questions and be willing to take the time to answer them. Devastating news may not sink in at once and may well need to be repeated. Most importantly, doctors should convey that they will not abandon their patients. They will still participate in their care, even when curative therapies are no longer possible. At the end of life, care is often "palliative," focused on relieving not only physical, but also emotional and spiritual suffering.

It may be replied that physicians don't have time for these lengthy conversations about values. Physicians get paid to treat, to do procedures, not to chat. These conversations, however, are not just chat but are some of the most important aspects of treating patients with serious and terminal illnesses. Teaching communication skills is now increasingly a part of medical education, though there are still many barriers to doctor–patient communication, including time pressures and continued emphasis on technology.

Is deception justified in some "hard cases"?

In the United States, at least lip service is paid to telling patients the truth, even if it doesn't always happen. But there are cases where it's not clear what should be revealed. What if the patient's family tells the doctor that they don't want their mother, say, to be told she has terminal cancer? What if the patient and her family belong to a culture in which truth-telling is not the norm—indeed, is regarded in such circumstances as unnecessary and cruel? Should the doctor go along with the family? Or should the doctor level with the patient?

If the patient tells the doctor that she does not want to hear her diagnosis or prognosis, the doctor is not obligated to force it on her. At the same time, it cannot just be assumed that the patient feels the same way as her family. It might be a delicate matter to ascertain the patient's attitudes toward being told the truth, but the physician has an obligation to try to find out. Ideally, this should be done earlier, before the patient has a fatal condition. Physicians should be wary of simply assuming that people from a particular culture or country have certain attitudes, which may be stereotypes. Also, cultures can and do change, and physicians will need to be sensitive to these changes. Finally, an individual patient may simply have a different attitude toward truth than her family or her culture generally. On balance, unless doctors know that a particular patient wants to be protected from knowing the truth, they should speak frankly, albeit sensitively, about the diagnosis, prognosis, and treatment options.

In most cases, telling patients the truth respects their autonomy. Hard cases arise when it can be doubted whether this is actually so. Consider the case of Monica, a 49-year-old divorced mother of two adult children and a heavy smoker.[9] Because she was having trouble breathing, she went to the hospital and was intubated, requiring that she be heavily sedated. A bronchoscopy was performed, and an inoperable cancer was found in her trachea. Radiation and chemotherapy were of unlikely benefit, with her life expectancy predicted to be about 3 months. Should doctors reduce her sedation enough to discuss treatment options with her ("wake her up") or maintain her sedation to keep her comfortable?

Perhaps the doctors were obligated to wake up Monica, since they cannot assume she would not want to be woken up. She may have things she wants to settle. She may want to say goodbye to her family. Those things may be more important to her than being spared the discomfort of the final months of her life. If so, then the fact that there are no good treatment options does not exhaust the possibility of respecting her autonomy since that is not limited to medical options.

On the other hand, why wake her up just for the purpose of letting her choose between horrible options? Not only would she experience considerable suffering without the sedation, but, in her condition, she would not likely be able to make informed, autonomous decisions. To wake her up would not demonstrate respect for autonomy; it would be a "charade of autonomy."

If they were available, should her children be consulted? They might know what their mother would likely want. But, of course, they might not know, they might disagree, or they might be wrong.

Cases like these bring out two aspects of many decisions faced in bioethics. First, it's often difficult to get the information one would need to make a good decision, and, second, the foundational principles of autonomy and beneficence may conflict. In real life, cases are often messy, and it may be difficult to know what is the right thing to do. There may not be a "right answer," just a choice between bad options. Those involved may just have to live with that.

Nevertheless, most cases are not hard cases. Medical professionals should be honest with their patients. Trust is diminished when doctors lie to patients or even shade the truth. Withholding the truth deprives patients of the opportunity to make their own decisions about what medical care they do and do not want. Patients need doctors they can trust but who are also sympathetic and caring. Even hard truths can be given in a kind and gentle way. Learning how to talk and listen to patients is as much a part of becoming a good doctor as technical proficiency and medical knowledge.

The importance of communication and empathy in the doctor–patient relationship is especially salient in the context of health disparities due to racism.

How should bioethicists and healthcare professionals address racism?

Although racism is not unique to the United States, it has played a significant role in US history, beginning with genocidal attacks on indigenous peoples and continuing with the kidnapping and enslavement of Africans. Racism and the core principle underlying it—white supremacy—is incompatible with American ideals of equality and democracy. Indeed, racism poses an existential threat to American democracy. It is incumbent on all Americans to be aware of this threat and to do something about it.

Simply as citizens, American bioethicists and healthcare professionals must fight against racial injustice. In addition, because the US healthcare system has played an important role in maintaining health disparities, and because racism can be such a fundamental failure to respect patients as persons, they have a special role to play in reducing such disparities. To do this, they must first understand what racism is.[10]

Racism can be either structural or personal. Structural "racism is a system . . . of structures, policies, practices, and norms . . . that assigns value and determines opportunity based on the way people look or the color of their skin. This results in conditions that unfairly advantage some and disadvantage others throughout society."[11] Unlike personal racism, which involves hatred of or contempt for people based on their ethnicity or skin color, structural racism does not depend on having these kinds of feelings. People who do not have racist prejudices can nevertheless get comparatively unfair advantages from a system of structural racism without even being aware that this is the case. The social institutions that comprise structural racism may simply appear to be "the way things are." In its extreme forms, it can involve lynching, segregation, and deprivation of civil rights such as voting. But structural racism is often much more subtle, determining where people live, work, and go to school, and how much wealth they accumulate. It can also determine how healthy people are and how long they live.

In the United States, racial and ethnic minorities have higher rates of chronic disease and premature death than do White people. Black patients have the worst health outcomes, and Black men have the lowest life expectancy of any demographic group. These disparities are partly due to socioeconomic factors, such as poverty. However, socioeconomic factors (which are often themselves the result of structural racism) are not the whole explanation for health disparities. Consider the disparity in premature births between African Americans and Whites. It was long believed that this was due to poverty, including poor nutrition and lack of access to prenatal care. However, researchers discovered that the chances of a woman giving birth prematurely are higher among Black women than among White women even when they controlled for education and socioeconomic status. One theory about why this is concerns hormones. "Stress hormones are part of the chemistry of pregnancy in normal conditions and can trigger labor when they reach a certain level. It stands to reason then that women who are already overloaded with stress hormones as a result of their day-to-day existence, are more likely to give birth prematurely."[12] Another example is pregnancy-related maternal mortality rates, which are three times higher among Black women than White women, even when researchers control for income and educational level.

The link between discrimination and stress and their effects on the body has been documented in other areas of medicine as well. One study found that merely anticipating having to deal with racism or prejudice leads to cardiovascular stress responses, which can cause high blood pressure. Studies consistently show a higher prevalence of hypertension in Blacks than in Whites, a main reason for the higher incidence of cardiovascular disease in Blacks. Chronic stress is also associated with inflammation, increasing the risk of cancer and kidney and heart disease. Racism can also affect mental health, causing depression, anxiety, and often leading to substance abuse and other unhealthy behaviors.

Bioethicists and clinicians need to become knowledgeable about the damaging health effects caused by racism, although for different reasons. Bioethicists determine the issues that are considered important in the field. They must be aware of the pervasive role that race and racism has played in healthcare disparities and unjust healthcare systems. Clinicians need to be aware of disparities in health outcomes due to structural racism. Medical schools can play an important role here, incorporating material about this in their curricula.

It is also important for providers to be aware of their unconscious assumptions or prejudices. For example, it has been documented that Black people are likely to receive less pain medication than White people who have the same medical condition. Doctors may be more likely to assume that Black people will abuse pain medication or simply believe that their pain is not as intense. "This suggests that racial bias is causing medical professionals to use different thresholds of pain for different racial groups, either inadvertently or purposefully, before administering care."[13]

Two large studies found that Black patients were two and a half times as likely to be described as noncompliant or noncooperative by their doctors in their electronic records as White patients. One doctor, not involved in the studies, suggested that providers tend to "label people in derogatory ways when we don't truly 'see' them—when we don't know them or understand them. The process of labeling provides a convenient shortcut that leads some physicians to blame the patient for their illnesses."[14]

Moreover, noncompliance may not be due to a lack of motivation on the patient's part. Instead of assuming that the patient doesn't care about getting better, the medical team should try to find out if there are other obstacles to adhering to treatment, such as financial barriers, transportation difficulties, illiteracy, or trouble with English. (The same approach could be taken with people who fail to show up for court appearances and parents whose children are not attending school.)

Part of the explanation for the disparity in maternal mortality rates stems from the failure of non-Black doctors to listen to their patients. As one doctor explains, "Pregnant women's complaints are often dismissed, and that is probably much more significant for Black and brown women."[15]

In addition to improving the compassion, empathy, and communication skills of White healthcare providers, the medical profession can do more to increase the number of Black physicians. African Americans make up 13% of the US population but only 4% of US doctors, a figure that has scarcely changed since 1940. African Americans often lack trust in the White medical establishment that has historically inflicted many abuses on them, including using them in harmful experiments (see Chapter 4, notable experiments). Because Black doctors are often better able to communicate with Black patients, increasing the number of Black doctors would likely ameliorate health disparities. For example, a substantial part of the difference in life expectancy between White and Black men is due to chronic diseases that can be prevented. In one study, researchers randomly assigned some Black men to Black doctors and others to White doctors. They found that Black men seen by Black doctors agreed to more, and more invasive, preventive services than did those seen by nonblack doctors. "By encouraging more preventative screenings, the researchers calculate, a workforce with more black doctors could help reduce cardiovascular mortality by 16 deaths per 100,000 per year—resulting in a 19% reduction in the black–white male gap in cardiovascular mortality and an 8% decline in the black–white male life expectancy gap."[16]

Concluding thoughts

The movement from paternalism to autonomy was motivated largely by respect for patients as persons and the recognition that patients have the right to make their own medical decisions, based on their own values and perceptions of their interests, so long as those decisions do not harm others. However, respect for patients means more than simply acknowledging their rights to make medical decisions. It requires carefully listening to patients in order to understand their choices and values. As previously noted, Emanuel and Emanuel argue that the preferred model of the doctor–patient relationship, the deliberative model, requires doctors to have a dialogue with their patients about health-related values. In addition, doctors need to be aware of the ways in which health outcomes are affected by structural racism and other inequities, as well as their own, perhaps unconscious, assumptions and stereotypes about individuals based on race or skin color.

3

DO ADVANCE DIRECTIVES PROTECT PATIENT AUTONOMY?

What is an advance directive for medical care?

In Chapter 2, we covered the movement in bioethics from paternalism to the right of competent patients to have a say in medical decision-making. In this chapter, we explore to what extent this right applies and should be respected even when a person's decision-making capacity is lost.

Advance directives (ADs) are written or recorded by people to preserve their moral right to make their own decisions about treatment and healthcare for later times when they have lost decision-making capacity. Because the directives are made in advance of the later situations to which the directives speak, they are called *advance* directives. Someone else—usually the healthcare agent or proxy—will need to speak for the incapacitated person, based in part on any AD they may have.

In the broadest sense, "advance directive" connotes both instructions about medical interventions they do or do not want (instructional directives, sometimes called "living wills") and the directives people make about who shall speak for them. We will use the term to refer to the former, and use "proxy appointment," or the legal term "durable power of attorney for healthcare," to refer to directives in which a person appoints her healthcare agent (proxy). Both instructional ADs and proxy appointments are important, and they need each other.

Without an AD, an agent exercising "substituted judgment" for the patient will have less to go on in making decisions that reflect the patient's wishes, and an AD without an appointed proxy to interpret and execute it is less likely to be effective.

The basic elements of a good AD are

1. *The measures to be withheld or withdrawn* (and in the opposite direction, discretionary measures that should be provided). Desires about the location of care may also be included, such as no hospitalization or admission to a long-term care facility.
2. *When those measures are to be withheld, withdrawn, or provided.* The medical or personal circumstances when the previous directions are to apply. Stipulating what should be withheld or provided without any mention of when can render an instruction impotent. Generally, any direction about what also needs to include a statement about when.
3. *The essential values that motivate the AD.* These provide guidance for the inevitable situations where the directive has no specific instruction. No AD can be written with foresight about all the situations that may arise. Though directives are thus always "incomplete," the person's proxy and providers still have to make decisions. Knowing something about the person's core values can provide helpful insights.

Some other general points about ADs are important. A directive is said to be *valid* if it has been made in the proper way: by a person with decision-making capacity at the time, with some basic understanding of the conditions to which the instructions apply, voluntarily (without pressure or coercion by others), and properly witnessed. A directive is *applicable* when the conditions to which its instructions were intended to apply obtain. The moral force of an AD is dependent on both its valid origin and its applicability at the time of implementation.

The legitimate scope of ADs is wide. The scope of the basic right usually being exercised through a directive, the right to refuse life-saving treatment, is as wide when carried forward through an AD as it is when the person has decision-making capacity. In neither situation is the right contingent on terminal illness, for example, or on any particular degree of suffering ("unbearable," say). Directives can also be written about matters other than medical treatment—mental health directives, for example, address financial issues and restraints on behavior.

The ethical basis of ADs is powerful: *People do not lose their basic rights when they lose decision-making capacity. Those rights just have to be exercised for them by someone else.*[1] An AD is simply a vehicle by which people guide the later decisions of others in accordance with this fundamental right.

Despite this strong ethical foundation, ADs can run into significant problems. There is a prima facie case for abiding by any valid, applicable AD that directs proxies and caregivers to do what people have a right to do when they have capacity, but in some instances the implementation of a valid and applicable directive can still be ethically questionable. One basis for doubt is that the person may have undergone a change of mind. Another is the "then-self versus now-self" problem. We explore each of these in the next two sections.

What constitutes a relevant change of mind?

Consider the following case[2]:

Margot Bentley. By 2016, Mrs. Bentley, an 84-year-old former nurse, had been diagnosed with Alzheimer's for fifteen years. For the last nine, she lived in a residential care facility, the last two in the most advanced stage of dementia. She did not recognize any friends or family, did not speak, and could make only very limited physical movements. She spent her days motionless in bed or slumped in a wheelchair with eyes closed. She required spoon-feeding. She would usually open her mouth, though sometimes only after repeated offers. She accepted different types and amounts on different days and seemed to prefer certain flavors.

Mrs. Bentley first executed an AD twenty-three years earlier: "If . . . there is no reasonable expectation of my recovery from extreme physical or mental disability, I direct that I be allowed to die and not be kept alive by artificial means or heroic measures." She listed specific instructions, including "no nourishment or liquids," and designated her husband and daughter as healthcare agents. Shortly after her diagnosis of Alzheimer's, and consistent with her earlier directive, she "repeatedly told her family that she wished to be allowed to die when she reached a stage of advanced dementia."[3]

In these last stages, when her AD clearly applied, but she would still accept food, had Mrs. Bentley changed her mind?

A person's genuine change of mind about her AD is always relevant. Any directive can be revoked, though legally valid revocation requires sufficient cognitive capacity to revoke. The person would have to understand the directive, the act of revoking it, and what may replace it, if anything. In none of her last years in severe dementia did Mrs. Bentley remotely have such capacity. As Ron Berghmans has trenchantly noted, at that point in dementia "you don't have enough of a mind left to change."[4]

Yet even if Mrs. Bentley lacked the capacity for the kind of change of mind that would constitute revoking her AD, the question remains: Didn't she have some kind of change of mind that should make her caregivers reluctant to go along with her directive? She was, after all, willing to eat. What, though, was that willingness? Was it a *decision*, or a merely an instinctual *desire or reflexive behavior* in the sensory presence of food?

Suppose we interpret it as a decision to eat. Then we might ask whether she had the requisite mental capacity to make that decision. Decision-making capacity is relative to the nature of what is being decided. A patient may have lost the capacity to decide about a complex course of therapy but still have capacity to make simpler decisions. If a person sees and smells food and wants to eat, she presumably has some at least rudimentary understanding of food and eating.

We would still need to ask, though, whether capacity to accept simple eating is the relevant capacity. Her act of eating is not just *eating*. In full context it is *eating when she had said in her AD not to be fed*. Does she have the capacity to decide to do *that*? Certainly not. She may in some sense understand food and eating, but she does not understand that what she is doing in her current context when she eats is what she said in her directive should not be done. Without the capacity to understand that, how can she have had a relevant change of mind?

A better way to understand such behavior, arguably, is to see it not as a decision but as either as merely a desire, or even just a reflexive physiological reaction to the presence of food. In the end stages of progressive dementia, the person may give no indication of recognizing food before it gets very close to her nose and touches her lips, and then opening her mouth and swallowing only if the food is patiently held there and then tipped into her mouth. This is certainly not a change of mind about her directive.

To sum up, "willingness to eat" covers a spectrum of behavior, from capacity to decide in the action's full context to merely reflexive mouth-opening. The former can constitute a full change of mind about the directive. Those on the latter end of the spectrum do not constitute a relevant change of mind at all, and caregivers should not interpret them as that.

Nevertheless, cases that do not qualify as a change of mind—there simply isn't "enough of a mind left to change"—can still present hard dilemmas. An especially hard case occurs when the patient who wrote an AD to withhold oral food and drink, upon getting to her current condition, seems happy to eat and expresses frustration when not fed. Those present a different and likely more difficult problem, the then-self/now-self problem.

What is the "then-self/now-self" problem?

This challenge to ADs goes to their core and reaches far beyond just cases of severe progressive dementia. It asserts that the very condition that activates them, the inability to participate in medical decision-making, undercuts their authority. Rebecca Dresser and John Robertson make this criticism of what they call "the orthodox approach" to ADs prevalent in American law courts and dominant in the outlook of many others.[5] In the orthodox approach, "respect for incompetent patients requires according such patients the same right to refuse treatment accorded competent patients." Refusal is based on the patient's own wishes, either stated in an AD or discerned by the patient's proxy in "substituted judgment" about those wishes. Allegedly this respects the autonomy of the person in avoiding treatment the patient does not want.

This orthodox approach, Dresser and Robertson argue, relies on a fiction. The now incompetent person is not an autonomous chooser. The autonomous chooser who made the AD no longer exists. Typically, the current patient does not remember writing her AD or care about either autonomy or the values that motivated her to write it. Respect for patient autonomy can therefore not be invoked as a reason for implementing a directive. Moreover, the current person may have quite different interests than the writer of the directive—no longer an interest in preserving control or dignity, being independent, or not being a burden to loved ones and caregivers, for example. Conditions that are regarded as unacceptable by people when competent may still be of value when they have lost decision-making capacity.

Critics of ADs then draw the conclusion that the current patient must be treated according to the patient's current best interests—the so-called *best interest standard*, not according to previous wishes expressed in a directive. Only best interest will respect the current patient and constitute good care. If the patient's current interests align with his AD, then the directive is superfluous, and, if the two conflict, the directive must give way. Either ADs are superfluous or they are irrelevant—bad news indeed for ADs.

Among the many cases that illustrate the problem of different interests and beliefs between the previous AD-writing "then-self" and the current "now-self" when a directive might be implemented, here, briefly, are two from the abundant literature on this problem.[6]

> *Ms. A.* As a religious group, Jehovah's Witnesses believe they should not accept blood transfusion even when it is critical to saving life. A lifelong committed Witness, Ms. A explicitly included refusal of blood transfusion in her AD. Later, when very senile, she develops bleeding ulcers. Without transfusion she will die; with it, she will likely survive for several, perhaps many, mostly contented years. She no longer has any recollection of her religion or her AD.

> *Ms. Snyder.* Ninety years old and diagnosed with Alzheimer's disease, Ellen Snyder has lived in a nursing home the past five years, with no living siblings and, never having married, with no children. Ms. Snyder had long been a foreign correspondent, appearing on television news from dangerous "hot spots." She fought to stay home, but as dementia progressed, her nephew Larry intervened and arranged nursing home placement.

Ellen had named Larry her healthcare proxy and written a detailed AD: if she were ever to become greatly cognitively compromised, she wanted her life not to be prolonged by any life-saving treatment, even the simplest and least invasive, citing antibiotics for pneumonia as an example.

Surprisingly, Ellen settled into the nursing home quite well. She liked the staff and often smiled at them, though she could not remember their names. When her nephew showed her a clip of herself on television, she showed no recognition whatsoever of herself. Then she came down with pneumonia. Larry reminded the staff of the clear terms of Aunt Ellen's AD: no antibiotics. The nurses and other caregivers were resistant, disturbed. They had no experience of the younger Ms. Snyder, only the recent pleasant, if limited, woman. If a burdensome therapy were being refused, they would understand, but a simple antibiotic? They were sure the present Ms. Snyder preferred to go on living.

What moral authority do Ms. A's and Ms. Snyder's ADs carry? Should Mrs. A's current lack of any awareness of religious identity allow a transfusion? Should Ellen Snyder's present contentment lead her nephew and caregivers to disregard her previous insistence and proceed with life-saving treatment for pneumonia?

How have defenders of advance directives responded to this problem?

Defenders of ADs have marshaled powerful responses to the Dresser/Robertson critique. We explore two. They do not entirely dispose of the then-self/now-self problem, but they go a long way toward preserving the moral force of ADs. [7]

Identity is not the problem

Perhaps the person who wrote the directive is not sufficiently the "same person" as the later person with dementia. David DeGrazia labels this the "someone else" problem.[8] If the basis for individual identity—what makes someone the same person over time—is psychological continuity, then radical changes in beliefs, desires, and concerns could affect identity itself and thus threaten ADs.

But are Ms. Snyder or Ms. A no longer the same *individual persons* they previously were? The unspoken assumption in the whole notion of an AD is that the later incompetent individual is the same person, for, with ADs, people wish to control *their own* later lives. Especially in the law, departing from this common assumption would create all kinds of difficulties. Pragmatically, bodily identity has huge advantages as a criterion for being the same individual compared to any psychological continuity standard. People just do use bodily identity when they uphold contracts, discern criminal and civil liability, or blame or praise each other, etc. People also, of course, speak of "becoming a different person," but their usual sense in doing that is a *personality* change, not the going out of existence of one person and the coming in of another.

Personality changes are still important, but as part of "narrative identity," DeGrazia argues. The inquiry "Who are you?" calls for a different response than the bodily focus used for individual identity: something of the history, experiences, beliefs, values, and other psychological features that make you "who you are." People in severe dementia may lose much of their narrative identity, but they remain the same numerical individual. People write ADs knowing perfectly well that they may not later have the same interests, but they will still be the same person. Ms. A is still Ms. A, the Jehovah's Witness, and Ms. Snyder still nephew Larry's Aunt Ellen.

People have *lives*, not just successive moments of being alive

Nancy Rhoden has articulated a powerful response to Dresser and Robertson. If we treat persons who have lost decision-making capacity only by the best interest standard, she noted, we treat them in the same way we would (and should) treat persons who have never had such capacity. But

> something is wrong . . . when we treat formerly competent patients as if they were never competent. Someone who makes a prior directive sees herself as the unified subject of a human life. She sees her concern for her body, her goals, or her family as transcending her incapacity. . . . One . . . component of treating persons with respect [is] that we view them as they view themselves. . . . To do this, we must not ignore their prior choices and values.[9]

The Dresser-Robertson position effectively erases the life of the person being treated.

There is a further point to be made in cases of greatly diminished cognitive capacity. For anyone with normal capacity, life is one of anticipation and memory. People think of their lives in temporally extended terms, future and past. This is so basic a feature of what we think of as *our lives* that it seldom rises to explicit consciousness. Yet if we ignore it, we are led into mistakes like thinking Ms. Snyder's AD is irrelevant because she is no longer aware of it or because she will never know that we have not followed it. What she cared about in writing her AD was *her life* and how it would end, for even when she loses capacity, it will still be *her life*.[10] Since it is hers, doesn't she have a right to control it?

These responses—retained identity and what a life is—strongly support the moral weight of ADs by effectively muting the then-self/now-self problem.[11] A somewhat different defense of ADs concedes more ground to the problem. To that view we now turn.

Can advance directives accommodate the then-self/now-self problem?

Though ADs survive the Dresser-Robertson critique, they are still problematic when it seems that survival is in the patient's current interest. Caregivers' and loved ones' loyalty to the person right before them, with his current interests as they are, should not be slighted. Might we acknowledge significant weight to the patient's current interests while still seeing directives as having considerable moral force? One attempt to do that is the "sliding scale" or "balancing" model.[12] It emerges from two observations.

The moral weight of ADs varies along a spectrum

ADs enable people to control how their lives end. They should generally be followed. Not all ADs, however, have the same moral force. Their strength varies with a number of factors. It is greater (1) when they are *based on realistic assessment* of the facts. People who write an AD wishing to avoid living years into severe dementia, for example, must inform themselves about the various stages of dementia and what life may then be like. They need to know that they might turn out to be relatively contented, though they could also be terribly frightened, anxious, and confused. Directives' force is also greater (2) when they *reflect the person's enduring values*, and those values are mentioned or even briefly explained. An AD's weight is greater (3) when the directive is *clear* about what should be withheld and when, and (4) when they have been *written, revised, or reiterated relatively recently*, not only decades ago.

The patient's current interest in living will vary

Even when a directive has many of these positive characteristics, the substantive question of whether to implement the directive may not admit of a simple Yes or No answer. The main complicating factor, already discussed, is that the writer of the directive, when he gets to the stage where he said life-saving care should be withheld, may still enjoy his life and have an interest in living. The stronger that interest is, the harder it is to justify following the instructions of even a knowledgeably written, clear, and recently reiterated AD.

The current interest in living of someone who has lost decision-making capacity can vary a lot. The interest in living is weakest, perhaps, when the individual is experiencing severe and irremediable suffering, but it can also be very weak in situations with little suffering. In her advanced Alzheimer's, for example, Margot Bentley was probably not suffering, but by then the value of her life *to her* was vanishingly low. What is the value to a person of her own survival in a condition where she cannot anticipate tomorrow, and, when she gets to tomorrow, she cannot remember yesterday? It is not nothing, but it is very little. When we value our *survival*, we are not just valuing the moment. We are valuing at least the next hour, or living until tomorrow, or next month. Similarly, appreciating that we have survived—valuing life retrospectively, one might say—involves some awareness of the past. In very severe dementia, with vanishingly little anticipation or short-term memory, the value of the person's survival to herself has withered to very little.

These two basic observations can be brought together by viewing decisions on following an AD in the face of a then-self/now-self problem as a "sliding scale" in which both the person's autonomous choice represented in the AD and his capacity for current enjoyment and appreciation of life are taken into account. The directive gains in authority to the degree that it is knowledgeable, reflects the person's enduring values, is clear, and has been written or reiterated relatively recently; conversely, its authority diminishes when those characteristics are weak. And the directive gains in authority as the patient gives little evidence that he still values surviving, and its moral authority to refuse life-saving care diminishes to the extent that the person gives indication of still enjoying his life.

Such a framework will sometimes yield "not yet" decisions—*don't yet* implement the directive because life is still of significant value to the person. Don't, however, disregard the directive; continue to attend to it carefully, ready to implement it as the person's ability to value her survival withers. Such "not yet" judgments are sensitive to the pull of the person's apparent desire to live while still honoring the person's AD by keeping it front and center.

What conclusions would such an approach generate in the cases described earlier?

Mrs. Bentley's directive was not clear about whether its "no nourishment or liquids" clause included food and water by mouth, not just medically delivered nutrition. Her agent daughter, however, had discussed her wishes and values with her, and she certainly understood the condition of dementia to which her directive spoke, as she had dealt with many such patients in her nursing career. Her acceptance of food when patiently spoon-fed indicated a nominal willingness to eat, but this acceptance was likely reflexive and instinctual. It is doubtful her survival had much if any value to her anymore. There were thus ample grounds for stopping oral feeding.

Ms. Snyder's AD was extremely clear and strong, specific about wanting no life-saving treatment of even the least invasive kind, citing antibiotics for pneumonia as an example. She also articulated her reasons and values for not wanting her life to end in years of dependence and passivity, and the subjective value to her of her own survival is low without much anticipation of tomorrow or memory of the immediate past. Not only Larry, her appointed proxy, but also her caregivers should probably abide by her instruction not to administer antibiotics. This is not, however, a simple case, for she is not in distress or pain, and she continues to experience some simple daily pleasures.

Ms. A's directive, as a long-time Jehovah's Witness, is clear: no blood transfusions, period. Now a transfusion is needed to save her for what will likely be several years of good life. How valuable, though, would that survival then be to her, knowing that it was due to the transfusion she had clearly refused? Her life is so linked to her religious identity that it cannot be said "she's no longer a Jehovah's Witness" just because she is no longer aware of her religious identity. As hard as it might be, the only way her caregivers can truly show respect for her and the life she has led is to follow her directive.

This nuanced approach to ADs, incorporating both their moral weight and the pull of any conflicting current interest, may not be the right one (we leave that to the reader). It is an example, however, of how a more complex view can emerge from wrestling with both sides of a difficult dilemma.

What communication challenges limit the use of advance directives?

In addition to these frequently debated issues about directives, challenges of a different sort—communication—confront their use at several levels: at the level of individual directives, provider practices, and systemic economic, ethnic, and racial disadvantage in the society.

Individual directives

We have noted the importance of appointing a healthcare proxy/agent, not just writing an instructional directive. It is not only that appointment which is important, but communication between patient and agent. The more an agent understands the values and larger orientation of the person who has entrusted her with this responsibility, the better she will be able to speak on his behalf, especially in situations not explicitly addressed in his AD. It is also important that the patient be able to trust that the appointed proxy will support his directive when the time comes. If she cannot, he should consider appointing someone else. The same sort of communication with the patient's primary provider is also important. Hopefully that will be a specific person with whom the patient can reach an at least general understanding about his directive. If it turns out that the provider cannot agree to support implementing the AD, it may be necessary to procure one who will.

Just as ADs can be woefully remiss in certain essential elements, like the when's for the various what's, so also failure to appoint a proxy, or appointing one who cannot support what is in the directive, or failure to communicate well with the agent can result in a directive not being followed.

Provider practices

Especially in emergency and intensive care situations, providers may not attend to a patient's directive. In the urgency of the moment, the tendency to act first and check things like ADs later is understandable. In addition, in high-tech professional medicine, an unstated mindset of "if we are able to do it, we should do it" tends to dominate. In the clinical culture surrounding hospital intensive care units (ICUs), for example, what Jessica Zitter has referred to as an "end-of-life conveyor belt" tends to operate once patients are seen to need intensive care.[13] Virtually automatically, they get conveyed to the ICU, and, once there, they routinely get put on ventilators. After all, isn't that what ICUs are for? Patients and their agents may not be informed of the frequently bleak prospects of getting out of the ICU, or of getting off a ventilator, or of what ventilator-dependent life is like in the rehabilitation center to which they will likely be moved if they do get out of the ICU. Many have no real opportunity to avoid the "do everything possible" mode.

ADs express patient choice and are meant to preserve it. Without adequate communication from and with providers, directives easily become irrelevant.

Economic, ethnic, and racial disadvantage

Separate from these communication deficiencies, structural inequities pose additional barriers. Interest in ADs—especially directives to refuse life-saving treatment—will understandably be higher among advantaged than disadvantaged segments of a population. Those with worse access to good care are generally less likely to have a continuous relationship with a primary provider who is willing to take time for consultation about prospective choices. And patients who perceive that they have not had access to good care may resent any suggestion that now they might instruct their providers and agents to withhold such care. In a context of understandable suspicion, forthright conversation is difficult to begin and sustain.

Unfortunately, providers and counselors can easily assume that "the problem" in such communication deficiencies is the patients from these populations, not themselves. This is itself an additional barrier. Providers may not realize that they tend not to listen as well to patients of a different racial, ethnic, or even economic demographic, or they may have practices, such as insisting on meeting alone with the patient without family in the room, that conflict with cultural assumptions about who should be there. For some patients, moreover, their pastor, priest, rabbi, or imam may be one of the most important persons to have in the room, but that can easily get overlooked in secular healthcare.[14]

These cultural and structural barriers are as important ethically as the change-of-mind and then-self/now-self questions about ADs that bioethicists have vigorously pursued. How to address effectively such barriers may not always be the province of bioethics per se, but getting them recognized as something that the health professions need to address certainly is.

Concluding thoughts

ADs, though problematic in various ways, are a necessary extension of a person's right to refuse treatment. People do not lose basic rights over their care when decision-making capacity is lost. Writers of ADs should be reasonably well-informed and not prejudiced about the conditions they address in their directives. Directives should be sufficiently clear about what is to be withheld or provided and when. They should be explained in terms of the person's basic values and should be relatively recently reiterated or revised. And they should always be supplemented with appointment of a healthcare agent/proxy.

Patients with decision-making capacity can always change their mind about their directive. Change of mind is often, however, no longer possible by the time to implement the directive has arrived. Especially with ADs to avoid living into severe dementia, the person will by then no longer have "enough of a mind left to change."

Directives also often face a then-self/now-self problem. In the face of it they retain the considerable moral weight they deserve, but the current interests of the patient that conflict with a directive also carry some weight. In most cases where the AD has been knowledgeably written and relatively recently reiterated, is reasonably clear about what to withhold and when, and is supported by a proxy who knows the patient well, a directive should be followed.

Inadequate provider–patient communication and barriers embedded in structural disadvantage hamper the access that many people have to ADs. Healthcare professionals are obligated to recognize and correct their own practices that impede productive communication.

4

WHEN IS EXPERIMENTATION ON HUMAN SUBJECTS UNETHICAL?

What principles for ethical research emerged in the Nuremberg Code?

Before the mid-twentieth century, ethical problems in biomedical research on human subjects were rarely a concern. For one thing, little self-conscious scientific experimentation was conducted, and much of what did occur was either not systematically organized into what we would now call "research," or it was regarded as part of medical therapy. For the West, and significantly worldwide, that changed momentously when war crimes trials after World War II, most notably those in Nuremberg, Germany, revealed shocking experiments on prisoners by so-called Nazi doctors. Concentration camp inmates were, for example, given typhus-infected blood to then test the effects of a vaccine (most died), infected with gangrene to observe various treatments, and submerged in freezing water to test how long it took to freeze to death, knowledge that would be useful in deciding whether to save downed pilots. In the end, sixteen doctors and their close associates were convicted for such experiments; seven were sentenced to death.[1]

The key principles articulated in the tribunal's decisions came to be known as the Nuremberg Code on experimentation on human subjects.[2]

1. *Informed voluntary consent* of the human subject is essential. This involves:
   - *Capacity to give consent.*
   - *Free power of choice*, "without . . . any element of force, fraud, deceit, duress, or . . . coercion."
   - *Sufficient knowledge and comprehension* of the experiment by its subjects to enable "an understanding and enlightened decision," including "the nature, duration, and purpose of the experiment; the method and means by which it is to be conducted; all inconveniences and hazards reasonably to be expected; and the effects upon his health or person."
2. *Sound experimental design*:
   - Designed to yield results "for the good of society" that cannot be procured by other means.
   - Based on sufficient knowledge of the disease.
3. *Death or disabling injury cannot be anticipated to occur from the experiment*, "except, perhaps, . . . where the experiment[ing] physicians also serve as subjects."
4. *Investigators must be prepared to terminate the experiment at any stage* if they have "probable cause to believe . . . that a continuation . . . is likely to result in injury, disability, or death."

The first principle quickly became known as "informed consent." All four are now included in official codes of research ethics used in virtually all institutional settings, including the Institutional Review Boards (IRBs) required in the United States and similar processes governing human subject research in most countries. As influential as they have been in the more than seven decades after their pronouncement, however, the Nuremberg Code's principles were hardly abided by in the decades before and several decades after 1949, even in the very countries that championed the trials. In the next section we consider experiments by reputable investigators, not "Nazi doctors," that attracted strong criticism. They raise a range of difficult and enduring questions. Some may represent a conflict between utilitarian considerations of the larger aggregate good that could come from well-designed experiments and Kantian respect for the persons who are research subjects, but the considerations involved go well beyond any conflict between utilitarian and Kantian ethics (see Chapter 1).

After the next section about specific trials, other sections will address issues raised by randomized controlled trials (RCTs), placebo-control trials (PCTs) when existing therapies are available, international trials in different cultural and medical circumstances, and "challenge" trials where subjects are deliberately infected in order to test treatments. Many of these issues have taken on extra importance with the COVID-19 pandemic, but none is unique to pandemics.

What notable experiments influenced the development of medical research ethics?

From among the many such experiments, we feature three, representing distinct issues.

Jewish Chronic Disease Hospital cancer cell injection studies

In 1963, at the Jewish Chronic Disease Hospital in Brooklyn, New York, Dr. Chester Southam and colleagues wanted to know whether cancer cells would be rejected by the bodies of people suffering from diseases other than cancer. [3] They knew that people with cancer take longer to expel foreign cancer cells than otherwise healthy people do, but would people who had diseases other than cancer also take longer? The results could be important for better understanding the human immune system. The study proposed to inject with foreign cancer cells elderly and debilitated patients who had other diseases. The researchers were confident this did not pose risks to the subjects since injecting foreign cancer cells does not cause cancer. The researchers were aware, however, that many people would refuse to participate if they knew they would be injected with cancer cells. Convinced they would not be able to disabuse potential subjects of their misconceptions, the researchers decided not to use the word "cancer" in describing what would be injected. If "cancer" is misleading information and injecting cancer cells is harmless, why should participants be told?

Eventually, at the highest level of state supervision, a committee of the New York State Department of Education's Board of Regents found the researchers overly confident in believing injected foreign cancer cells did not risk cancer. The fact that Dr. Southam was unwilling to inject himself with cancer cells revealed that he thought there was some risk, a risk he was not willing to take. The committee also found the word "cancer" to be "material" to the subjects' decision: "any fact which might influence the giving or withholding of consent is material" regardless of whether the influence of that information on the subject is considered by physicians to be irrational. It rejected the paternalistic model of physicians and researchers determining what information is needed for subjects to make a rational decision, replacing it with what information is material to—could make an actual difference in—their decisions.

In the decades since, a primary task in research ethics has been to refine the standard that emerged from this decision: What is the scope of the *material information* owed to subjects to make their consent adequately informed?[4]

The Willowbrook State School hepatitis studies

In the 1950s and 1960s, Dr. Saul Krugman and colleagues conducted a series of experiments on thousands of residents of the Willowbrook State School for mentally disabled children on Staten Island, New York. [5] Eventually, by injecting subjects with both live hepatitis virus and gamma globulin, a component of blood plasma rich in antibodies, Krugman was able to more clearly distinguish hepatitis A and B, spurring significant advances. The process Krugman used involved isolating many newly admitted residents in a separate wing and conducting the experiment only on them. Since hepatitis and other infections were prevalent in the institution, the separate wing provided some protection for its children from infections other than hepatitis. As for the hepatitis that they contracted in the experiment itself, they would likely have contracted that anyhow just by residing in the School. In addition, with the greater attention they got, many received better general care.

These benefits and the alleged absence of net comparative harm to the subjects provided Krugman his ethical justification. The participating children were no worse off—perhaps even better off—than they would have been had they not participated by being in the separate wing. Much of the resultant criticism of this defense focused on whether Willowbrook *as it existed*, with infectious disease rampant within its walls, was the proper comparison for determining harm. Critics argued that the pathetic conditions in Willowbrook were a terrible wrong to the children living there and that the research could not be justified by the existence of such conditions.

Nevertheless, the conditions in the School would not have improved had Krugman never done his experiment. Was he exploiting an egregious institutional situation to justify his research, or was he making the best of an unfortunate situation by advancing the understanding of that disease? Perhaps we should say he is doing both, but this provides no answer to whether his experiment violated a central principle of ethical experimentation—not to cause subjects serious harm.

In the end, the defense of the Willowbrook experiments— that they created no net harm to their subjects—stumbled on one of the study's own elements. Krugman's very own research "demonstrated that gamma globulin [serum] provided some protection [against hepatitis], and yet he [continued to infect the] . . . control groups with the virus *and withheld the serum from them* in order to fulfill the requirements of his research design."[6] The real net harm to the children from injecting live virus may have been negligible, if harm at all, but then to withhold potentially effective treatment crossed a different line. The obligations of clinical physicians acting as researchers are still their obligations as clinicians. They are not ethically permitted to withhold effective treatment from patients just because the patients are also research subjects.

The Tuskegee Syphilis Study

The scandalous issues of inadequate, less than "material" information, of questionable estimates of harm, and of withholding treatment that marked the two experiments just discussed were all present in the infamous Tuskegee Syphilis Study, greatly exacerbated as well by racism.[7] From 1932 to 1972 in Tuskegee, Alabama, the United States Public Health Service (PHS) conducted a study of the natural course of syphilis in African American males. In syphilis's acquired form, bacteria enter the body through skin or mucous membranes, usually during sexual intercourse. They multiply rapidly in the nearest lymph glands and spread into the bloodstream. The course of the disease varies in different individuals, but it usually results in bone and joint pain and highly infectious skin ulcers. Sometimes, after that, it becomes latent for up to thirty years, but usually for only two or three. In the final tertiary stage the disease eats away bone structure, including nasal and palate bones. The tumors it causes may affect liver, heart, optic nerves, and brain. It is an awful disease.

The US PHS devised the study to establish the incidence of syphilis in Black males in the county around Tuskegee, men who typically had little access to medical care. The study was also designed "to learn whether Blacks could be treated successfully . . . if treatment programs were made available to them." Tests would be administered to a representative portion of this population, and those who tested positive would be offered free treatment. The prevailing treatments at the

time were arsphenamine and mercury, both of dubious efficacy. But, even if these treatments had been successful, they
would not have been given to the subjects as that would destroy the experiment's aim of discerning the natural course
of syphilis in this population. Being promised treatment and
then being given only inadequate amounts certainly violated
the informed consent requirement; in addition, subjects who
tested positive were not told they had syphilis, only that they
had "bad blood," a term used by rural Blacks for a range of
ailments.

It might be argued that withholding full doses of the dubious mercury and arsphenamine treatment did not violate the
Nuremberg Code's prohibition on foreseeably causing death
or serious injury since, in the absence of the study, the vast
majority of this Black and impoverished population would not
have received this treatment or, indeed, any treatment. Any
conceivable defense of the study on this ground, however,
collapsed with the discovery of penicillin in the early 1940s and
its use in World War II on US and other Allied troops. Penicillin
was much more effective than the previous treatments—a
cure, in fact—yet it was not offered to the Tuskegee subjects.
Worse yet, the PHS intervened with local military draft boards
to prevent potential draftees among the subjects from being
given effective treatment that would have made them eligible
for military service. And, even worse, for decades after the war
the PHS continued the study and withheld penicillin. Even
Black medical professionals in the area who were involved
with the study showed no more concern for the men than the
White doctors and health officials did who launched and ran
the experiment. Only after explosive exposure by courageous
dissenting personnel within the PHS and considerable attention in the media did the Service end the study in 1972.

The legacy of Tuskegee is not only its egregious violation
of informed consent and the causing of foreseeable harm, but
also its deeply racist character. It was falsely believed that
syphilis ran a different course in Black men than in White. And

even if White and Black men were believed to be equally sus-ceptible, would the PHS have ever seriously considered doing this experiment on White males? It is especially doubtful that penicillin treatment would have been withheld from White males after the war. Unfortunately, the terrible effects of this discriminatory use of Black subjects have continued to rever-berate in the United States ever since. Vaccination efforts for COVID-19, for example, are hampered by the understandable distrust of government-provided medicine by many African Americans, distrust stemming in great part from the infamous Tuskegee Study.

Racial and ethnic bias is a threat to ethical experimentation well beyond the Tuskegee study. Antisemitism fed the ter-rible experiments in Nazi Germany, bias against the already ill and elderly arguably fed the Jewish Chronic Disease Hospital experiments, and prejudice against disabled children likely explains some of the ethical lapses at Willowbrook. The in-tersection of a vulnerable subject population with racial and ethnic bias is a lethal combination.

Are randomized clinical trials ethically questionable?

Clinical experimentation in medicine became greatly more sci-entific in the late 1940s with the development of the *randomized controlled trial* (RCT, also known as *randomized clinical trial*). Before then, the chances that most therapies a patient received were actually effective were not great. The RCT brought a huge advance in the scientific and evidence-based status of medicine, one of the major life-extending improvements in the history of medicine, and it did not come until the late 1940s.[8]

In an RCT, similar participants, chosen as appropriate for the therapy being tested, are randomly assigned to different "arms" of the trial. In one arm they receive the experimental treatment; in the other, usually a placebo that has no thera-peutic effect (e.g., a "sugar pill") or sometimes another, ex-isting therapy for the same condition. If the second arm uses an existing treatment, the RCT is an *active-control trial* (ACT); if it uses a placebo, it is a *placebo-control trial* (PCT). By comparing the experimental treatment against a placebo, it is possible to determine if it is more effective that something that is known to have no therapeutic effect. By comparing the experimental treatment against an existing treatment, it is possible to determine if it is at least as effective as existing treatment. Both active-control and placebo-control trials are now typically randomized.

Soon after its advent in the mid-twentieth century, a refinement beyond randomization became standard: the *blind* RCT, where the subject does not know in which arm of the trial she has been placed. A further refinement is the *double-blind* RCT, where neither the researcher and all persons administering the treatment or placebo nor the subject know which of these the individual participant has received. Blinding ensures that the results are not affected by the preconceptions of either subjects or researchers. The double-blind RCT is now the gold standard for medical research.

For *first-in-class* new therapies—the first for treating the condition targeted—placebo-control trials are standard. The reason is the well-known *placebo effect*. Through psychological mechanisms that we may not understand, the patient's view that he is now receiving treatment can itself spur improvement. The therapy won't be producing the effect; the patient's belief that he is getting therapy will. A PCT tests for this using a placebo such as a sugar pill. Clearly, experimental therapies should not become approved standard practice if they are no better than a sugar pill. (For new *next-in-class* therapies, however, where an existing therapy regarded as at least somewhat effective is already available, simply doing PCTs without also comparing the new therapy to the existing therapy remains controversial. This is pursued in the next section.)

At first glance randomization itself seems not to pose an ethical problem as long as participants are adequately informed of this structure of the trial. When RCTs are used in therapeutic research, however, ethical doubts arise. When it is therapies that are being investigated, some of those directly involved are clinicians, not just scientists, and the subjects of the experiment are their patients. Since a clinician's foremost obligation is to her patients, then if a relatively effective therapy already exists, how can the clinician fulfill her obligation by inviting patients into a trial with a new treatment whose effectiveness is unknown? Moreover, if the new treatment is highly promising, can a good clinician place her patients into a trial that exposes them to getting not the promising treatment, but only a placebo? Within a Kantian ethic of respect for persons (see Chapter 1), randomization will then be unethical: though an imperative of good scientific medicine, it amounts to sacrificing current patients for the benefit of future ones. Obtaining participants' fully informed consent may still provide ethical justification, but that consent will have to be extremely well informed.

In response to this basic ethical problem inherent in RCTs, one may simply depart from the Kantian framework of respect for individual persons and make a utilitarian argument: for the maximum long-term good of everyone affected, scientifically sound RCTs are needed. Otherwise, clinicians will be flying relatively blind in judging what therapy is best. Interestingly, though, a defense of RCTs can be mounted using one of the very elements that Kantian critics use against them. The whole point of a clinical trial is to find out which therapy is better. In the history of medicine, so many "standard" therapies regarded as effective have subsequently turned out not to be. The clinician will often have little scientifically sound reason for preferring the existing over the experimental therapy. She is in "equipoise," and being exposed to receiving either the existing or experimental therapy is not a comparative harm for her patient.[9] Clinicians can then in good conscience enroll their patients in a randomized trial.

The ethical road for a RCT, though, may still not be clear. Suppose distinctly positive results appear midway through the trial. A notable case of this occurred with the first trials for extracorporeal membrane oxygenation therapy (ECMO) for infants with respiratory failure, now standard of care in some of these situations. In some initial trials in the 1990s, researchers saw distinctly positive results most of the way through, but the trial had not been completed and the sample was small. Between the two trial groups, 30 of 93 infants receiving ECMO died, compared with 54 of 92 who received conventional care—a roughly 50 percent increase in survival with the new therapy (UK Collaborative ECMO Trial Group 1998).[10]

In such a circumstance, what should a conscientious clinician, loyal to the patients involved in the trial, do? Arguably, she should stop the trial and administer the new treatment to everyone who wants it. But the situation thus created would hardly be ideal: with the trial not completed, we gain less certain knowledge about the effectiveness of the new treatment. Benjamin Freedman has argued that, for this reason, clinicians can ethically continue a trial because they are still effectively in equipoise—they still do not really know that the new therapy is more effective. When honest, professional disagreement still exists among clinicians about what is most effective, a trial can still continue. If the trial is not brought to its design completion, doubts about effectiveness of the therapy will just continue, precisely the situation that the RCT is designed in the first place to alleviate.[11]

In summary, how can RCTs be justified? (1) Subjects should be well informed of the randomization before they consent, with adequate information on what will be provided in all arms of the trial. The risks of error about effectiveness in both directions should be described as accurately as possible, not glossed with "hopefulness" and "promise." (2) "Equipoise," if it really does characterize clinicians' situation, can reconcile randomization with their fundamental obligation to patients. The effectiveness of the new therapy is not yet known, but the evidence for the effectiveness of existing therapy may not be very good either, especially if that therapy has not itself been subjected to a good clinical trial. (3) This justification of an RCT is harder to make if, before the trial has been completed, positive results make the new therapy appear to be distinctly more effective. On the other hand, unless most trials are run to their completion, medicine will become less evidence-based, with real costs in human lives and health. Perhaps those costs in life and health over time in the society create a culture of accepting RCTs and typically their completion with few moral qualms. At the edges, utilitarian considerations may soften a stricter view of what Kantian respect for persons requires. The ethical tensions remain, but we live with them, with most people gaining from the scientifically better research.

When do placebo-control trials violate basic principles of medical ethics?

When no standard therapy for a disease exists (first-in-class therapy trials), randomized PCTs of new treatments with properly informed and consenting participants are ethically acceptable. The situation is very different for next-in-class therapy trials when there is already a presumably effective standard therapy. Then, as the well-known Declaration of Helsinki on research in medicine stated in 1989, "the use of a placebo control is inappropriate, and the novel intervention ought to be compared with an active control" (an existing approved therapy).[12] The reasoning is patient-focused: How can it be ethical to enroll patients in an RCT with a placebo control arm if an existing therapy is already known to be better than a placebo? Absent some special circumstance, the use of a placebo arm violates the obligation of healthcare providers to serve the best interests of their patients.

Could a defense of PCTs in these situations rely on patients' informed consent to be part of such a trial? They would have to be informed not just that they might be in the trial's placebo arm, but that, if they were, they would be getting an almost certainly inferior "treatment" (the placebo). Some patients might want to consent to that in the interest of contributing to the development of effective new therapies, but even that altruistic goal is largely a delusion. The primary purpose in developing the therapy being tested is for it to qualify as another next-in-class drug, not a first-in-class, initial effective drug for the condition. If potential participants are fully and not misleadingly informed of the situation, how likely is it that a sufficient number will volunteer to generate convincing trial results? Moreover, in addition to the informed consent that must be obtained, the subjects must also not be harmed, according to the Nuremberg and Helsinki Declaration principles. If they end up being randomized into the placebo arm, won't they suffer harm compared to getting standard treatment?

These considerations constitute an extremely strong ethical case against using placebo controls to test new next-in-class medicines where effective therapies already exist for the targeted condition. This ethical judgment, however, has hardly limited the use of placebos in actual research practice. The US Food and Drug Administration (FDA), for example, has been adamant in not limiting PCTs to first-in-class therapies. It is understandable why major pharmaceutical firms want to be allowed to use PCTs without active controls for testing next-in-class therapies, for they can then gain approval for potentially lucrative new drugs that add nothing better to patients' therapeutic options. But why would an agency that authorizes medicines as safe and effective so readily accept PCT results without requiring active controls as well?[13]

A PCT in these situations puts participating clinicians in the ethically dubious position of deliberately not providing patients an existing effective therapy. Why would they do that? Perhaps because many others do it. Or because some relatively hidden or indirect self-interest is present. In any case, the larger picture is that excessive use of PCTs in effectiveness trials leads to weaker evidence about best therapy. Real, clinically usable, evidence-based medicine suffers. The Helsinki

Declaration was correct in generally limiting the ethical use of PCTs to trials of first-in-class therapies.

How do international contexts affect the ethics of trials?

Controversies about PCTs' ethical justification arise in another context, too: international variation in standards of care. Though a PCT to test a new and less expensive treatment or dosage may not be ethical in a high-income country where an already available treatment is standard of care, could a PCT trial be justified if done in a low-income country where that treatment is not standard of care and simply not affordable? Would it be justified if done by researchers from the low-income country, though not when done by researchers from the high-income country?

These questions came to the fore in trials for a shorter course of zidovudine (AZT) to prevent maternal–child transmission of human immunodeficiency virus (HIV) in the 1990s. The "076 protocol" that had emerged as standard of care in high-income countries involved considerable prenatal testing, five pills a day for twelve weeks prenatally, intravenous administration during delivery, followed for six weeks by a four-times-a-day regimen and no breastfeeding during that period. The $800–1,500 cost was as much as a hundred times the annual per capita spending on all healthcare in some low-income countries.[14] How many of the benefits of the full 076 course of treatment would still be produced by a shorter and more affordable course of AZT? Good scientific study design required a placebo arm since the most relevant comparison was between the current situation of no AZT in the low-income country and the experimental short course.

The ethical tension here is between exploitation and realistic opportunity. If such PCTs would be unethical in high-income countries, would conducting them in a low-income country exploit the meager resource situation of that country? It arguably would if the research was being done to see whether the short course might work well enough to be used even in high-income populations. But if the trial is conducted to develop a feasible treatment for low-income countries, particularly the country in which the trial is conducted, why isn't a PCT permissible? Compared to no trial at all, no participant would end up worse off for participating even if she received a placebo, for her realistic alternative is no treatment at all.

Perhaps this conflict can be resolved by requiring that any PCT providing participants less than the best standard of care meet four conditions: (1) the condition the new treatment addresses must be of significant concern to the host community where the trial is conducted; (2) the need to develop such treatment can only be addressed by a study design using placebo controls; (3) the trial, if it succeeds in revealing a new feasible treatment, would benefit the host community; and (4) there is no credible evidence that the trial would expose its participants to greater risk of harm than if they never participated.[15] Under these conditions there is no exploitation. In the vein of Kantian ethics, every individual in the trial is respected as a moral equal (see Chapter 1). Utilitarians, too, can support such trials if better knowledge that benefits other persons, present and future, is likely to be produced.

We should not be under the illusion, however, that these conditions will be readily met if the actual research is done in low-income countries by companies or agencies from high-income countries, including pharmaceutical companies. The economic incentives to use low-income populations are powerful. The four conditions articulated above will need to be followed scrupulously by the pharmaceutical development institutions themselves and checked by reputable watchdog agencies.

When are "challenge" trials for new vaccines acceptable?

Ethical questions are posed as well by so-called *human challenge studies*, also known as the *controlled human infection* model.

Investigators administer an infectious agent to volunteers, either to refine understanding of the properties of that agent or to then test treatments for it. A major advantage of challenge trials is that they often shorten the time needed for a well-designed trial. They are especially useful during a pandemic, such as COVID-19 (SARS-CoV-2), when vaccine development is urgent. They can also be useful in determining the causes of particular maladies.

Sometimes "challenge" research is also self-experimentation (*auto-experimentation*). Primary investigators test treatments on themselves, believing that it would be unethical to expose subjects to the risks that an experimental treatment may involve. Auto-experimentation by commendably conscientious and brave researchers has a distinguished history in medicine. Very significant advances in the treatment of gastritis, peptic ulcer disease, and adenocarcinoma, for example, were spurred by the discovery that the *Helicobacter pylori* (*H. pylori*) bacterium often caused these conditions, not stress, as had been thought before. In 1984, Barry Marshall, one of the two discoverers, underwent gastric biopsy to make sure he did not carry *H. pylori* and then he immediately infected himself. In 2005, he and his collaborator were awarded the Nobel Prize for Medicine.[16]

In the case of vaccines, the aim of challenge trials is not to discover the virus that causes an illness (that is already known), but whether a vaccine is effective in preventing it. The vaccine is administered to the trial group, who are then exposed to the virus. Compared to ordinary vaccine trials, challenge trials typically allow more careful selection of participants to control for confounding variables (e.g., other disease conditions). Challenge trials also enable investigators to control the amount of infectious agent to which participants are exposed. In situations where an effective treatment for the condition exists, such trials are not so controversial, for if the vaccine does not successfully prevent contracting the disease, participants can be effectively treated. Challenge trials become much more questionable when no very effective treatment exists. COVID-19 presented precisely this situation. To be sure, most of the few participants who got infected despite having had the vaccine survived with the help of extraordinary hospital care. Some of them, however, suffer from "long COVID."

In 2021, the Human Challenge Programme of the British government's Vaccines Task Force comprehensively addressed the ethical as well as technical considerations involved in running challenge trials. Among the considerations that emerged, in addition to well-informed consent, two were key: (1) challenge trials must be justified by a need for them that cannot be met with a different, less questionable trial design, and (2) the risks to participants must be minimized and manageable. The Task Force argued that the careful challenge trials being readied at the time qualified on both scores. Especially important was that participants could be selected to minimize their risks—for example, confining participants to those thirty and younger with no other risk factors. Their risk of death was calculated to be 1:250,000 and of hospitalization 1:4,900. That does not seem an unacceptable risk, as participants already had some of that risk just living amid the pandemic. And if the trial were to reveal an effective vaccine, they themselves, not only the general population, would likely benefit.[17]

In such carefully managed circumstances, why would a challenge trial be unethical? The mere *act of exposing* well-informed volunteers to the virus is no sound objection unless that exposure creates a greater risk than we believe it is responsible to ask any volunteer to take or unless a better-designed and -managed trial would lower that risk. Medical research needs to be very careful in using challenge trials, but this can be said of virtually all trials. With challenge trials, we do not end up in a sharp clash between a "No" from a Kantian ethic of respect for individual persons and a "Yes" from utilitarians pointing to aggregate benefits.

When do exclusions and priorities unjustly affect disadvantaged groups?

Many ethical violations in biomedical research involve improperly *including* people in clinical trials, often by failing to obtain adequately informed and voluntary consent. Injustices in research can also occur by *excluding* people from research or failing to devote sufficient research attention to them.

Insufficient numbers of women have been involved in notable research, and the different effects of medications on women have gone undetected and ignored. The adverse effects on women of Ambien, a popular sedative and sleep aid, went undetected when fewer were involved in its clinical trials and no one thought to look for differences in women's and men's reactions. As it turned out, the proper dose for women is only half that prescribed for men. For years women suffered the ill effects of being prescribed too high a dose.[18]

The distribution of research funding is also a problem, adversely affecting Black and other populations of color. The 90/10 ratio of research funding for diseases dominant in higher-income countries compared to diseases of lower-income nations has long been noticed (see Chapter 12). A similar disparity likely afflicts comparative research efforts within high-income nations. In the United States, for example, the greater healthcare needs and poorer health of Black Americans as a group can be significantly attributed to social determinants of health—income, housing and location, and education. Yet research related to the social determinants of health generally receives much less funding than research on direct medical determinants. These matters need more attention if health disparities between Black and White populations are to be narrowed, but they do not receive it. No wonder improvements in Black citizens' health driven by good research come more slowly.[19]

Many Native American/Alaska Native tribes have experienced research conducted in questionable ways, creating distinct mistrust of research investigators in these communities. Stereotypes and lack of respect for native culture and beliefs add to the problem. In repairing these breaches and lapses, some tribal voices advocate ethical treatment of communities in addition to the individual participant focus of protections provided by the Belmont Report's principles. In this view, justice in research activities should focus on reciprocity: the "group receives fair compensation in return for what its individual members contribute to research activity."[20] That can be done by prioritizing research on the issues most affecting tribal health. That will easily not occur if so much of the research is driven by outside funding and the interests and perspectives of those who provide it.

These injustices warrant the concerted, sustained attention of everyone involved in biomedical research.

Concluding thoughts

Medical research on human subjects can easily violate ethical norms. The basic principles established in the Nuremberg Code of 1949 have held ever since: human beings must not simply be used for the greater good of medicine. Over the ensuing decades, however, the Code's principles have required refinement and have harbored many new controversies.

RCTs contributed greatly to the advance of evidence-based medicine. Initial ethical doubts about them have been persuasively handled by a careful restriction: subjects should not be randomized into an arm of what is known to be inferior treatment when that would risk significant harm to participants. In particular, it is rarely permissible to randomize subjects into placebo-control arms when an effective therapy for the condition already exists. Even if the new treatment might be more effective, have fewer side effects, or be less expensive, existing therapy, not a placebo, should be used in a control arm.

Variation in standard of care between low- and high-income countries raises special issues. PCTs can be conducted in a low-income country if the condition being treated is significant for that country, if scientifically sound findings cannot be obtained without a placebo arm, if advances developed through the trial are likely to benefit and be affordable for the host country, and if there is no credible evidence that trial participants will be any worse off from participation than if the trials were never conducted.

Challenge trials in which participants are deliberately exposed to a dangerous contagious disease may seem highly dubious ethically. In particular circumstances, such as vaccine development in a pandemic, however, and with careful selection of subjects to minimize risk, they, too, can be justified from a Kantian as well as utilitarian perspective.

The basic anchoring principle of research ethics—the need for subjects' genuinely informed consent—still leaves many decisions open. What is adequate information? Should a trial be stopped if early results are good? What is true "equipoise" for conscientious physicians in an RCT? In what circumstances may placebo arms still be used when there is already a good therapy? Moreover, injustices to women and disadvantaged minorities need to be repaired, and, given the inertia of the status quo, improvements for these groups will not come soon enough.

The debates and refinements in research ethics will certainly continue.

5

HOW SHOULD DEATH BE DEFINED AND DETERMINED?

What is death?

What is death, and how can we determine when someone has died? The answers have implications in medicine, notably for organ donation and the removal of life-sustaining treatment. The topic of death also raises deep philosophical questions about the nature of human beings.

Before addressing current controversies regarding the determination of death, we need to note three related but distinct ways of talking about death.

The first is the *concept* or *definition* of death. Death is defined as the end of life or the opposite of life or the termination of life. That concept has not changed.

By contrast, the *criteria* for determining that death has occurred have been affected by advances in medicine. The traditional criteria are cardiovascular: irreversible cessation of the functions of the heart and lungs. The newer criteria are neurological: irreversible cessation of neurological activity, often referred to as *brain death*. In the past, there was no need to distinguish between these two sets of criteria because they occurred virtually together. Catastrophic brain injury would quickly lead to respiratory failure, followed by permanent cardiac arrest. Conversely, when the heart and lungs completely ceased functioning, the brain also stopped functioning. The two sets of criteria diverged in the 1950s with the development of mechanical ventilators to assist breathing. Cardiopulmonary resuscitation (CPR) combines techniques to restart a stopped heart (by chest compressions or defibrillation) with artificial respiration provided by a ventilator. The aim is often to preserve intact brain function until spontaneous circulation and breathing occur. However, they may not occur, raising the question: Should patients whose hearts are beating and who are breathing, though with mechanical assistance, be considered alive or dead?

The third issue concerns the *clinical tests* to determine if the criteria have been met. Older, traditional tests included checking for a pulse to determine if the heart was pumping blood or checking to determine if the person was still breathing, perhaps by putting a mirror in front of the mouth or nose. The clinical tests for neurological criteria are more advanced technologically, such as lack of activity (flat-lining) on an electroencephalogram (EEG).

What is brain death?

Brain death is determined by the use of neurological criteria. It goes back to 1968, when a committee chaired by Henry Beecher issued a report entitled, "A Definition of Irreversible Coma: Report of the Ad Hoc Committee of the Harvard Medical School to Examine the Definition of Brain Death." The Beecher report essentially said that patients on life support whose brain function has completely and irreversibly ceased should be declared dead and removed from respirators.

In 1981, the US President's Commission for the Study of Ethical Problems in Medicine and Biomedical and Behavioral Research issued a landmark report, *Defining Death: Medical, Legal, and Ethical Issues in the Determination of Death*. That report was the basis for the Uniform Determination of Death Act (UDDA), a model state law. The UDDA offers both cardiovascular and neurological criteria for the legal determination of death. It states that an individual who has suffered *either* (1) irreversible cessation of circulatory and respiratory functions, *or* (2) irreversible cessation of all functions of the entire brain, including the brainstem, is dead. The latter is called "whole-brain death."[1]

In all 50 US states, whether by statute, regulation, or judicial decision, physicians may declare patients who have sustained irreversible cessation of all brain functions to be dead. All states and the District of Columbia have adopted the UDDA. Nevertheless, critics have maintained that there is ongoing confusion about the legal standard of death by neurological criteria: "medical standards of determination vary, public acceptance is inconsistent, and responses to family objections have ranged from continuation of organ support indefinitely to unilateral discontinuation of organ support. . . . Because of medicolegal variations, a person could be considered 'dead' in one state and 'not dead' in another."[2] This happened in the case of Jahi McMath, a matter that we address below.

Are neurological criteria a better indicator of death?

One reason for the shift to neurological criteria for determining death was the development of techniques that can restart the heart and mechanical ventilation. CPR can sustain patients who have suffered cardiac arrest due to, for example, a heart attack. Such patients are clearly not dead since heart and lung function can be restored. The mere absence of breath or a pulse does not indicate *irreversible* cessation of heart or lung function. By contrast, once the brain stops functioning, there's no way to mechanically take over its functions or restart it. For this reason, neurological criteria may seem a better indicator of death than cardiovascular.

That does not necessarily mean that diagnoses of brain death are always correct. In a 2009 Hong Kong case, Suzanne Chin, a lawyer in her forties, suffered a heart attack, was taken to the hospital, went into a coma, and was declared brain dead.

(Hong Kong, like the UK, regards brain death to occur when the brainstem irreversibly ceases to function.) The head of the intensive care unit, two neurologists, and a cardiologist advised her husband to take her off life support because, "simply put, there was no hope."[3] Her husband refused. Three days later, she woke up from her coma. She recovered within a week and left the hospital. As of 2017, the latest information available, she is fully recovered, still practicing law, and living in Singapore.

What do we learn from the case of Suzanne Chin? She believes that a miracle occurred, that she recovered from brain death. However, it is entirely possible that Ms. Chin was improperly diagnosed. We need to remember that, in addition to needing criteria for death and clinical tests for these criteria, the tests must be administered and interpreted. Doctors can improperly perform or interpret the tests, even in high-quality medical centers.

What are the practical advantages of neurological criteria?

Other reasons for the shift to neurological criteria are practical, rather than medical or scientific. Should we be spending huge amounts of money to keep patients for whom the chance of recovery is practically nonexistent on life support indefinitely? If death is defined as the total loss of all brain function, it allows the removal of such patients from ventilators, freeing them up for other patients who could benefit from them.

Another practical reason for the movement to neurological criteria has to do with organ donation. More than 100,000 solid organ transplants are performed worldwide every year. In the United States alone, more than 106,000 people are on the national transplant waiting list as of January 2021; seventeen people die each day waiting for an organ transplant. Cadaver organ donation can potentially save hundreds of thousands of lives, but it also poses a dilemma. Transplant surgeons need to remove vital organs as quickly as possible before they deteriorate and become unusable. However, removing vital organs from living patients would cause their deaths, which would violate both laws against homicide and the presumptive ethical principle against the intentional killing of innocent human beings.

A neurological standard for death solves the dilemma. Once there is irreversible loss of brain function, indicated by a flat EEG, the patient is determined to be dead. The deceased donor is kept on a ventilator to continue respiration and circulation, necessary to keep the organs viable until surgery to remove the organs can be arranged and performed. The maintenance of respiration and circulation by mechanical means is not evidence that the patient is alive because it is the irreversible loss of brain function that determines death. Furthermore, once the brain dies, the death of all the other organs inevitably follows, usually fairly quickly. It is hard to see the point of waiting for the cessation of respiration and circulation, which will render perfectly good organs nonviable, when death is inevitable in any case.

Are there scientific arguments in favor of brain death?

Defenders of brain death argue that while it has practical advantages, this is not the only reason for adopting neurological criteria. Indeed, it would be ethically objectionable to characterize individuals as dead just because you want to transplant their organs! However, defenders of brain death maintain that there are independent scientific reasons for regarding neurological criteria as superior to cardiovascular criteria in determining death.

Dr. James Bernat[4] argues that, for numerous reasons, whole-brain death should be the medical and legal standard for determining death. First, whole-brain death fits best with the common, ordinary meaning of death. Second, death is a biological concept, and it is biological organisms that die. Third, death is an all-or-nothing concept. Although one may be recently dead or long dead, no one is a little bit dead, any more than anyone is a little bit pregnant. Fourth, death refers to an event, not a process. Just as the moment of birth is recorded, so is the time of death. For both medical and legal purposes, we need a conception of death as an event that occurs at a particular moment in time.

Bernat's argument does not rest solely on common sense or social needs. He also argues that the whole brain is the organism's "critical system." The brainstem, or lower brain, controls automatic functions such as heart rate, breathing, sleeping, and swallowing. The neocortex, or higher brain, controls sensory perception, consciousness, and thinking. When all of these functions are irretrievably lost, the organism is no longer functioning as a whole. That is what explains and justifies regarding the irreversible loss of the functioning of the whole brain as the death of the organism.

What are the arguments against brain death?

Alan Shewmon[5] rejects Bernat's claim that the whole brain is the organism's critical system, making its death the death of the organism. According to Shewmon, there is no one critical system of an organism, but rather multiple important systems. In addition, brain dead individuals exhibit several functions of living organisms. If they are fed artificially, they digest food and excrete waste. Their wounds heal, they grow, they may undergo sexual maturation. Some brain-dead women have gestated fetuses while on life support and even given birth. Can someone who undergoes processes like these, and who retains some essential neurological functions, such as regulated secretion of hypothalamic hormones, be said to be dead? A related point is that people who are declared brain dead while attached to ventilators do not appear dead. Their skin is moist and warm. Their color is normal. Their hearts continue to beat, they continue to breathe. For this reason, it is often very difficult for their families to accept that they are actually dead.

Shewmon also disputes the notion that brain death is inevitably and quickly followed by the death of the patient. It depends on how much support they are given. He relays the story of TK, who survived for nearly two decades after being diagnosed as brain dead after contracting meningitis. His doctors suggested discontinuing life support, but his mother refused. Eventually he was transferred to his home, where he remained on a ventilator and a feeding tube, requiring only routine nursing care. According to Shewmon, "TK has much to teach about the necessity of the brain for somatic integrative unity. There is no question that he became 'brain dead' at age four; neither is there any question that he is still alive at age nineteen."[6]

What is the significance of the case of Jahi McMath?

Jahi McMath was a 13-year-old Black girl from Oakland, California who underwent a tonsillectomy, a standard treatment for sleep apnea in children. Shortly after waking up, she started coughing up blood. The nurses at UCSF Benioff's Children's Hospital assured her mother that this was normal and showed her how to suction blood from her daughter's mouth. However, within a few hours she began to hemorrhage. Repeated pleas for medical attention from family members were to no avail. After several hours, her grandmother, who was a nurse, noted that Jahi's oxygen saturation levels had dropped to seventy-nine percent. She yelled to the medical staff, who ran to intubate Jahi. She heard a doctor say, "Oh, shit, her heart has stopped."[7]

Two days later, on December 12, 2013, two hospital tests showed that she was brain dead. California follows a version of the UDDA which says that someone who has suffered irreversible cessation of all functions of the brain is dead. Accordingly, Jahi was pronounced dead; the following month a coroner in California issued her death certificate.

California law also requires hospitals to permit "a reasonably brief period of accommodation" before disconnecting a ventilator. This period should be long enough to allow the family to gather, while taking account of the needs of other patients and potential patients for life support. Over the next few days, a social worker repeatedly urged the family to make a plan for taking her off the ventilator. She also suggested that they consider donating her organs. They refused. Her mother, Nailah, "didn't understand how Jahi could be dead when her skin was moist and soft, and she occasionally moved her arms, ankles, and hips."[8] The family believed that the diagnosis of brain death by physicians and the hospital was an attempt to cover up their negligence. "No one was listening to us. I can't prove it, but I really feel in my heart: if Jahi was a little White girl, I feel we would have gotten a little more help and attention."[9]

On January 5, 2014, Jahi was moved to St. Peter's University Hospital in New Brunswick, New Jersey. New Jersey was specifically chosen because it is the only state where death cannot be declared "in violation of an individual's religious beliefs." While some US states, including California, Illinois, and New York, require hospitals to make "reasonable accommodations" to give the families some time to accept the death and decide whether to donate their child's organs, only New Jersey makes a blanket exception for those who reject brain death on religious grounds.

When Jahi arrived in New Jersey, she hadn't been fed for more than three weeks and her organs were failing. The chief of pediatrics at St. Peter's wrote in her notes that there was no hope of brain recovery. Nevertheless, she received a tracheal tube and a feeding tube that provided nutrition and vitamins. She remained in intensive care at St. Peter's, her treatment costs, approximately $150,000 a week, covered by Medicaid.

Had Jahi suffered "irreversible cessation of all functions of the brain"? Her mother noted that Jahi's heart rate, which tended to be high, lowered when a music therapist played the harp in the intensive care unit. Tests performed by a Cuban neurologist, Calixto Machado, revealed that her heart rate also responded to her mother's voice. Her mother recorded videos of Jahi moving her hands and feet, allegedly in response to her mother's commands, and said, "I knew that Jahi was in there."[10]

In addition, Jahi began menstruating in the hospital, a process mediated by the hypothalamus, a part of the brain, suggesting that not all neurological function had ceased. A magnetic resonance imaging (MRI) scan showed that, while her brainstem was nearly destroyed, large areas of her cerebrum were structurally intact. Alan Shewmon, interviewed in *The New Yorker* article cited above, wondered if she might have a condition known as *ischemic penumbra*, where cerebral blood flow is so diminished that it cannot be detected by standard tests, leading to a misdiagnosis of brain death. Shewmon speculated that Jahi might be in a minimally conscious state, in which patients are partly or intermittently aware of their surroundings.

This was a tragic story. First, the death of a healthy 13-year-old girl after what should have been a routine tonsillectomy is shocking. Second, the hospital staff failed to respond to the family's pleas for medical attention, which the family was convinced was because of their race. Finally, the family suspected that their daughter was declared dead to cover up the hospital's negligence, or to harvest her organs, or both. The failure of communication between the hospital staff and the patient's family led the family to feel dismissed and disrespected, making trust, which is foundational to the doctor–patient relationship, impossible.

There is another reason why the story of Jahi McMath is important in bioethics. In addition to maintaining that Jahi was incorrectly diagnosed as brain dead, the family did not accept brain death as the correct criterion of death in the first place. Some have ascribed the family's denial that Jahi was dead to a simple failure to understand that brain death is real death and that Jahi was now a corpse, not a severely brain-injured patient. Noted bioethicist Arthur Caplan said that the doctors in the facility where Jahi was transferred were "trying to ventilate and otherwise treat a corpse." He also predicted—wrongly—that "she is going to start to decompose."[11] This dismissal of the family's view ignores a real debate in the bioethics community about what death is.

In late August 2014, Jahi was discharged from St. Peter's. She moved into an apartment with her family, where she received round-the-clock care from her mother and from nurses paid for by Medicaid. Her family hoped that she could eventually recover from her catastrophic brain injury. However, in June 2018, she began to bleed internally and was taken back to the hospital for exploratory surgery. When more surgery was proposed, her mother decided to "let her go." Jahi was removed from life support and died in the hospital on June 22, 2018. The New Jersey death certificate cites liver failure and hypoxic brain injury as the causes of death.

Jahi McMath is in the unusual position of having two death certificates: one dated December 12, 2013, and the other June 22, 2018. Is one of these false, as her family claimed? Or are both correct, making her death a matter of location and jurisdiction? Should we say that, prior to the irreversible cessation of cardiovascular functioning on June 22, 2018, Jahi was not actually dead, but rather "as good as dead"? Or was she neither dead nor as good as dead, but rather a seriously ill patient in need of treatment?

In part, our responses to these questions depend on whether Jahi McMath had been correctly diagnosed as brain dead. There is also the further question of whether brain death is the right standard for determining death. Should we acknowledge that brain death is not biological death and revert to cardiovascular criteria?

What would happen if we gave up brain death?

Some argue that neurological criteria are now so entrenched both in law and medicine that it would be impossible to go back to cardiovascular criteria. They also argue that a return to cardiovascular criteria would greatly reduce the number of organs available for transplant, costing countless lives. Others protest that brain death can be viewed as "conceptual gerrymandering,"[12] implemented "for purely utilitarian purposes."[13]

A different solution to the problem of organ donation comes from Robert Truog and Franklin Miller.[14] They agree with Shewmon that brain death is not biological death. However, even if the brain dead are not actually dead, they will never recover even minimal consciousness. From their own subjective perspective, we can say that they are "as good as dead" because they have permanently and irreversibly lost all cognitive function, resulting in the permanent loss of any awareness of themselves or their surroundings. Although they are biologically alive, as Shewmon correctly argues, Truog and Miller maintain that those who are brain dead no longer have a life in an experiential sense. The basic claim is that continued biological life is simply not beneficial to someone whose biographical life has ended. And if they are not benefited, does it make any sense to insist that they nevertheless remain on life support, at great expense, depriving those who might be restored to function by ventilators? In light of these considerations, Truog and Miller argue that we should treat those who are brain dead *as if* they are dead, for legal purposes.

This is not a unique idea in law. For example, there is the notion of someone being "legally blind," which is defined as corrected visual acuity of 20/200. People who are legally blind are not literally blind. They can see. But we acknowledge that their sight is so poor that we are justified in imposing on them certain restrictions, such as refusing to issue them a driver's license, or providing certain benefits to compensate them for their loss of vision. We treat the legally blind *as if* they were blind, for legal purposes. Analogously, we could treat the brain dead who are biologically alive as if they were dead, for legal purposes, such as removal from life support and organ donation.

One potential problem with the "as good as dead" approach is that it might expand the category of those we may treat as if they were dead, in particular, patients in permanent vegetative states (PVS). PVS patients have suffered an irreversible loss of all conscious experience due to extensive damage to the "higher brain," consisting of the cerebrum and the cerebellum. However, their "lower brain" or brainstem, which controls involuntary functions, such as breathing, heartbeat, sleeping, and blood pressure, remains largely intact. Unlike those who are brain dead, some PVS patients can be weaned from respirators and breathe on their own.

On either whole-brain or cardiovascular criteria, PVS patients are alive. To treat them as dead would be to adopt a higher-brain standard for death. While no jurisdiction has adopted the higher-brain standard, it has been supported by a number of scholars. Truog and Miller do not explicitly adopt a higher-brain standard. However, it is hard to see why their account would not apply as much to PVS patients as to those who are brain dead. After all, with the irreversible loss of the capacity for consciousness, defined broadly as including any subjective experience, PVS patients have lost what is valuable in life as much as brain dead patients have.

Should a higher-brain standard be adopted?

In contrast with both the whole-brain and the brainstem standards, higher-brain standard is the view that when the higher brain has irreversibly lost the capacity for consciousness, the patient is dead. One of the most interesting defenses of the higher-brain standard is given by philosopher Jeff McMahan.

McMahan rejects all of Bernat's assumptions. He denies that death is necessarily a biological phenomenon, that it is paradigmatically something that happens to organisms, that we are human organisms, and therefore that our death will be the death of an organism. McMahan defends the claim that we are not human organisms by appeal to a thought experiment.

> If my cerebrum were successfully grafted onto the brain stem of my identical twin brother (whose own cerebrum had been excised), I would then exist in association with what was once his organism. What was formerly my organism would have an intact brain stem and might, therefore, be idling nicely in a persistent vegetative state without even mechanical ventilation. Since I can thus in principle exist separately from the organism that is now mine, I cannot be identical with it.[15]

If we are not human organisms, what are we? McMahan answers that we are embodied minds. If my brain, or specifically the part of my brain that is responsible for my thoughts, my personality, my emotions, etc. could be transplanted into someone else's body, I would continue to exist in that body. The intuition is that we go where our minds go. We die, or cease to exist, when our brains die, or rather, when there is irreversible loss of function in the parts of the brain in which consciousness/mind is realized. This, McMahan stresses, is not a scientific, but rather a metaphysical or philosophical claim about what we essentially are. Given that you and I are essentially embodied minds, *we* die with the permanent loss of function of the higher brain which enables conscious experience. By contrast, an *organism* dies when it irreversibly loses the capacity for integrated functioning. Probably, McMahan says, the best criterion for this is a circulatory-respiratory one, but this is a matter of science, not philosophy.

What are the practical implications of McMahan's embodied mind account? Would it be permissible to remove organs for transplantation from those who have irreversibly lost all capacity for consciousness? McMahan says it would be. "[I]f the person had consented in advance, there would be no moral objection to killing the unoccupied organism in order to use its organs to save the lives of others."[16]

Some who welcome the practical implications of McMahan's view for organ donation reject his metaphysical claim about what we essentially are. David DeGrazia says that the embodied mind account implies that none of us is an animal, which is contrary to scientifically informed common sense. DeGrazia thinks that we are essentially human animals, that our death is the death of the human organism, and the best criterion for human death is the circulatory-respiratory standard, which asserts that "human death is the permanent cessation of circulatory-respiratory function."[17]

Is death an event or a process—and does it matter?

Amir Halevy and Baruch Brody think that the debate between those who defend whole-brain death and those who reject it on the grounds that brain dead individuals display characteristics of living organisms can never be resolved because there isn't a sharp line between life and death that can be identified by one criterion or another. The reality, they argue, is that "different aspects of brain functioning cease at many different times."[18] Any point that is chosen as the definitive moment of brain death is bound to be arbitrary. Therefore, we should give up the quest for a criterion of death and instead address on their own merits practical questions about when life support may be withdrawn and organs may be harvested, as well as when bodies are ready for burial or cremation. They propose that care may be unilaterally withdrawn once there is irreversible cessation of conscious functioning, or higher-brain death. This is not because the permanently unconscious patient is biologically dead, but because "the need to rationally use societal resources outweighs the desire of some persons for unlimited care."[19]

The second question, about when organ harvesting is permissible, should focus on balancing the number of lives saved through increased organ donation against the need for public acceptance of organ donation. It is very likely that the public would not accept the harvesting of organs from PVS patients who were breathing on their own, much less from anencephalic infants. Therefore, Halevy and Brody recommend that organs may be removed for donation when there is irreversible cessation of consciousness combined with apnea which, they say, is close to the point at which we currently harvest organs.

Some theorists balk at the notion that death, as opposed to dying, is a process. Whether or not it is, the "death-is-a-process" account proposed by Halevy and Brody does not seem essential to the proposal of using different answers to the practical questions. For example, DeGrazia and Truog and Miller support current policy for harvesting organs, even though they reject brain death as biological death. They do this by suggesting that we should give up the dead-donor rule, the rule that donors of vital organs must be dead prior to the donation process. Giving up the dead-donor rule is independent of the idea of death as a process.

At this point, it will be helpful to review the numerous issues that have arisen in connection with the definition of death. It is important to note that sometimes people who disagree on one issue agree on another.

Concluding thoughts

Bernat, Shewmon, and Truog and Miller all agree that death is a biological concept. They disagree on whether neurological or cardiovascular criteria should be used to determine that death has occurred. There are also debates within these two camps. Some in the neurological camp favor whole-brain; others, brainstem criteria. Within the cardiovascular camp, some favor a return to traditional criteria; others have proposed various updated accounts.

Another issue is whether individuals should be able to choose between neurological and cardiovascular criteria.

The only state that allows this is New Jersey, which says that neurological criteria cannot be used if this would violate the individual's religious beliefs. Robert Veatch agrees, although he would not limit the choice to religious beliefs. He thinks that, given the persistent disagreement among proponents of whole-brain, cardiocirculatory, and higher-brain criteria, and the reasonableness of all three, individuals and their surrogates should be able to choose among them.[20]

Some argue that the need for a single legal standard of death is more important than allowing individuals to choose their own concept of death based on religious, cultural, or philosophical ideas. A related issue, more technical than appropriate for this chapter, is whether apnea testing is a reliable means of diagnosing brain death and whether it should require the informed consent of the patient's proxy decision-maker.

The move to neurological criteria was motivated, at least in part, by utilitarian considerations about saving lives and conserving resources. Some, like Truog and Miller, think that, while such considerations are important for deciding social policy, they are not relevant to determining death, which is a matter of biology. Others, like Halevy and Brody, think that the quest for one criterion, or set of criteria, for biological death is based on the mistaken idea that death is an event. Once we understand that death is a process, they say, we can decide at which point in the process different actions are appropriate based on social needs.

The debate over the criteria for death depends on a philosophical or metaphysical debate about our nature. Are we essentially organisms, as DeGrazia maintains? If so, then our death should be no different than the deaths of other animals, or at least higher invertebrates. It doesn't matter whether we're talking about the death of a hamster or a human being; the criteria for death should be the same.

Or are we essentially persons, or embodied minds—conscious, feeling, thinking beings: that's what some philosophers, including Robert Veatch and Jeff McMahan think, leading them to adopt a higher-brain criterion of death. As McMahan explains it, when the portion of our brain that enables consciousness, the higher brain, is permanently destroyed, we cease to exist, although our empty organism may continue to live in a permanently unconscious state.

The continuing debate over the definition of death has implications for law, medicine, and policy. In addition, it reflects deep philosophical differences about the nature of personal identity, and when an individual human being's life begins and ends, that go beyond end-of-life care and organ donation.

6

IS PHYSICIAN-ASSISTED DYING AN ETHICAL CHOICE?

In this chapter, we discuss whether and under what conditions individuals should have the right to die and to seek medical help in dying. First, the meanings of important terms are explained. Next, we examine the law in jurisdictions where some form of physician-assisted dying (PAD) is legal. Then we turn to the moral arguments for and against PAD. In our view, there is a strong moral and legal case for permitting PAD. However, there remains the difficulty of deciding which safeguards are legitimate. We end the chapter with a brief discussion of the expansion of PAD in some controversial cases and a brief description of alternative ways of hastening death.

What is euthanasia?

The word "euthanasia" comes from the Greek *eu* which means beautiful or good, and *thanatos* which means death. A good death is understood as one in which there is not undue suffering. However, as Philippa Foot points out, simply causing a death without suffering is not the same as euthanasia.

> For "euthanasia" means much more than a quiet and easy death, or the means of procuring it, or the action of inducing it. The definition specifies only the manner

of the death, and if this were all that was implied a murderer, careful to drug his victim, could claim that his act was an act of euthanasia. We find this ridiculous because we take it for granted that in euthanasia it is death itself, not just the manner of death, that must be kind to the one who dies.[1]

Euthanasia, then, has two necessary elements: the act and the motive. The action is killing, that is, causing the death of another person. The motive or reason for the act is to benefit the one who is killed because, in the circumstances, death is regarded as beneficial or good for that person. In other words, although death ordinarily is regarded as a great harm to the person who is killed, causing someone's death can be merciful, as implied by the term "mercy-killing."

What is the difference between voluntary and nonvoluntary euthanasia?

In *voluntary euthanasia*, the patient requests to be killed. Moreover, for the request to be voluntary, the person must be competent; that is, have the cognitive capacities necessary for making this momentous and irreversible decision. This includes understanding the medical situation; the alternatives to euthanasia, such as hospice care; and the finality of death. In addition, the request cannot be made under pressure or coercion.

Like all euthanasia, *nonvoluntary euthanasia* is done for the sake of the one who is killed, but, in nonvoluntary euthanasia, the individual is incapable of requesting death or giving consent. Examples include infants and young children. Euthanasia would also be nonvoluntary if performed on those with advanced dementia[2] or severe cognitive impairment. Note that we are not speaking at this point of whether nonvoluntary euthanasia is ever justifiable, or under what circumstances, but simply explaining what the category includes.

Theoretically, there can be a third category: *involuntary euthanasia*. Involuntary euthanasia would occur when competent patients who want to go on living are killed for their own good. It might seem that if individuals do not want to die, then it is impossible to kill them for their own good. After all, if they want to go on living, can ending their lives be done "for their sake"? Perhaps. Imagine a case where death would clearly be better for the person than continued life—perhaps where a horribly painful death is imminent and unavoidable—and his desire not to be killed stems from ignorance or an irrational fear. In such a case, we might plausibly speak of involuntary euthanasia. (Again, whether involuntary euthanasia could ever be justified is a separate question from how to categorize the act.) But such a scenario, while possible, is very unlikely. In real-life cases, as opposed to philosophical thought experiments, killing people who want to go on living is not euthanasia, but murder.

What was the Nazi "euthanasia" program?

Some of the opposition to euthanasia stems from the fact that the Nazis used "euthanasia" as a euphemism to describe a program, codenamed Aktion T4, that aimed at killing individuals with mental and physical disabilities. Historians estimate that Aktion T4 claimed the lives of 250,000 persons. It is an irony of history that originally Jews were not eligible for the program, which was limited to "Aryans" who had "incurable" diseases. The Nazis began with the killing of children with genetic diseases and disabling conditions. Such children were taken from their parents, ostensibly for "treatment." After they were killed, their parents were told that they had died natural deaths.

This program was extended by a directive from Adolf Hitler in 1939, to allow physicians to kill people who were considered incurable, including adults with a range of conditions, including deafness, mental illness, alcoholism, and "congenital imbecility." They were poisoned, starved to death, and eventually killed in gas chambers like those that were later used in Auschwitz and other concentration camps. "For that reason, the so-called euthanasia program is often characterized as a 'trial run' or 'dress rehearsal' for the Holocaust."[3] It demonstrated to Nazi officials that they could carry out mass killings of Jews and others in a systematic and efficient way without raising too much opposition.

One result of this tragic history is that the term "euthanasia" has become taboo in some places. However, the fact that the Nazis used the term "euthanasia" as a euphemism for mass murder is not an argument against genuine euthanasia. The Nazi program was never, even at the start, *euthanasia*; that is, the compassionate ending of life for the individual's own good. People were not killed because they experienced unbearable, unmitigable suffering or because they wanted to die but rather because those who had disabling conditions or incurable diseases were considered "unworthy of life" and a drain on society: "useless eaters" in the repellant Nazi terminology.

What is self-administered physician-assisted dying?

In the United States, euthanasia is prohibited everywhere. However, in several US jurisdictions, physicians are permitted, under certain carefully delineated conditions, to write prescriptions for lethal medication, usually pills, that the person then administers herself. This form of assisted dying goes by various names: death with dignity, aid-in-dying, medical aid in dying (MAID), and PAD. In this chapter, we use the term "self-administered PAD" for this kind of hastened death, although we recognize that "PAD" is also used to cover both self-administered PAD and voluntary euthanasia in jurisdictions where both are allowed. In euthanasia, the physician typically administers a lethal injection, although sometimes the physician gives the patient a lethal drink. In self-administered PAD, by contrast, the physician does not directly cause the patient's death but rather writes a lethal prescription which patients can then use to end their lives.

Are there good reasons to prohibit voluntary euthanasia while allowing self-administered PAD? In our view, there is no *intrinsic* moral difference between them. In both cases the physician does something intentionally to bring about the patient's death out of compassion for the patient who requests it. Writing a prescription is more remote in time from the death than giving a lethal injection, but that does not negate its role as a causal factor. Moreover, the conditions justifying euthanasia apply equally to self-administered PAD. If, for example, the request was not voluntary, or death was not in fact in the patient's interest, the prescription for self-administered PAD would be as wrong as euthanasia. The fact that it is the patient, and not the physician, who administers the lethal dose in self-administered PAD does not lessen the physician's moral responsibility for the outcome.

There could be a pragmatic reason for banning euthanasia while permitting self-administered PAD: namely, concerns about voluntariness. If someone requests a prescription for lethal pills, deliberately puts them into her mouth and swallows them, that is a clear indication of her intention to die. By contrast, if someone else gives her a lethal injection, we have less evidence of her desire to die. Lethal injections could also be given to sleeping or unconscious patients. Thus, self-administered PAD may seem safer than euthanasia.

It may also give more room for a change of mind. We know that not everyone who asks for and receives a lethal prescription ends up using it. In 2020, 370 prescriptions were reported to have been given to dying Oregonians who qualified for the Act; 245 people died using the prescribed medications. Some died before they had the chance to take the medication; others decided against using it. This suggests that some terminally ill people ask for the prescription not because they are sure that they want to die, but because they want to preserve this option if life becomes unbearable. It is possible that it would be harder to change one's mind after scheduling a home visit for euthanasia than simply not taking the prescribed pills. Certainly, we want to make it easy for people to change their minds, so if self-administered PAD accomplishes that better than euthanasia, the former would be preferable.

However, patients who request euthanasia can also change their minds. This is demonstrated in the documentary, *24 & Ready to Die*,[4] in which a young Belgian woman, Emily, is granted her request for euthanasia for unbearable suffering from severe, untreatable depression. In the film, the psychiatrists explain to Emily that, on the day of the appointment, they will come to her home and have another chat where they will ask her explicitly if this was really, really what she wanted. They stress to her that she can say "No" until the last moment. "Even after the needle goes in, you can still say, 'no.'" This is because the first injection is just a sedative that renders the patient unconscious. It is the second injection that causes death. They also emphasize that no one would think less of her if she changed her mind.

In fact, Emily did change her mind, deciding not to have euthanasia on the day of her appointment. Her life did not seem so terrible during the two weeks between deciding to have euthanasia and the date when it was scheduled, perhaps because she knew her suffering would come to an end. Sadly, her feelings of hopefulness did not last. Emily died peacefully by euthanasia on August 25, 2018, surrounded by those she loved. Nevertheless, her story reveals that doctors can emphasize to their patients who request euthanasia that they can change their minds. If euthanasia is given only to patients who request it, and if they understand that they can change their minds at any time, even after the first needle goes in, then euthanasia allows for a change of mind as much as PAD. It is the creation and implementation of the eligibility and due care criteria, not the method of causing death, that matters.

There is another reason in favor of allowing euthanasia and not merely self-administered PAD. Some patients who are

terminally ill and experiencing unbearable suffering may be
unable to self-administer the lethal medication, due to paral-
ysis, for example, or an inability to swallow. Why should eligibility for assisted dying depend on something as irrelevant
and arbitrary as the ability to place pills into one's mouth or
to swallow? If all the other criteria are met, it seems absurd to
limit the right to die to those with the physical ability to self-
administer the medication.

What is the equal protection argument for PAD?

The right of competent patients to refuse medical treatment,
including life-prolonging treatment, is well-established in US
law. However, the culture of medicine, which tends to focus
on aggressive treatment to cure illness and prevent or forestall
death may be in opposition to this legal right. Terminally ill
patients, in particular, often find themselves on an "end-of-
life conveyor belt," resulting in treatment that does not benefit
them and which they do not want.[5]

The legal right of competent patients to refuse medical
treatment, even when the refusal is made in order to die, has
led some commentators to argue that competent patients
also have a legal right to die by self-administered PAD. They
reason that for the law to allow some patients to choose death
by refusing life-saving treatment while denying the same right
to choose death to patients for whom there is no life-saving
treatment to refuse is simply discriminatory. Either both
groups of patients have the right to die or neither does. This
is known as the "equal protection argument." It has been used
by a number of litigants, commentators, and judges, including
Chief Justice Barbara Rothstein of the US District Court for the
Western District of Washington,[6] when she ruled that terminally ill, competent, adult patients have a constitutional right
to at least self-administered PAD (referred to at the time of her
decision as "physician-assisted suicide").

Ultimately, the Supreme Court of the United States rejected the equal protection argument of the lower courts.[7] The Court unanimously ruled that a right to assisted suicide is not protected by the Constitution's guarantee of due process and equal protection and that there is no federal constitutional right to MAID. At the same time, the Court left open the possibility that state legislatures should be permitted to debate the issue and decide for themselves if the benefits of legalizing such assistance outweighed the risks.

Where is self-administered PAD legal in the United States?

The first US state to legalize self-administered PAD was Oregon. Its 1994 Death with Dignity Act (DWDA) has been the model for all the subsequent legalizing states. It restricts self-administered PAD to competent, terminally ill patients. Patients must request a prescription for lethal pills in writing, twice over a period of two weeks. The physician must ascertain a patient's competence, though there is no requirement for an evaluation by a psychiatrist.

The attending physician must get a second opinion from another physician who is not involved in the patient's care that patient is terminally ill—death is predicted to occur within six months—and that the request is voluntary (i.e., the patient understands that the pills will cause death and is not under any kind of external pressure or coercion).

Oregon has now been joined by ten jurisdictions in the United States. Nine passed laws legalizing self-administered PAD: Washington (2009), Vermont (2013), California (2016), Colorado (2016), District of Columbia (2017), Hawaii (2019), New Jersey (2019), Maine (2019), and New Mexico (2021). In addition, PAD became legal in Montana by court decision when its Supreme Court ruled in *Baxter v. Montana* (2009) that the Rights of the Terminally Ill Act protects from liability a physician who prescribes aid in dying.

What is the legal status of PAD elsewhere in the world?

Canada legalized PAD in February 2015, by decision of its Supreme Court in *Carter v. Canada*, which struck down criminal laws prohibiting assisted suicide as contrary to the Canadian Charter of Rights and Freedoms. The Court ruled void the parts of the Criminal Code that prohibited PAD to competent adult persons who clearly consent to the termination of life and have grievous and irremediable medical conditions that cause enduring suffering that is intolerable to the individual. In March 2021, the eligibility requirements of Canada's law were expanded to include individuals whose death is not reasonably foreseeable. In Canada, MAID allows both self-administered PAD and euthanasia.

PAD is legal, under certain circumstances, in five of Australia's six states, Austria, Belgium, Finland, Germany, Luxembourg, the Netherlands, Spain, and Switzerland. In Colombia, euthanasia is legal, but self-administered PAD is not. In Belgium, Luxembourg, the Netherlands, and Spain, both euthanasia and self-administered PAD are legal. Euthanasia is more common in the Netherlands because most physicians consider lethal injection more reliable and therefore more likely to result in the desired end—the death of the patient—than prescribing pills. A unique feature of Dutch law is that it is not based on the patient's right to die, but rather on the right of physicians to help their patients to die. Assisted suicide remains a crime in the Netherlands, but if physicians follow the due care requirements, they are exempt from criminal liability.

In Switzerland, assisted suicide, whether through the aid of a physician or nonphysician, is legal if it is not done from a selfish motive. The legalization of assisted suicide in Switzerland was based on the following argument: if suicide is not a crime, then assisting a suicide cannot be a crime. This argument has nothing to do with physicians and their role in the care of grievously ill patients. Switzerland is unique in the world in not requiring the participation of a physician as a safeguard in assisted death laws.[8]

What are the moral arguments in favor of PAD?

As mentioned earlier, the term "physician-assisted dying" can be used to cover both self-administered PAD and voluntary euthanasia. Since the moral arguments in favor are the same for both, that is how it is used in this section. Supporters of PAD maintain that when people have incurable illnesses that cause them great suffering, they should have the right to medical assistance that will provide them with a good death. This can be broken down into two arguments: the argument from suffering and the argument from autonomy.

The argument from suffering is based on the idea that someone who is terminally ill and is going to die soon anyway should not be forced to go through unbearable and unrelievable suffering if that individual prefers a quick and painless death. We regard euthanizing pets to prevent suffering as the right thing to do. Why shouldn't people be entitled to the same consideration? On this argument, it is cruel to force people to suffer in this way, which is why the argument from suffering is sometimes called the argument from cruelty.

The argument from autonomy says that, in general, people should be able to make the most important decisions about how their lives go so long as they do not harm others or violate their rights. This includes decisions about how one's life ends. Most people regard how they die as having special significance. They want their deaths to reflect their values: that is, they do not want to go on living when that would contradict their deepest convictions. As Ronald Dworkin has eloquently expressed it, "Making someone die in a way that others approve, but he believes a horrifying contradiction of his life, is a devastating, odious form of tyranny."[9] Basing the right to choose how one dies on respect for autonomy is independent of whether or not the person is suffering.

In some jurisdictions where PAD is legal, such as the Netherlands and Canada, unbearable and unrelievable suffering is an eligibility requirement. In these places, suffering is interpreted broadly to include both physical and mental suffering. Suffering is not mentioned in Oregon's DWDA or in the law of the states which have followed Oregon's lead. This may be because suffering is regarded as physical in nature. The data from Oregon indicate that a desire to avoid physical suffering is not the main reason people want medical assistance to hasten death. They are more likely to say that they want to have control, or it's a question of dignity, or their lives are devoid of things that make living worthwhile. This suggests that some would opt for PAD in the face of terminal illness even if, as the hospice movement claims, physical suffering in terminally ill patients can almost always be controlled or managed. It also leaves open the possibility that some would want to hasten their deaths, even if they were not experiencing any physical suffering, to avoid living into severe dementia.

These arguments in favor of PAD are strong and persuasive. Are there equally strong and persuasive arguments against?

What are the moral arguments against PAD?

Opponents of PAD generally agree that suffering is to be avoided and individuals should be able to make their own choices about how their lives go. However, they maintain that there are cogent moral reasons why people should not be able to decide when and how to die.

The first has to do with the role of physicians and the professional responsibilities that flow from it. Physicians, it is said, are supposed to be healers, not killers. To allow them to kill their patients would be inconsistent with their role as healers. In addition, this could result in a loss of trust on the part of patients who might be afraid that their doctors would be all too willing to kill them if they could not be cured. This would be devastating to the doctor–patient relationship, which is a central foundation of medical ethics.

A second argument is related to the first. It acknowledges that physicians cannot always be healers since not all conditions can be cured. However, when healing is not possible, then doctors should manage pain and suffering not by participating in hastening death, but rather by providing comfort care, also known as *palliative care*. Some argue that legalizing PAD could weaken society's commitment to providing palliative care to dying patients. After all, excellent palliative care can be time-consuming and expensive; in comparison, assisting death is faster and cheaper. The argument is that the very existence of PAD as a legal option would undermine palliative care.

A third argument is that giving the option of PAD to dying patients imposes a terrible burden on them. Might they not feel that it is selfish for them to go on living, imposing serious burdens on their families and/or society when they have the option to die? Is this really a choice we want to offer people who are gravely ill?

The fourth argument against PAD is that it is likely to put us on the first step of a very slippery slope. Slippery slope arguments have the following general form: we start with something that seems perfectly reasonable, but leads, little by little, to an outcome that was not intended and is generally regarded as morally wrong. Moreover, if we take the first seemingly innocuous step, it will be difficult if not impossible to prevent the slide to the wrongful outcome. Law professor Yale Kamisar gave a slippery slope argument when he said that legalizing euthanasia poses "the danger that legal machinery initially designed to kill those who are a nuisance to themselves may someday engulf those who are a nuisance to others."[10] In other words, if we allow killing people who are *in pain*, we may end up killing people who are *a pain*.

Can these objections be met?

Is PAD inconsistent with the physician's role?

Physicians ought to promote the well-being of their patients, curing when that is possible, caring when no cure is possible. However, even if providing palliative care is part of a physician's role, why is the physicians' role *limited to* palliative care? It is not enough to say, "Doctors do not kill," without explaining why providing patients with a good death, the kind of death the patient wants, is inconsistent with the physician's role. If the patient's request is informed and voluntary, there is no reason to think that acceding to the request will result in a loss of trust. Indeed, trust might be strengthened if patients know that they will not be abandoned by their doctors when they are dying but will be helped to have the kind of death they want. It seems, then, that the appeal to the physician's role is not, by itself, an argument against legalizing PAD.

Would legalizing PAD undermine palliative care?

The second argument was that legalizing PAD would undermine palliative care. But will it? Some terminally ill patients will want palliative care that enables them to live as long as they possibly can. Others will decide that life is not worth living even with the best palliative care available. Legalizing PAD doesn't get rid of the need for palliative care. It just provides another option.

Of course, we do not want to create a situation where patients are subtly encouraged to choose PAD instead of palliative care in order to reduce healthcare costs. However, there is evidence that in states where PAD has been legalized, palliative care has not been undermined and may even have improved. Oregon's DWDA requires doctors to inform their patients who request aid in dying of the "feasible alternatives, including, but not limited to, comfort care, hospice care and pain control." Prior to the adoption of the DWDA, physicians were not required to inform their patients of these options, and, indeed, many were not informed about them. The DWDA served to educate doctors who passed on this information to their patients, thus strengthening palliative care.

The emergence of palliative care as a specialty has been a great advance for patients who too often experience serious pain at the end of life. However, even the best palliative care in the world will not be sufficient for some patients. Consider the tragic case of Brittany Maynard, a young California woman who had recently married and was looking forward to starting a family when she was diagnosed with aggressive and terminal brain cancer. At that time, California had not legalized aid in dying. After being told that she had probably only months to live, Brittany was offered palliative care to control her pain. However, understanding that she was going to lose significant physical and cognitive function to the point where she would not be Brittany anymore, she said that she did not want to end her life that way. With her parents and her husband, she moved to Oregon where she could get aid in dying. Before she died, she became a vigorous advocate for aid in dying. She is probably singlehandedly the individual most responsible for self-administered PAD being legalized in California.

Does legalizing PAD create a slippery slope?

To be a valid objection to a law or policy, the claim of a slippery slope requires evidence both that the alleged unwanted outcomes are likely to occur and that they really are undesirable. For example, it is not enough to point to the Netherlands and say, "They allow euthanasia for *infants*." Instead, we should ask whether allowing infant euthanasia in certain restricted cases is a bad outcome of their policy or its logical and acceptable extension. Of course, infant euthanasia should not be a first or an easy option, but that does not mean that it could never be justified. The Dutch have concluded that it should be available in those rare cases when doctors and parents agree that the child's suffering is so great, and incapable of being controlled, that death would be in the child's best interest. Are the Dutch right to preserve this option, and, if not, why not? Once we decide which outcomes really would be unjustifiable, then we can attempt to determine whether there are effective safeguards to prevent such outcomes. The claim that a slippery slope is likely or inevitable should be based on the available data, not pure speculation about what might happen.

Despite predictions of a slippery slope, there does not seem to be any evidence of it, at least in the United States. Since Oregon passed the DWDA in 1994, and reaffirmed it in 1997, it has been collecting and publishing yearly data about the program. The fears of its leading to a slippery slope do not seem to have materialized. The number of people who request and receive prescriptions is relatively small: "During 2020, the estimated rate of DWDA deaths was 65.5 per 10,000 total deaths."[11] Concerns about the potential for exploitation of especially vulnerable groups also do not seem to have occurred. Those using the DWDA are not typically impoverished or come from marginalized groups. Virtually all had some form of health insurance; most died at home. It has not expanded beyond the terminally ill; the majority had cancer and were on hospice.

Reports from Belgium and the Netherlands are mixed as regards a slippery slope. Some say that in these countries, something that was originally intended as a relief from unbearable suffering in late-stage cancer patients has been expanded to people who may live for many years; who have long-term, but not terminal illnesses; who suffer from mental illness; or who are simply tired of life.[12] In 2021, Canada also expanded its eligibility requirements in an Act of Parliament known as C-7. The law allows individuals with chronic illnesses and disabilities that cause enduring, intolerable, and irremediable suffering to have access to MAID, whether or not their death is reasonably foreseeable. At present, persons with mental illness as their sole underlying condition are not eligible for MAID in Canada. The exclusion of psychiatric illness from MAID eligibility will be automatically repealed on March 17, 2023. This temporary exclusion gives the government and other health bodies time to consider how MAID can be safely provided to people whose only medical condition is a mental illness.[13]

The mere expansion of eligibility criteria does not necessarily indicate a slippery slope. Consider the terminal illness requirement. If the reasons for allowing people access to PAD are respect for autonomy and prevention of unbearable suffering, why should it be limited to cases of terminal illness? Some diseases causing unbearable suffering do not kill the patient within six months. An example is amyotrophic lateral sclerosis (ALS, also known as motor neuron disease or Lou Gehrig's disease), a degenerative, incurable nervous system disease. About three-quarters of patients in late-stage ALS report taking pain medication to help ease the physical pain associated with ALS. However, the suffering caused by ALS is not restricted to physical pain. "Emotional pain becomes a major issue in the last months of life and can be heightened by increased physical pain."[14]

People with ALS may have greater suffering than those who are terminally ill simply because they live longer. If the goal of assisted dying is to prevent intolerable and unrelievable suffering, the limitation to those predicted to die relatively quickly seems arbitrary and unjustified. This is reflected in the fact that terminal illness is no longer a requirement—outside of the United States—in any of the countries that now permit PAD, although it is a requirement in a UK bill before Parliament, introduced in 2021.

Is there really a need for PAD?

Kamisar's opposition to euthanasia is not that it is always or in principle wrong. Indeed, he explicitly says that if someone had an incurable illness, intolerable and unmitigable suffering, and an unchanging and rational desire to die, he "would hate to have to argue that the hand of death should be stayed."[15] He doubts, however, that we can know with certainty that these conditions are satisfied. More importantly, he is skeptical that we can create legislation that will cover all and only the cases where the conditions are satisfied. In addition, he doubts that the need for legalized euthanasia is sufficiently great to justify running the risk of mistake and abuse. For one thing, he thinks that in most cases medication can take care of intolerable suffering. For another, Kamisar argues, in those few cases where suffering cannot be alleviated, even with the best palliative care, doctors can and do quietly help their terminally ill patients to die. Sometimes this is accomplished by allowing a secondary illness, such as pneumonia, to kill the patient. Or a doctor, knowing that a patient is ready to die, may write a prescription for sleeping pills with a "warning" that taking a certain number will kill the patient. The idea here is that we don't need to legalize PAD; we have other subtler ways of accomplishing the same end. Moreover, if doctors know they face criminal liability for helping their patients to die, they will only do it in the few cases where it is really warranted.

In response, it may be said that it is safer for patients if PAD is done openly and with clear guidelines, rather than leaving the decision completely up to doctors. It is also safer for doctors if they are not forced to conceal what they are doing but can be assured that they are acting legally so long as they comply with the statutory guidelines. Admittedly, before Death with Dignity laws were passed, very few physicians were convicted in the United States for helping terminally ill patients to die. (An exception is Dr. Jack Kevorkian, who was convicted of second-degree murder and spent eight years in prison.) Nevertheless, some doctors and nurses have faced criminal charges even for providing palliative care to patients who died.[16] It is unfair to ask medical personnel to risk of serious criminal charges to help their suffering patients achieve the kind of death they want. Most physicians would be reluctant to break the law or do something widely viewed as unethical even if they thought it would be justified in the particular case. For this reason, the claim that legalized PAD is unnecessary because doctors do it anyway seems dubious.

Concluding thoughts

The moral arguments from suffering and autonomy support a strong prima facie right on the part of individuals to end their lives, and receive medical help in doing so, in accordance with their own values. At the same time, society has an obligation to protect individuals from being killed against their will or pressured or coerced to choose death. The debate over the legalization of assisted dying depends on how these two values should be balanced. It is a debate likely to continue for some time. At present, relatively few jurisdictions allow assisted dying, but that appears to be changing.

In addition to the basic question—should assisted dying be legalized—there are many unanswered questions. Should assisted dying be limited to self-administered PAD, or should euthanasia also be an option? Should terminal illness be a qualifying condition, and, if so, should terminal illness be defined in terms of having six months to live? Or should those with degenerative, incurable, and debilitating illnesses also have access to assisted dying?

How should the voluntariness requirement be understood? In the United States and Canada, PAD is available only to those who are competent at the time of their request. Yet many people are more concerned about living into severe dementia, perhaps for years, than a few months of suffering at the end of life.[17] Should they be able to request assisted dying by advance directive, as permitted in Belgium and the Netherlands? What about those with psychiatric illnesses, such as severe, treatment-resistant depression?[18] Should they have access to PAD? They may suffer just as much as people with physical illnesses and for a longer time. What about people who do not have a physical or psychiatric illness, but who feel they have lived long enough and are "tired of life"? Are such expansions evidence of the danger of a slippery slope or a logical extension of the right to die? All of these questions have been raised and need to be resolved.

PAD is not the only way to hasten death. In contrast to PAD, voluntarily stopping eating and drinking (VSED) is legal in virtually all jurisdictions. While not an attractive option for everyone who wishes to hasten death, with proper palliative support, VSED almost always provides a peaceful, comfortable, and time-predictable way to die (7–14 days).[19]

Medically assisted dying should be a last resort. It should not be provided *instead of* providing decent healthcare to everyone; it should be integrated into palliative care for those who want it. Its goal should be preventing unmitigable suffering and respecting individual autonomy, not a means of saving money or sparing families from emotional burdens. One more thing is needed to make legalization of assisted dying morally acceptable: namely, a culture of respect and care for the elderly, the sick, and the dying. This is perhaps less common in the United States than in some European and Asian cultures.

7

IS ABORTION AN ETHICAL CHOICE?

While restrictive abortion laws have been relaxed in many countries over the past fifty years, abortion remains ethically controversial and politically divisive, especially in the United States. Some regard abortion as murder. Others think that access to safe and legal abortion is a matter of reproductive justice and that decisions about abortion belong to pregnant women who can make the best decisions for themselves and their families.

Although most Americans support keeping abortion legal, the legal right to abortion has come under serious attack in the United States (even as abortion has been legalized in traditionally conservative countries, most recently in Mexico, Argentina, and Colombia). In June 2022, the United States Supreme Court overturned the constitutional right to abortion established in 1973 by *Roe v. Wade*, returning the matter of abortion to the states. It is expected that about half of the states will continue to allow abortion, while the remaining states will ban or restrict it.

Abortion can be approached from many different perspectives: legal, medical, religious, political, historical, sociological, and ethical. In this chapter we discuss the morality of abortion, which turns primarily on two distinct though related issues: the moral status of embryos and fetuses and whether a pregnant woman has a moral obligation to sustain the life of the fetus.

The issue of moral status is a general one in philosophical ethics. Broadly speaking, the question is: Which beings count morally? That is, when we are considering what we ought morally to do, which beings must we consider and why? Until relatively recently, it has been assumed, without argument, that full moral status belonged to all and only human beings. In the 1970s, the question of the moral status of animals began to be seriously addressed. This led to questions about other "marginal cases," including human embryos and fetuses, and beyond the human species, to animals, plants, the natural world, entire species, and future generations.

What is the conservative view of the moral status of the unborn?

Opponents of abortion, known as conservatives on this issue, consider abortion to be the killing of an innocent human being and therefore seriously morally wrong. This view depends on categorizing the fetus as a human persons. In *Roe v. Wade*, the Supreme Court noted that fetuses have never been treated in the law as full persons. That status depends on live birth.

The conservatives claim, to the contrary, that a fetus is a human person with a moral right to life and therefore ought to have a legal right. This claim may be based on religious belief, namely, the possession of a soul, which leads many in secular societies to object that social policy should not be based on religion. However, the opposition to abortion of, for example, the Roman Catholic Church, is not solely derived from religious teachings and so cannot be rejected on that ground. Instead, the teachings of the Church also stem from what modern genetic science tells us about embryology. "From the time that the ovum is fertilized, a new life is begun which is neither that of the father nor of the mother; it is rather the life of a new human being with his own growth. It would never be made human if it were not human already."[1]

In other words, because the genetic code exists at conception and directs the development of the new human being, it is at conception that the new human being comes into existence. All successive stages that have been held to have moral significance—such as heartbeat, brain waves, fetal movement, the capacity to feel pain (sentience), viability (the point at which the fetus can survive independently of the pregnant woman)—are, on the conservative view, just developments from the beginning. None of those stages can count as the point at which one can say, "Oh, now we have a human being with a right to life, and now it is impermissible to kill it, but before it was permissible." The conservatives say that the only point at which it makes sense to draw a line is at the very beginning of a human life.

Why do moderate conservatives think human life begins after conception?

Extreme conservatives maintain that a human life begins at fertilization, also called *conception*. By contrast, moderate conservatives put the beginning of an individual human life at implantation, which occurs about two weeks after conception when the fertilized egg, or zygote, travels down the fallopian tube into the uterus, where it implants itself.

What is the reason for regarding implantation, rather than conception, as the beginning of the life of a human being? One reason is that a clinical pregnancy begins at implantation. Before a pregnancy starts, there is no possibility of abortion.

Another reason is that, after implantation, the chances that the embryo will go on to become a born human being dramatically increase. Prior to implantation, there is a huge amount of embryo wastage. As many as fifty to seventy-five percent of pregnancies end prior to a positive result on a pregnancy test.

The third reason to place the beginning of an individual human life at implantation is that, prior to implantation, there is the possibility of twinning (i.e., the division of the fertilized egg into two or more embryos, each of which has the possibility of developing into a child). After implantation, twinning is no longer possible. The preimplantation embryo might split into multiple embryos, resulting in twins, triplets, quadruplets, or even quintuplets. None of these individuals can be uniquely identified with the preimplantation embryo, making the claim that every human life begins at conception not obviously true. If twins do not have their beginning at fertilization, but rather later, at implantation, perhaps we should say that all of us begin as distinct individuals only after twinning is no longer possible. Indeed, some suggest that the preimplantation embryo should be regarded not as an individual, but rather as "a community of possibly different individuals held together by a gelatinous membrane."[2]

Whether one regards the beginning of a human life at conception or implantation has implications for the permissibility of a morning-after pill, which prevents the implantation of a fertilized egg in the uterus. Extreme conservatives are opposed to the morning-after pill, but moderate conservatives regard it as a form of contraception, and moderate conservatives generally do not oppose contraception.

Is abortion always wrong for conservatives?

Extreme conservatives think abortion is virtually never justified, not even in the case of rape, fetal indications, or to preserve the life of the pregnant woman. On their view, to kill the innocent child because its father was a rapist would be seriously unjust. Aborting a fetus because of severe deformity is no more justifiable than killing an infant with a severe defect. Nor is abortion justifiable to save the life of the pregnant woman because the killing of an innocent human being is never permissible, not even to save the life of another equally innocent human being.

Moderate conservatives allow some exceptions. In the case of rape, the idea is that a woman who has been raped has already been a victim of a terrible injustice. To force her to carry and bear her rapist's child asks too much of her. Moderate conservatives also would allow abortion when it is necessary to save the pregnant woman's life, and perhaps also when continuing the pregnancy poses a serious threat to her health. This is justified on the principle that no one is morally obligated to sacrifice their own life or risk their own health in order to save the life of another person. To do so would be supererogatory: that is, above and beyond what is morally required. This is especially so when the life of the fetus cannot be saved, but the woman's life could be saved by abortion.

As for abortion for fetal indications, moderate conservatives think it depends on how severe the defect is. There are some defects that are incompatible with continued existence: that is, the fetus is likely to die in utero, or, if the child survives birth, it is likely to die soon after. An example is anencephaly, a neural tube defect in which a major portion of the brain, skull, and scalp is missing. Typically, anencephalic infants die within the first year of life. Other examples of severe fetal indications include trisomy 13 (Patau syndrome) and trisomy 18 (Edwards syndrome). Only fifty percent of babies with trisomy 18 who are carried to term are born alive. Once born, their average lifespan is three days to two weeks. Many infants with trisomy 13 die in the first days or weeks of life. Fewer than twenty percent live past their first year (see Chapter 8).

Moderate conservatives think that abortion is not justifiable if the child can have a life worth living—that is, a life that, despite severe impairments, will be of value to the child. An example of a fetal indication that would not justify abortion for conservatives is Down syndrome (see Chapter 8 for further discussion).

What is the liberal view of the moral status of the unborn?

Those who support the right to abortion are known as liberals on this issue. Liberals base their support of abortion primarily on the devastating effects on women of restrictive abortion laws. Liberals regard such laws as violations of women's rights to control their own bodies and inimical to the full equality of women.

Nevertheless, such arguments do not justify abortion if, as conservatives maintain, the fetus has the same moral status as any born human being. Important as the rights to bodily self-determination and equality are, surely they do not justify murder. The liberal response is that abortion is not murder because the fetus differs from a born child in morally significant ways. Throughout most of gestation, the fetus cannot feel or experience anything and is therefore not the kind of being who is owed protection. Indeed, on a liberal view, an embryo is more similar to an egg or a sperm than a born baby.

One of the best-known liberal accounts has been given by Mary Anne Warren.[3] Warren argues that the conservative's argument depends on the conflation of two quite different senses of "human being," making the argument fallacious. One sense is biological and refers to species membership. A human being is a member of the species *Homo sapiens*. It is a matter of fact that a human fetus is a human being in the biological sense of the word.

However, there is another sense of "human being" that is used in making the claim that it is wrong to kill innocent human beings. Here, the term is used normatively, not descriptively. That is, the term "human being" in this context has moral significance. It refers to members of the moral community who deserve to be treated in certain ways. To avoid confusing the two senses, Warren suggests that we reserve the term "human being" for the biological sense and use the term "person" to refer to full-fledged members of the moral community.

According to Warren, it is in virtue of certain psychological characteristics that we are persons. These characteristics
include sentience, self-consciousness (an awareness of oneself
as existing as the same being through time, with a past and a
future as well as a present), rationality, and moral agency (the
capacity to be motivated by and to act on the basis of moral
reasons). Importantly, she maintains that species membership
does not necessarily determine whether a being is a person. If
we were to come across space aliens, who are obviously not
biologically human, and we found that they, like us, could
feel, think, empathize, and act on moral reasons, we would
not think it would be okay to eat them or put them in zoos.
We would—or should—regard them as persons, possessed
of the same moral rights we have. For that matter, it is possible that some nonhuman animals are sufficiently personlike
to count as full-fledged members of the moral community.
Examples might be great apes, elephants, whales, dolphins,
and octopuses.

A conservative might agree that there could be persons with
rights who are not genetic humans. If we ever come across intelligent aliens, perhaps we should acknowledge their membership in the moral community. Perhaps we should extend
moral and legal rights to gorillas and chimpanzees. However,
a conservative is likely to think that even if being biologically
human is not *necessary* for personhood, it is *sufficient*. That is,
all human beings are full-fledged members of the moral community. But, Warren asks, why should this be? Why should
we regard humans who have *none* of the characteristics of personhood, not even a capacity for sentience, as persons with
moral rights simply because they are biologically human? The
basis for moral rights, she maintains, is personhood, not species membership.

What are the implications for abortion? In early gestation,
the fetal nervous system is so undeveloped that there is no
possibility of any kind of conscious awareness or ability to
experience anything. By the eighth week of pregnancy, brain

waves are detectable, but brain waves, while necessary for experience, are not sufficient. In addition to a functioning brain, experience, of which pain perception is the most basic kind, requires neural pathways that transmit pain messages to the cerebral cortex. These neural pathways are not sufficiently developed until twenty to twenty-four weeks of gestation, making pain perception highly unlikely much earlier than near the end of the second trimester. The early fetus cannot feel, hear, or think. In Warren's terms, it has no person-making characteristics. To regard the early fetus as a person, she says, is simply to *confuse* the moral sense of human being with the biological sense. Since the early fetus is not a person, not yet "one of us," abortion at least in the first trimester is permissible whenever a woman does not want to have a child.

Some conservatives would simply insist that what matters for full moral status is that a being is human and alive. However, a conservative could make another response that acknowledges the importance of person-making characteristics: while the fetus does not have any person-making characteristics *now*, it has all of these characteristics potentially. If you leave the fetus alone, if you do not abort it, it will most likely acquire all of the characteristics that make it a person, a full-fledged member of the moral community. This differentiates the case of the fetus from that of the infant with anencephaly or the patient in PVS. The fetus is potentially a person; an anencephalic or PVS patient is not. The view that abortion is seriously morally wrong because of the potential of the fetus to become a person is called "the potentiality principle."

What is the potentiality principle?

The potentiality principle holds that if a being potentially has the characteristics of a person, then it now has the rights that persons have. The usual objection to it is that potential persons have only potential rights, not actual ones. For example, before the President-elect takes the oath of office, he or she is a potential President of the United States. But a potential president does not now have the right to command military forces or sign bills into law. Similarly, before the fetus becomes a person, it potentially has rights, including a right to life, but it does not yet have actual rights, including a right to life, based on that potential.

A defender of the potentiality principle might try to avoid this criticism by weakening the principle. Instead of saying that the potential person has a right to life, we can say that its potential to become a person confers value on its life now. That is, if we value the lives of persons, then we have good reason to protect the lives of potential persons.

Another objection to the argument from potentiality is that there doesn't seem to be a reason to limit potential personhood to the embryo or fetus. Why isn't a sperm or an egg also potentially a person? If you put viable sperm into a petrie dish with viable eggs, there's a good chance one of the sperm will fertilize one of those eggs and the fertilized egg will become an embryo. Why can't we regard all of the gametes in the petrie dish as potential persons? Virtually everyone who puts forth the potentiality argument wants to draw the line at fertilization, but it's not clear that this is defensible.

Does the person view justify infanticide?

Warren uses the person view to argue that abortion is justified throughout pregnancy, on the ground that fetuses are not persons. Clearly, an embryo or early gestation fetus has no person-making characteristics, but what about the fetus toward the end of pregnancy? In late gestation, the fetus can feel, it can hear, it can suck its thumb. It is much closer in appearance and capacities to a born baby than it is to an embryo. However, Warren maintains that even in late gestation, the fetus is less of a person than the pregnant woman, and therefore her interests in not continuing the pregnancy outweigh the fetus's claim not to be killed.

This leaves Warren open to a serious objection. She justifies abortion on the ground that, even in late gestation, a fetus is less personlike than a woman, or even a mature mammal. But isn't that also true of a newborn human? The person view, it seems, does not merely justify abortion, but also infanticide, implying that parents should be permitted to kill unwanted newborns. That conclusion seems completely unacceptable. An argument that entails an unacceptable conclusion is called a *reductio ad absurdum* or a reductio, for short. Philosophers often use the method of trying to show that an argument is a reductio in order to refute it.

Some philosophers, such as Michael Tooley[4] and Peter Singer and Helga Kuhse,[5] have responded to this criticism by arguing that the alleged unacceptable conclusion is not unacceptable after all. They maintain that newborns, like fetuses, do not have a serious right to life. In fact, Singer and Kuhse regard this as an advantage of their view because many of the conditions revealed by prenatal testing have a range of disability. If we allowed infanticide at birth, or shortly thereafter, parents could choose not to abort a fetus if a prenatal test revealed a disabling condition, but instead wait until the baby was born, when the prognosis would be much more accurate and might be less dire. Allowing for infanticide within a month after birth might actually save lives.

Warren acknowledges that her view commits her to accepting that newborns do not have a serious right to life. Nevertheless, she tries to avoid the conclusion that infanticide is permissible by giving consequentialist reasons against it. One important difference between abortion and infanticide is that, after birth, babies can be given up for adoption, relieving the burden on parents who cannot or do not want to care for them while bringing joy to those who do want them. Admittedly, some babies may be unlikely to be adopted, in particular, those with severe disabling conditions, but infanticide would still not be justified, according to Warren, because most people would prefer to pay taxes for state institutions than to allow unwanted infants to be killed. However, are these sorts of preferences really an adequate basis for regarding the killing of unwanted infants as seriously morally wrong?

At this point, we may have come to a standstill. The conservative is convinced that the fetus is a person, with a right to life, in virtue of being biologically human. The liberal is convinced that the conservative has confused two very different senses of human being. Is there a way to move forward?

How does the "future-like-ours" theory offer a new approach to abortion?

In "Why Abortion Is Immoral," Don Marquis argues for a new approach, maintaining that both conservatives and liberals have given inadequate arguments.[6] Conservatives argue that it's wrong to kill fetuses because they are *human*, but, as the liberal persuasively points out, species membership seems a very arbitrary basis for moral standing. The liberal says that it isn't wrong to kill fetuses because it is only wrong to kill persons (human or otherwise) and fetuses are not persons. But, Marquis says, this could justify killing not just fetuses, but people with severe dementia and severe cognitive defects, something most people would find very hard to accept. Marquis suggests that we start over by going back to the fundamental question: Why do we think that killing is wrong?

According to Marquis, what makes killing wrong is that it deprives the one who is killed of its future, and not just any future, but a future of value. A future of value is one that includes relationships with others and plans and projects. Marquis also refers to a future of value as a "future like ours," abbreviated as FLO. If the individual's future has no value to that individual, then that individual is not deprived of anything of value by being killed, and killing the being is not seriously wrong, or not as wrong as killing a being with FLO. Killing a being with FLO deprives that being of everything—relationships, projects, and plans—in its future, and that is what makes killing such beings seriously wrong.

We should note that Marquis's theory of moral status is not based on genetic humanity; it is not limited to human beings. His theory is thus not speciesist. It applies to any beings with FLO, including extraterrestrial aliens. If chimps, dolphins, and elephants have FLO, then, according to Marquis, it's also seriously wrong to kill them.

Nor does Marquis claim that all human fetuses have FLO. He acknowledges that a fetus could have a disease or defect severe enough to prevent it from having a valuable FLO. In that case, killing it might not be wrong; at least it would not be wrong because it deprived the fetus of a valuable future. Since most fetuses do have FLO, however, most abortions are seriously wrong, according to Marquis.

The description of what it is to have a future of value or a FLO sounds awfully close to Warren's analysis of what it is to be a person. However, there is an important distinction. Warren thinks that abortion is permissible because the fetus is not now a person, only a potential person. Marquis does not claim that the fetus is now a person nor is his argument based on the fetus's potential personhood. Rather, his claim is that the fetus *right now* has a future of value, in exactly the same way that you or I have a future of value. If the fetus is killed now, it is deprived of that valuable future. Moreover, its having a future of value does not depend on any capacities or properties it presently has. It is irrelevant, he says, that early fetuses can't feel or think. They do not need to be personlike now in order to have a valuable future. This is precisely what Jeff McMahan denies.

How does the embodied minds view affect the debate?

In Chapter 5 we discussed McMahan's view that we are essentially conscious beings: that is, embodied minds.[7] This means that we die when we permanently lose the capacity for consciousness. His view also has implications for abortion. If we are essentially embodied minds, then our lives begin, not with the beginning of our organism, but with the beginning of consciousness. I come into existence when my mind does. Therefore, the fetus, which is an earlier stage of my organism, is not *me*, and therefore it does not have my future. What, then, is my relationship to the fetus from which I developed? The fetus is my empty organism, in exactly the same way that my body is my empty organism after brain death. On McMahan's view, *I* was never a fetus, just as *I* can never be in a permanent vegetative state.

Are McMahan's conclusions—that I was never a fetus, and we are not human organisms—plausible? David DeGrazia thinks not.[8] When parents see an ultrasound photo of the fetus, they regard it as a picture of their baby. After the baby is born, they may put this photograph into the baby's album and label it "baby's first picture." They may show the child the photo and say something like, "This is you when you were inside Mommy's tummy." When they do this, are they lying to the child? Surely not. Moreover, if we are not human organisms, then our biology teacher was lying when she told us that we are human animals, which is equally implausible. DeGrazia maintains that a biological view of human identity—that we are essentially organisms—is more plausible than McMahan's mind essentialism.

Both McMahan and DeGrazia think that we have to be essentially something, whether an organism or a mind, if we are to know when we come into (and go out of) existence. However, perhaps the important question is not what am I essentially, or when did I begin, but rather when did I acquire the features that endow a being with moral status?

To say that a being has moral status is just to say that the being counts morally. This means that its interests count. That is, when moral agents are deciding how they ought to act, they are morally required to consider the interests of all beings who will be affected by the decision. If a being *has* no interests, it cannot be affected. It cannot have moral status; that is, it would make no sense to ascribe moral status to it. This view that connects moral status and interests—the interest view—has been elaborated by Steinbock in *Life Before Birth*.[9]

What are the implications of the interest view for abortion?

On this view, what endows a being with moral standing is the possession of interests. Having interests is a necessary condition for having moral status; beings that do not have interests cannot have moral status.

We can see why interests matter to moral status if we consider beings that do not have interests. Mere things—rocks, tables, jewels—do not have interests of their own, though they may have value of various kinds (monetary, aesthetic, historical, or sentimental, for example) and thus be of interest to us. We may have all kinds of reasons for taking care of or protecting or preserving mere things, but these reasons do not imply that we do these things for their sake. For example, I have a reason to take care of my car because, if I don't, it won't run as well. I do not change the oil and go in for routine maintenance *for the car's sake* because the car is a thing and it doesn't have a sake of its own. It does not matter to the car if it runs smoothly or stops working.

Cars are different from pets in this respect. Both can be owned, but our reasons for taking care of our pets are not solely derived from our interests. While it would be very odd for someone to say to you, "Well, even if you don't care if the car runs well, you should take it to a mechanic for *its* sake," but not at all odd to say, "Even if you don't care about the dog, you should take it to the vet, for its sake." A dog, unlike a car, can suffer when it is ill and untreated. It matters to the dog whether it gets fed or is left to starve, whether it is protected or out in the cold, whether its wounds are treated or it is left in pain. Dogs have interests because it matters to them what happens to them. They have the ability to care because they can feel. Dogs, unlike cars, are sentient. The interest view links moral standing to interests and interests to sentience.

The interest view is similar to the person view in that it bases moral status on psychological characteristics, not species membership. However, the interest view regards sentience as the most basic element and sufficient for minimal moral status. All sentient beings have moral status, although the possession of other characteristics, such as self-consciousness and moral agency, can endow persons with a higher moral status and greater moral importance than the lives of nonpersons.

Marquis thinks that simply having FLO gives the fetus—indeed, the implanted embryo—a stake in its future. By contrast, on the interest view, even if embryos and early fetuses have FLO, they do not have a stake in that future. An early fetus is no more harmed by abortion than sperm is harmed by coming into contact with a spermicide or an embryo is harmed by being prevented from implanting in a uterus.

To review, on the interest view, prior to the onset of sentience, fetuses have no moral standing any more than gametes do. This does not, of course, mean that women who become pregnant do not care about their fetuses. Women who want to have a baby care deeply about their fetuses, but this is because they do not intend them to stay fetuses. Ultimately, they care about their babies. That is why prospective parents talk about "their baby" during pregnancy. No one paints a nursery or buys a crib for "their fetus." Moreover, to increase the chances that you have a live, healthy baby, you need to take precautions during the fetal stage. While fetuses do not have moral standing prior to becoming sentient, they have great importance and moral value to expectant parents who have a strong stake in their survival.

How does the interest view support a gradualist approach?

The interest view holds that, prior to the onset of sentience, the fetus has no interests, and so no interest in the continuation of its life. As the fetus develops, it becomes more like a newborn in morally relevant ways, the most important of which is its ability to experience pain. Once a fetus can experience pain, it has an interest in not experiencing pain, and we have a reason to do what we can to avoid the unnecessary infliction of pain on the fetus. For example, even the possibility that the fetus can feel pain would be a reason to use anesthesia in the case of late abortions. On a gradualist view, the reasons for having an abortion should be stronger in the case of late abortions than in the case of early abortions. Simply not wanting to have a child is a perfectly good reason to terminate a pregnancy in the early stages, but in the later stages, a stronger justification, such as a risk to the woman's health from continuing the pregnancy, would be required. Thus, the interest view is a gradualist view that has the advantage of cohering with the most people's strong intuition that late abortions require more justification than early abortions.

Interestingly, however, the extremely plausible gradualist approach is not taken by either conservatives or most liberals. The conservative cannot regard late abortions as worse than early ones because the conservative regards the unborn *at all stages* as a human being, with a right to life. The extreme conservative places the beginning of a human life at conception, the moderate places it two weeks later at implantation, but, for both, the fetus is a human being in the moral sense throughout gestation. If that's true, then late abortions are not morally more problematic than early abortions.

Warren also cannot take a gradualist view. She holds that abortion is morally permissible *at every stage* in pregnancy because only persons have full moral standing and rights, and the fetus, even in late gestation, is not a person. On her view, late abortion is no worse than early abortion. Both conservatives and liberals seem committed to the view that abortion is morally the same throughout pregnancy, a view that conflicts with most people's views and common sense.

What about late abortions?

On the interest view, the sentient fetus has moral standing, but so does the pregnant woman. In general, her interests count for more because she is a full-fledged person, with interests that go far beyond not experiencing pain. Her interests stem from her projects, values, and relationships with others. These are not the kinds of interests that a fetus can have, and they give a greater value to the life of the woman. Nevertheless, the sentient fetus begins to have a life that has subjective value to it. We can ascribe to the sentient fetus not merely an interest in avoiding pain, but also an interest, albeit a weak one, in continuing to exist. While its weak interest in continuing to exist does not justify ascribing to it anything as strong as a right to life, it does provide a reason for preserving its life when this does not conflict with the woman's important interests.

Late abortions are rare. In fact, in the United States, only 1.2 percent of all abortions occur at or after twenty-one weeks. The reasons women have abortions after twenty weeks are quite similar to the reasons women have abortions after the first trimester. They may delay having abortions because of the roadblocks to access, or because they do not realize they are pregnant, which could be due to obesity, lack of pregnancy symptoms, or simply youth. Some late-term abortions occur in the case of *wanted* pregnancies where a serious threat to the woman's life or health is discovered, or where prenatal testing reveals a serious health problem in the expected child. The woman or the couple then has to make a very difficult and often emotionally wrenching decision. The decision is not made easier or better by legal prohibitions.

So far, we have been discussing the morality of abortion in terms of the moral status of the unborn. However, the right of bodily self-determination plays a unique role in the morality of abortion.

What role does the right to bodily self-determination play?

Fetuses do not exist floating in space. They have to grow and develop inside a particular woman's body. In essence, the pregnant woman serves as a life support system for the developing fetus. This means that the justifiability of abortion rests not only on whether the fetus is a person, with a right to life, but also on whether the fetus has a right to what it needs to stay alive: namely, the body of the pregnant woman. Even if the fetus is a human person, there remains the question of whether pregnant women are simply "fetal containers"[10] or whether pregnant women retain the right to bodily self-determination.

The first person to distinguish the right to life from the right to use another person's body when necessary to sustain life was Judith Thomson in her groundbreaking and now classic article, "A Defense of Abortion."[11] Thomson begins by saying that people have simply assumed that once the moral status of the fetus is determined, the abortion argument is over. If the fetus is a person, then it has a right to life, a right not to be killed. Since abortion kills the fetus, abortion violates its right to life and so is seriously morally wrong. To show that we can differentiate between the right to life and the right to use another person's body, Thomson assumes, for the sake of argument, that the fetus is a person with a right to life. Does it follow that abortion violates its right to life?

To show that this is not obvious and, indeed, false, Thomson comes up with a novel example, the Famous Violinist. It goes like this. You wake up one day and discover that you are in bed, attached to an unconscious violinist. He has a fatal kidney ailment and the Society of Music Lovers has determined that you alone have the right blood type to help. They kidnapped you and plugged his circulatory system into yours, so that your kidneys can extract poisons from his blood as well as your own.

The director of the hospital comes to see you. He acknowledges that it was very wrong of the Society to kidnap you. Still, he says, he cannot now unplug you from the violinist, for to unplug you would be to kill him. But not to worry; you only need to stay plugged into him for nine months. By that time, the violinist will have recovered and can be safely unplugged from you. Thomson asks, is it morally incumbent on you to stay attached to him? It would be very nice of you to do so, but do you have to—that is, are you morally obligated to do so? Do you have to stay plugged in as long as his life depends on it because the violinist is a person and all persons have a right to life? Thomson says that you would be outraged by this suggestion, which shows that simply having a right to life does not entitle you to whatever you need to stay alive.

Some think that the Famous Violinist example is too fanciful to be helpful to our thinking about the morality of abortion. However, we need not rely on fantastic examples to demonstrate her central point. What if I will die unless you donate a kidney to me? Does the fact that I need your kidney for life itself mean that I have a moral right to it? I clearly don't have a legal right to it, but it does not seem plausible to claim a moral right either. Again, it would be very nice of you to give me a kidney but, absent special circumstances, such as your promising to give me your kidney, I do not have a valid claim on you to give it to me.

However, even if the fetus does not have a right to use the pregnant woman's body, any more than the Famous Violinist has a right to use your kidneys, maybe she ought to allow the fetus to remain inside her out of kindness? However, that depends on how much is required for her to continue the pregnancy. Pregnancy can impose serious burdens on the woman: physical, emotional, economic.[12] We may have moral obligations to others to keep them alive when we can do so without undergoing serious burdens, but making huge sacrifices to save someone else's life is above and beyond the call of duty.

At this point, it may be objected that the fetus *does* have the right to the woman's body because she is (partly) responsible for its being there. By engaging in sexual intercourse, knowing that pregnancy is a possible result, she tacitly or implicitly gives the resulting fetus a right to use her body, to remain inside her. However, this would be true only of voluntary intercourse. If she did not voluntarily have sex—if the pregnancy was due to rape, for example—then she could not be said to have given the fetus even a tacit right to remain inside her. Thus, Thomson's Famous Violinist can be used to support the claim that abortion is permissible in the case of rape. It is one of the ironies of the abortion debate that one of the most famous articles defending abortion has been adopted by moderate conservatives who oppose abortion but seek to justify their exceptions in the case of rape.

Of course, most pregnancies do not result from rape. Can Thomson claim that even when the pregnancy results from voluntary intercourse, the woman still has not given the fetus-person a right to use her body? That depends, she says, on whether the woman is responsible for its presence. Doing something voluntarily that has a foreseeable outcome is not enough to show that the person is responsible for the outcome; it depends on what the person did to prevent the outcome. Suppose, for example, that the woman used a reliable contraceptive and still got pregnant. People who use the diaphragm, an IUD, or even are on the pill do sometimes get pregnant. Would the fact that she voluntarily engaged in sexual intercourse make her responsible for the presence of the fetus and mean that now it has a right to stay? Here, intuitions divide. Some agree with Thomson that if the woman has acted responsibly and done what is reasonably expected of her to prevent the existence of the fetus (i.e., has used contraception), then she cannot be held responsible for its presence. She has not given it a right to remain in her body: abortion is permissible. Others think that she is responsible since contraceptive failure is known to occur. Therefore, the fetus has a right to remain: abortion is impermissible.

One more point should be made. If the fetus is a person, then it is a person who has a special relationship to the pregnant woman: it is her child. She is its mother. Mothers, or parents generally, have special obligations to their children, obligations of care and protection. So even if the fetus-person doesn't have a *right* to its mother's body, she surely ought to let it stay. In the same way, a child might not have a right to bone marrow or a kidney from a parent, but what would we think of parents who would refuse to donate, at the cost of their child's life?

Even if Thomson's argument all by itself does not constitute a general defense of abortion, it can justify abortion in general if it is combined with a view of the moral status of the fetus. In early pregnancy, the fetus has no moral status and abortion is justifiable if the woman does not want to have a child. In later pregnancy, the fetus begins to acquire moral status, and its weak interest in survival must be considered. This does not mean that abortion is impermissible, but the reasons for having late abortions should be stronger than the reasons for early ones.

Concluding thoughts

Thomson's defense of abortion contributes an essential element missing from the standard liberal position, namely, the importance of the fetus's dependence on the pregnant woman's body. Thomson makes it clear that the morality of abortion does not depend solely on whether the fetus is a person and has a right to life, but also on whether that right to life gives the fetus a right to use the body of the pregnant woman, necessary for its survival, in light of the burdens and risks imposed by pregnancy. Thomson's argument provides a very limited defense of abortion, however, since in most cases the woman is (partly) responsible for becoming pregnant. Combining the view of moral status provided by the interest view with bodily self-determination provides a stronger justification for

abortion than either argument alone. Moreover, while reasonable people can differ on whether a particular abortion is morally justifiable, in our view the choice of abortion should not be
legally restricted. Because the decision is so personal and has
such far-reaching physical and emotional effects on the bodies
and lives of pregnant women, the decision whether or not to
continue a pregnancy must ultimately be theirs.

8

WHAT ARE THE IMPLICATIONS OF THE DISABILITY CRITIQUE?

In the past few decades, disability activists have criticized prevailing misconceptions about disability in what has become known as "the disability critique" (DC). The DC rejects the notion that life with a disabling condition is miserable and filled with suffering. It also rejects the "medical model" that views disability primarily as a medical problem to be fixed by medical means. Disability activists deny that all disabilities need to be fixed. For example, many Deaf people have no desire to become hearing. They live independently, have jobs, and also have their own language and rich culture. Moreover, although disability activists acknowledge that there are real obstacles faced by people living with disabling conditions, they argue that these obstacles are socially constructed and can be socially removed so that all people, regardless of disability, can lead good lives and participate fully in society.

The DC has significance in many areas in bioethics, including experimentation on human subjects, physician-assisted death,[1] advance directives,[2] the demands of social justice,[3] and genetic modifications of humans. In this chapter, we focus specifically on what the DC has to say about prenatal testing and selective abortion: that is, abortion to prevent the birth of a child with a disabling condition. Although we do not cover what the DC has to say on all the areas where it is relevant, what we say in this chapter will help readers to apply the perspective of the DC to other issues in bioethics.

In Chapter 7, we discussed the morality of abortion in general, where the aim is to prevent having any child. In this chapter we consider whether selective abortion to prevent the birth of a child with a disabling condition or disease is morally permissible. Those who regard all abortion as morally impermissible will, of course, oppose selective abortion. However, some who are generally pro-choice on abortion have moral objections to selective abortion, stemming from the DC. We will say more about the DC in a subsequent section, but the basic idea is that thinking that disability is a good reason for terminating a wanted pregnancy reflects incorrect beliefs about, and discriminatory attitudes toward, disability.

Ultimately, we reject this conclusion about selective abortion. We do not accept the view that disability is merely a form of difference, but can reasonably be seen as something that should be prevented. There is nothing objectionable in the desire of many—though not all—prospective parents to avoid disabling conditions in their offspring. Moreover, we argue that selective abortion is a permissible means of achieving that end. At the same time, we appreciate the insights of the DC about the ways in which society needs to adapt to be welcoming to people of all abilities and disabilities.

What is prenatal testing?

Prenatal testing (PT) includes a range of techniques performed on the fetus during pregnancy to screen for congenital disorders and check on fetal development. It began in the 1950s, with ultrasound imagery, a noninvasive procedure that today is commonplace in obstetrics. Nearly all women in the United States receive one or more ultrasounds during pregnancy. Another technique, available since 2012, is noninvasive prenatal testing (NIPT), a blood test performed during pregnancy that screens for trisomy 21 (more commonly known as Down syndrome), trisomy 18 and trisomy 13.

If a fetal disorder is detected during NIPT, it usually will be followed up with a diagnostic test, such as amniocentesis and chorionic villus sampling (CVS). Both of these procedures remove and test cells for chromosomal and genetic disorders. In amniocentesis, a needle is inserted into the uterus to remove a small amount of amniotic fluid, which contains fetal cells. Amniocentesis is usually done between fifteen and twenty weeks of pregnancy. It carries a small risk of causing miscarriage, but that risk—about 0.6 percent—is only slightly higher than the normal risk of miscarriage at this stage in pregnancy. In CVS, cells known as *chorionic villi*, which share the fetus's genetic makeup, are removed from the placenta for testing. CVS can be done earlier than amniocentesis, usually between the tenth and twelfth weeks of pregnancy, which has the advantage of allowing for a first-trimester abortion, earlier than is available using amniocentesis. However, CVS carries a slightly higher risk of miscarriage than amniocentesis—about 1 percent.

Prenatal testing can detect over a thousand fetal disorders. They include neural tube disorders (such as spina bifida), genetic diseases (such as Tay-Sachs and cystic fibrosis), and chromosomal abnormalities, including trisomy 13, 18, and 21.

What is preimplantation genetic testing?

Preimplantation genetic testing (PGT) is another technique for detecting and preventing congenital disorders. Unlike PT, PGT is done prior to the establishment of a pregnancy, and must be done in conjunction with in vitro fertilization (IVF). As we will see in Chapter 9, in IVF mature eggs are removed from the woman's body and fertilized with sperm in a petri dish. The resulting embryos remain in vitro for a few days to determine that they are developing normally. Once the embryo reaches about 100 cells, one or two cells can be removed for screening without any damage to the embryo. Unaffected embryos can be transferred to the woman's uterus or frozen for future use. Embryos with disorders are discarded or may be donated for use in research.

Because PGT results in the discarding of affected embryos and does not involve the termination of a pregnancy, it is regarded by many people as morally less troubling than abortion. Of course, it would not be less troubling for those who regard even early, not-yet-implanted embryos as full human beings with a right to life (see Chapter 7 for a discussion of the moral status of embryos). In addition, as we will see, some apply the disability critique to PGT as well as PT.

What is the purpose of PT and PGT?

Both PT and PGT provide the prospective parents with information about whether their baby is likely to have a genetic or chromosomal disease. While such testing is generally very reliable, no testing is perfect. There is always the risk of false positives (i.e., results that indicate a fetal disorder when there is none) or false negatives (i.e., results that miss a disorder). Moreover, some disorders will not be detected until the baby is born.

Each year, more than eight million babies born worldwide are affected with a serious congenital disorder, including one in every thirty-three babies in the United States.[4] Nevertheless, only two to three percent of patients undergoing prenatal screening will receive results indicating a fetal disorder. Thus, for the vast majority of expectant parents who use them, prenatal tests are a source of reassurance. Indeed, PT and PGT can result in the births of children who would otherwise not have been born because such testing enables people who are unwilling to take the risk of having a child with a serious congenital disorder to attempt a pregnancy.

Not all individuals who opt for PT use the information of an affected pregnancy to terminate it. Some choose PT to prepare themselves for the birth of a child with special needs. There may also be medical reasons for learning about a disorder prior to birth, as this might affect the method of delivery. For example, a cesarean section may be safer if the baby has been diagnosed with spina bifida.

However, the reason most people opt for PT is to avoid the birth of a baby with a congenital disorder. A British study found that "Between 81 and 90% of parents terminate pregnancies identified with lethal, life limiting, or severely debilitating disorders."[5] The number is undoubtedly smaller for conditions that are not generally lethal or severely debilitating, such as Down syndrome (DS), the most common disorder detected by PT. No one really knows how many American women who receive a prenatal diagnosis of DS choose to terminate because this kind of data is not collected in the United States. It has been estimated to be about sixty-seven percent, a number that has gone down as more is learned about DS. We will return to this topic below.

Because the risk of chromosomal abnormalities increases with maternal age, testing used to be offered only to women with particular risk factors, such as a family history or over a certain age: thirty-five in the United States, forty in the United Kingdom. In 2007, the American College of Obstetricians and Gynecologists (ACOG) recommended that all pregnant women, regardless of age, be offered PT for conditions like DS. The rationale was that, while the risk of having a child with DS is considerably greater for older women, most babies with DS are born to younger women simply because younger women are having the most babies.

ACOG has been very clear that while PT should be offered to all pregnant women, the decision whether to accept the offer belongs to the woman herself. This differentiates PT from other kinds of obstetric procedures and advice on such matters as the number of prenatal visits, the use of prenatal vitamins, diet and exercise in pregnancy, and the avoidance of tobacco, alcohol, and recreational drugs. Advice in these matters is given because we know that the future child's health can be significantly impaired by what happens during pregnancy. For example, a deficiency of folic acid in the pregnant woman's diet can result in a neural tube disorder in the child. If she takes a folic acid supplement, she can avoid this outcome. Smoking during pregnancy can cause low birth weight and associated medical problems. Drinking, especially binge drinking, can cause fetal alcohol syndrome, resulting in cognitive impairments. Medical recommendations on these matters are given to protect the health of the expected child.

Sometimes PT is presented in a similar way. For example, a March of Dimes website alludes to the value of PT as follows: "Prenatal tests are medical tests you get during pregnancy. They help your health care provider find out how you and your baby are doing. . . . These tests make sure you and your baby are staying healthy." The impression this gives is that PT is like taking prenatal vitamins or avoiding alcohol during pregnancy: something the expectant mother ought to do to safeguard her baby's health. This is seriously misleading. Getting a prenatal test does nothing to *protect* the fetus from developing a disorder. It simply reveals the likelihood that the fetus *has* a particular disorder. In most cases, nothing can be done to improve the condition. Rather, PT gives the pregnant woman information on which she can base a decision whether to terminate the pregnancy. The claim that PT can give prospective parents the chance to have a healthy child is true so long as we understand that such testing does not protect or improve the health of the fetus in *this* pregnancy. Rather, it provides the opportunity to replace this fetus with a *different* fetus in a subsequent pregnancy. Because changing the identity of the fetus is the only way to protect the health of a future child, this issue is often called "the non-identity problem."

By contrast, not taking prenatal vitamins or engaging in binge drinking can cause *this* fetus, which could have been born "healthy and whole," to develop a disabling condition. The choice to have PT does not change the condition of the fetus, but only gives the prospective parents the chance not to have a child with the detected disability and (perhaps) to have a different child without the disability. If we fail to understand the difference between PT and other measures aimed at having a healthy child, we will not be able to understand the objections of the DC to PT and selective abortion.

What is the DC's objection to selective abortion?

Not all disability activists or people living with disabling conditions oppose selective abortion. As one participant in the annual meeting of the Society for Disability Studies explained, "Why would I want to force people who do not want to raise a child with a disability to do so? How would that be good for the child?" However, many in the disability community have serious misgivings about selective abortion to prevent the birth of a child with a disability.

It is important to understand the reasons for their opposition and to distinguish their reasons from opposition to abortion based on the claim that a human fetus is a human person with a right to life (see Chapter 7). Anyone who regards fetuses as morally equivalent to infants will of course object to PT and selective abortion. After all, if killing newborn babies with serious disorders is morally wrong and illegal, and fetuses have the same moral status as born babies, then what justifies killing "unborn babies"? Dr. C. Everett Koop, who was Surgeon General of the United States under President Ronald Reagan, expressed this attitude to PT when he referred to it as a "search and destroy mission."

This objection to PT hinges on the moral equivalence of embryos and fetuses to born infants. Undoubtedly, some disability activists are generally opposed to abortion. However, the DC does not entail an objection to all abortion. The DC's objection specifically to selective abortion is based on two factors. First, that the general acceptance of abortion to prevent the birth of a child with a disability stems from widespread misinformation about what life is like for people who have disabling conditions. Second, that the choice of selective abortion reveals something wanting in the characters of people who use it and displays a regrettable understanding of the parent–child relationship.

Many people think that life with a disability must be filled with suffering and limitations. They may justify selective abortion as sparing the child a lifetime of suffering. But this is simply not true. Research shows that most people with disabling conditions, even serious ones, do not lead lives of unremitting suffering. They do not regard their lives as "not worth living." In fact, they are nearly as happy as people who are not disabled, and any dissatisfaction with their lives does not stem from the disabling condition[6]—more about this below. This is surprising since most people think that if they were to become disabled—to go blind, to go deaf, to become paralyzed, to lose their cognitive abilities, and so forth—they would be devastated and extremely unhappy. They extrapolate from their own contemplated misery to a generalization about the lives of people living with serious disabling conditions.

However, this is mistaken on two counts. First, although people who become disabled often do experience a severe drop in happiness and well-being, they do not in general remain miserable. They typically adapt to their new circumstances and eventually regain the level of happiness they had prior to becoming disabled. This phenomenon of adaptation has been well documented in the literature.[7]

Second, while the lives of people living with severe disabling conditions may be limited in various ways—for example, in achieving higher education, finding employment, or living independently—disability activists maintain that these obstacles to full participation in society are not, for the most part, the result of their medical condition. Rather, the obstacles are *socially constructed*. That is, it is a social choice whether or not to provide accommodations for various kinds of disabling conditions, such as ramps and elevators for wheelchairs or sign language interpreters on television. Indeed, most nondisabled people may be completely unaware of the ways people with disabling conditions are prevented from engaging in full participation—until legislation requiring access gets passed. Disability advocates argue that instead of seeking to prevent the births of people who could have lives well worth living and contribute a great deal to society, we should focus on removing the obstacles to their full participation in society.[8]

What responses can be made to the DC?

While it is true that the obstacles that prevent some people living with disabilities from having full participation in society are often socially constructed, it is an exaggeration to say that they always are. Consider, for example, trisomy 18 or 13, chromosomal disorders that are usually fatal before birth or within the first weeks or months of life. Some children do survive, with support, even as long as ten years. "Although survival rates are improving, most infants are likely to die before their first birthday."[9] Because they die so early, no amount of social support will enable them to participate fully in society. However, these conditions are quite rare. Trisomy 18 occurs in about 1 in 5,000 live births. Trisomy 13 is even rarer. It has been estimated to occur in about 1 in 5,000 to 12,000 births. Most conditions detected by PT are both less rare and less severe.

Consider, for example, Down syndrome. Intellectual and developmental problems may be mild, moderate, or severe. Some people with DS have significant health problems, such as serious heart defects, while others do not. Today, children with Down syndrome usually stay at home with their parents, they go to school, some graduate from high school, and a few go on to postgraduate education. In the United States, many are able to live semi-independently and about twenty percent have jobs, although support in financial and legal matters is often required. With proper healthcare, life expectancy is fifty to sixty years. Attitudes toward DS today are very different from sixty or seventy years ago, when families were often advised to institutionalize their children. Institutionalized children often have severe cognitive defects, but today we understand that this was often a result not of the extra chromosome that causes DS, but rather of the institutionalization itself.

It is clear that the lives of children with DS, by and large, are well worth living. It is simply not true that continuing a pregnancy after learning that the child will have DS is "unfair to the child" or that such children are "better off not being born."[10] Yet termination may be sought because the prospective parents seek to avoid the extra financial, physical, and emotional burdens that come with having a child with a serious disability.

Some disability advocates maintain that there are no additional burdens that come with being a parent to a child with a disability or that the burdens are no more onerous than the burdens that come with having a gifted child. While we should not overemphasize the burdens, neither should we trivialize them. About half the children with DS have a congenital heart defect, which may require surgery in early infancy. Some have gastrointestinal defects and develop digestive problems. People with DS are at increased risk of developing an autoimmune disorder, some forms of cancer, and infectious diseases. In addition, they are likely to require parental support longer than children without developmental delays. This is a source of concern for people who worry about who will take care of their child after they die. It is not unreasonable for individuals to want to avoid having a child under these conditions.

To say that the desire is not unreasonable is not to say that it is required by reason. Some prospective parents will be committed to *this* pregnancy and *this* child. So long as the child will have a life that is worth living, there is nothing wrong with their choice to continue the pregnancy. Our claim is simply that neither is there anything wrong with the choice of prospective parents to terminate a wanted pregnancy on learning that the child will have a serious disability.

Can prenatal testing be regarded as a preventive measure?

Some congenital disorders can be prevented by protective measures taken by the pregnant woman. We have already mentioned not smoking, not drinking alcohol, and eschewing recreational drugs. In addition, neural tube defects, such as spina bifida, can be prevented by getting enough folic acid in the diet. Presumably, no one in the disability community objects to these kinds of measures for preventing disability. The question then is, why is selective abortion regarded differently?

If the reason is that abortion is morally wrong, or morally problematic, then the issue is the moral permissibility of abortion in general and not selective abortion in particular. Nonetheless, some disability activists who are pro-choice in general think abortion should not be used to prevent the birth of a child with a disabling condition, or at least not a disabling condition compatible with a life well worth living. Their argument against PT, followed by selective abortion, is based on what has become known as the "any-particular distinction." The any-particular distinction is between seeking an abortion because the pregnant woman does not want *any* child (at least not now, under these circumstances) and seeking an abortion because the pregnant woman does not want to have *this* child—that is, a child with certain characteristics. Most selective abortions terminate wanted pregnancies. That is, the woman intentionally became pregnant or was happy on learning that she was pregnant. She wants to be a mother (or to be a mother again, if she already has children). However, she does not want to have *this* child because of the risk that the child will have a disability.

Does the choice of selective abortion display a bad parental attitude?

Chris Kaposy, a bioethicist, has written about his family's decision to continue a pregnancy after a prenatal diagnosis of DS.

He acknowledges that the first days after the diagnosis were hard. He and his wife went through a period of grieving. But they came to accept that their son would have DS and to accept him as a member of their family. Today, their son, Aaron, is an affectionate boy who is passionate about hockey and animals. If the lives of people with DS can be good ones, and they can bring joy, not heartache, to their families, why is it, Kaposy asks, that so many people are unwilling to have a child with DS? Kaposy writes,

> One explanation shows up repeatedly when parents re-count the early days after receiving their child's diag-nosis. They feel a sense of loss because they no longer dream that their child will get married, go to college or start a family of their own one day—in other words, that they will not meet the conventional expectations for the perfect middle-class life. In fact, some people with Down syndrome do accomplish those things. Nonetheless, hopes and dreams of perfection might be a strong motive for parents to choose abortion.[11]

He goes on to say that, after the initial phase of grief, parents "leave behind concerns about perfection" and instead embrace "acceptance, empathy and unconditional love of their chil-dren." This is not merely a psychological description of what some parents in fact experience after a prenatal diagnosis of DS. It is a normative judgment about what attitudes prospective parents *should* have on receiving this diagnosis. Prospective parents who opt for abortion are, in his view, seeking perfec-tion. Kaposy offers them this advice, "If you value acceptance, empathy and unconditional love, you, too, should welcome a child with Down syndrome into your life."

We disagree. One need not be a perfectionist to prefer not to have a baby that may have serious medical problems. Indeed, such a preference is not only common among prospective parents, but expected of them. Parents who failed to take steps to protect their children from medical problems would be seriously inadequate. Moreover, when babies are born with serious conditions that were not discovered prior to their birth, most parents will love their children unconditionally—despite the fact that they would have terminated the pregnancy if they had known about the medical problem. This implies that, for most people, it is born children who receive unconditional love, not fetuses. Are prospective parents morally required to have the same attitude toward the fetus as they have toward the born child? We think not.

In Chapter 7, we argued that abortion is a morally permissible choice because there is a moral difference between the born child and the fetus. If that is correct, then it is entirely acceptable for a woman to regard her fetus quite differently from her baby. A woman who learns at ten weeks that the fetus she is carrying has DS may not yet have formed a parental bond. She may think that she still has a choice about becoming a mother, and she may think that the difficulties of raising a child are great enough without taking on extra burdens. To show that selective abortion is wrong, one would need to claim that the pregnant woman is already a mother and the fetus is already her child. However, if one could show that, it would follow that most abortions, not merely selective abortions, are wrong. The DC of selective abortion seems incompatible with a generally pro-choice attitude toward abortion.

A few disability activists[12] even reject PGT and embryo selection. They suggest that parents undergoing IVF should refrain from testing the preimplantation embryos and simply implant any of the viable embryos. However, this view is even less persuasive than opposition to selective abortion because embryos with chromosomal or genetic abnormalities are much less likely to be viable. They are less likely to implant, and, if they do implant, they have a much higher risk of miscarriage. Given that PGT is now routinely used in IVF because it improves the chances of successful pregnancy, it is unthinkable that any fertility doctor would deliberately take the risk of implanting an embryo with a chromosomal or genetic disorder.

Concluding thoughts

The DC provides an important perspective in many issues in bioethics. It highlights the prejudice and discrimination against people with disabilities once rampant and still prevalent in society today. It reminds us of how far we still need to go to make society more accessible to people living with a variety of disabling conditions.

It also provides a useful counterbalance to misinformation about the lives of people with disabilities. It reminds that many conditions range in severity. Being blind or deaf or using a wheelchair is compatible with being a fully functional member of society so long as necessary accommodations, such as those required by the Americans with Disabilities Act (ADA), signed into law in 1990, are provided. Other kinds of disabling conditions, in particular those with cognitive implications, may limit what an individual can expect to do or achieve, but they do not rule out having a full, worthwhile life.

All too often, members of the medical profession have simply assumed that prospective parents who receive a prenatal diagnosis of DS would *of course* want a termination. Disability activists are right to criticize this assumption. It is crucial that women be given clear and adequate information, that they have access to nonjudgmental counseling, and that they are not under any pressure to accept or refuse PT. Better information about disabilities, combined with better services offered to individual and families, may lead some individuals to forego PT altogether or to reject abortion as the solution. Those who decide not to have testing or to continue a pregnancy after a prenatal diagnosis of a disability should be supported in their decision. They should not be made to feel that their decision is irresponsible or selfish because of the monetary costs it imposes on society.[13] No one should be bullied or coerced into having an abortion. At the same time, many people will prefer to have a child without a serious disabling condition, no matter how much social support they might receive or how inclusive the society is. They are entitled to make this choice.

If wishing to avoid a disability in one's future child is a reasonable preference, and if abortion is a permissible choice, then the choice of abortion to avoid having a child with a serious disability is also a permissible choice and one that should be respected. It does not indicate selfishness, a lack of empathy, or an incapacity for unconditional love for one's children. It just means that the individual does not think of the fetus, much less the preimplantation embryo, as already one's child to whom unconditional love owed.

On the individual level, being willing to terminate a pregnancy after learning of a disabling condition in the fetus is completely compatible with being a wonderful parent if one has a child born with a disability that was not detected during pregnancy. On a societal level, there is no conflict between respecting the rights of existing people with disabilities and making society more accessible to them, and respecting the rights of women and couples to make their own choices about whether to have PT and what to do with the information gained.

Respecting the rights of people with disabilities means listening to them and incorporating their views into law and policy. In the phrase of disability activists, "Nothing about us without us!" It means respecting their rights as competent adults to make their own medical decisions while understanding that the fact of disability does not translate into a monolithic position on such issues as selective abortion, advance directives, and physician-assisted death. Above all, it means recognizing and avoiding all-too-common discriminatory misconceptions about living with disabling conditions.

9

WHAT ETHICAL ISSUES ARE RAISED BY ASSISTED REPRODUCTIVE TECHNOLOGY?

In Chapters 7 and 8, we examined the permissibility of abortion when a woman does not want to continue a pregnancy. In this chapter, we take up the opposite issue: the use of assisted reproductive technology (ART) to help infertile people to achieve pregnancy. Infertility, which affects millions of people of reproductive age worldwide, can be as distressing as the inability to control fertility. ART also raises issues beyond infertility. It enables LGBTQ individuals to have children, which some allege constitutes an attack on traditional families. Gamete donation and surrogate motherhood involve more people than the individuals who intend to be rearing parents, which has been criticized as creating confusion about kinship and identity in the children created. Payments to gamete providers or gestational carriers are alleged to commodify reproduction. Finally, preimplantation genetic testing (PGT), which is routine in ART today, gives prospective parents the ability to choose the sex of their children, which some reject as reinforcing sexist stereotypes. We will consider each of these issues after gaining a basic understanding of ART.

How is infertility defined, and what are its causes?

What causes infertility, and why is it rising worldwide? The media sometimes give the impression that infertility is primarily a problem for older, middle- or upper-class White women who have been so focused on their careers that they put off childbearing until they were no longer fertile. In fact, infertility in the United States is more prevalent among poor people and minorities than among middle- or upper-class Whites. Increasing exposure to environmental pollutants, work-related stress, and the rise in obesity due to unhealthy diets and lifestyles are all contributing factors. Sexually transmitted diseases (STDs), such as chlamydia, can cause infertility, especially when people do not have sufficient access to decent healthcare and these diseases go untreated.

A public health approach to infertility focuses on diagnosing and treating STDs and educating people about infertility's causes. While these preventive measures can reduce the prevalence of infertility in a population, they cannot help those who are already infertile. They need medical assistance if they are to have biologically related children.

What medical procedures are used to treat infertility?

Treatment begins with a work-up to determine the cause of infertility. The problem could lie with the male partner, the female partner, or both. If the man does not produce sufficient sperm, or if his sperm do not swim fast or long enough to reach and fertilize the egg, he cannot biologically reproduce. The couple may then decide to use a sperm donor.

Infertility may be due to the failure of the woman to ovulate (i.e., produce eggs). This can be treated with drugs to promote ovulation. Sometimes the problem is not ovulation, but blocked fallopian tubes, where the released egg is prevented from traveling through the fallopian tubes where fertilization occurs. Surgical repair may then be indicated.

These approaches to infertility, known as conventional therapies, are used to treat eighty to ninety percent of cases. If they do not work, the next step is in vitro fertilization (IVF), a reproductive technology in which sperm fertilize eggs outside the body, in a petrie dish. IVF may also be used by women who do not have trouble getting pregnant but whose pregnancies end in miscarriage caused by chromosomal abnormalities in her eggs due to age.

To remove eggs from a woman's body requires considerable preparation. The woman must be injected or, increasingly, inject herself, every day for two weeks with drugs that cause her to super-ovulate (i.e., produce many eggs, not just the one or two she would naturally produce). When the eggs are ripe, they are retrieved in a transvaginal surgical procedure. Afterward, most women experience cramping, which can range from mild to severe.

It is much easier to retrieve sperm from a man than to retrieve eggs from a woman. All the man has to do is masturbate into a cup. A high concentration of his sperm is placed around each egg in a growth medium in a petrie dish. If all goes well, fertilization will occur within two to six hours. The fertilized egg then begins to divide until, in about five days, it reaches 100 cells and is then technically known as a *blastocyst*, though commonly called an *embryo*. At this point, the blastocyst is usually tested for any chromosomal abnormalities that might prevent implantation or normal development. Typically, the blastocysts are frozen until they are transplanted into the woman's uterus.

The first IVF baby, Louise Brown, was born in the United Kingdom in 1978. Her parents knew that the procedure was experimental, but they did not know that it had never before resulted in a human baby. Critics said that this prevented them from giving genuinely informed consent to the procedure. At first the success rates of IVF were very low, resulting in the birth of a live baby in only about ten percent of cases. Clinics varied tremendously in their success rates, and no reliable data were available on how successful individual clinics were. Concern about the exploitation of "desperate" couples led to calls for more accurate data collection and regulation of ART.

Approximately 1.9 percent of all babies born in the United States every year are conceived using ART. Before embarking on IVF, which is physically burdensome and expensive, most women want to know their chances of success—that is, of having a "take-home baby." This is hard to determine because it depends on many factors, including the age of the woman, her medical history, whether she uses her own or donor eggs, and how many cycles of IVF she undergoes. A woman younger than thirty-five who uses her own eggs has a better than fifty percent chance of having a baby after her first egg retrieval and any embryo transfers following that retrieval. Her chances improve to seventy percent if a second egg is retrieved that year, and to eighty-two percent with a third retrieval. However, the picture is much less good for older women. Fewer than twenty percent of women older than forty, using their own eggs, will have a live birth after IVF, and the chances of a live birth for women forty-five years old is under three percent. Moreover, advanced maternal age is a risk factor for pregnancy loss, fetal anomalies, and obstetric complications. According to one fertility doctor,

> Reproductive medicine specialists and obstetrician/gynecologists should promote more realistic views of the evidence-based realities of advanced maternal age pregnancy, including its high-risk nature and often compromised outcomes. Doctors should also actively educate both patients and the public that there is a real danger of childlessness if individuals choose to delay reproduction.[1]

What ethical arguments favor ART?

The basic argument for ART is respect for procreative liberty: the moral right of individuals to make their own decisions about reproduction. Just as individuals have the moral right to avoid having children, so, too, they have a moral right to medical treatment that will enable them to have children. The inability to have children does not preclude a desire to have them, any more than the inability to hear or see or walk precludes a desire to do those things. Moreover, for many people, the desire to have children is not merely one desire among many but a profound and fundamental one connected to the meaning of becoming an adult. For many, having children is an important part of self-identity. Some regard having progeny as providing a kind of immortality. If medical assistance can enable infertile people to have children, is there any reason why they should not have access to it? We turn now to some of the objections that have been made to ART.

Is adoption a better alternative than ART?

Some object to ART on the ground is that it is both unnecessary and less socially responsible than adoption. Adoption provides people who want a family with a child while also providing children who need parents with a family. This, it is alleged, is better than using ART to create more children in an already overpopulated world.

This is, at least initially, a persuasive argument. Adoption can be a wonderful option for many people. However, before deciding that adoption is more socially responsible than ART, we need to consider three points.

First, adoption is not less expensive than ART. Adoption costs between $20,000 and $50,000, about the same as IVF. Second, if adoption is more socially responsible than ART, isn't it also more socially responsible than natural reproduction as well? In other words, if there are all those children out there who need parents, shouldn't adoption be the preferred method of acquiring children? Why does the obligation to adopt, rather than have biologically related children, apply only to people who happen to be infertile?

Third, there aren't as many adoptable babies as is sometimes thought. The number of healthy newborns available for adoption in the United States began to decrease in the 1970s and 1980s, due to the legalization of abortion and access to reliable contraception. In 2013, the most recent year for which there are data, only four percent of American women with unwanted pregnancies placed their children for adoption. In addition, the increasing acceptability of unpartnered women raising their children has decreased the number of babies available for adoption. "Contrary to common belief, . . . domestic infant adoption is actually rather rare, with only roughly 10 percent of hopeful parents being placed with a baby. The wait is often long and full of disappointment and heartbreak."[2]

Frustrated by waits of two or more years, many Americans have turned to international adoptions. These, too, have become less common, having dropped seventy-two percent since 2005. In recent decades, South Korea, Romania, Guatemala, China, Kazakhstan, and Russia, all leaders in foreign adoptions, have also banned or cut back on them. In part, the reason has been a growing awareness of coercion and exploitation in adoption transactions. Rather than finding parents for children who needed them, private attorneys were conducting a business. "Unknown to the adoptive parents, these attorneys would use all sorts of tactics to acquire Guatemalan children for adoption—from buying and kidnapping kids to defrauding and coercing women to give their babies up."[3]

Adopting a child in the United States is easier and quicker if the couple is willing to accept an older child or one with special needs. However, this often poses additional challenges that add to the already daunting challenge of parenthood. The children may have emotional problems stemming from having been put in foster care and then put up for adoption or from institutionalization. They may have physical or cognitive problems that led their parents to give them up. As much as these children need families, and as rewarding as it may be to become their parents, adopting older children or those with special needs isn't for everyone.

As with the adoption of older children or children with disabilities, transracial adoption (usually White people who adopt Black, Asian, or mixed-race children) also poses challenges. The National Association of Black Social Workers (NABSW) opposes such adoptions as not being in the best interest of the children, believing that Black children belong in Black families. Even if they are wrong about this and children can thrive in mixed-race families, the complexities of transracial adoption must be realistically faced. Before embarking on a transracial adoption, the prospective parents need to ask themselves if they have family and close friends of other racial, cultural, or ethnic groups, and, if not, how they can develop such relationships. They will need to think about where they will live, what schools the child will attend, how they will meet the child's needs in developing self-identity and esteem, and how they will support the child when he or she experiences racial prejudice and discrimination. After reflection, some prospective parents may conclude that they would not be good candidates for a transracial adoption.

Adoption is problematic in another way, an aspect expressed by the sociologist Barbara Katz Rothman, herself an adoptive mother. Adoption creates a family, but it also destroys a family, the birth family. In the 1940s and '50s, unmarried women were often made to feel guilty about getting pregnant, and putting their babies up for adoption was both an atonement for their sin and widely regarded as giving the child the best opportunities in life. Such attitudes are much less prevalent today. It is widely acknowledged that social policies that support women who want to keep their babies are preferable to coercing them into giving them up.

Finally, unlike adoption, ART allows for the experiences of carrying, delivering, and nursing a baby, experiences which are important to many women. ART also enables couples to have a child that comes from both of them—the child they would have had but for their infertility. Even if the child cannot have a genetic connection to both parents, it may allow a genetic connection to at least one rearing parent.

The desire for a biological connection with one's child has been characterized as exemplifying "biologism."[4] This term suggests that the desire for a biologically related child is somehow deficient or trivial, something that really good parents would not care about. But why should that be? Kinship has profound significance for people all over the world. The fact that adoptees who love their adoptive families often want information about, and even contact with, their biological families is testimony to the power of biological relationship and its connection with identity and selfhood.

To acknowledge the importance of kinship is not to denigrate adoption or to suggest that adopted children are less valued or loved. Adoption, when done without coercion, is a wonderful alternative and the best way for some people to create a family. So is ART.

What are the health risks of IVF to women?

The drugs used to make women produce large amounts of eggs often cause considerable discomfort, including enlarged, tender ovaries and uterine cramping. In severe hyperstimulation, the ovaries become very large and painful. Swelling may occur and fluid may leak into the abdomen and chest resulting in serious fluid and electrolyte imbalance, with potentially significant complications, including death, though this is now extremely rare. Even without complications, the procedure is onerous. After egg retrieval and prior to embryo transfer, progesterone must be taken to support implantation. In the past, women were given tablets or suppositories. However, recent research indicates that better results are obtained by intramuscular injection. Increasingly, IVF patients are required to give themselves progesterone injections every day for two months.

Are there perhaps also long-term health effects on women from IVF treatment? We don't really know. In the United States, part of the problem is lack of follow-up data, largely a feature of the fragmented healthcare system that collects relatively little national medical data. Most existing research compares outcomes of women who have conceived using fertility treatments with those who have conceived naturally. But this is a very crude comparison, making it all but impossible to tell if the long-term health problems were caused by the fertility treatments or by the underlying causes of the infertility itself. For example, some early studies found a link between fertility drugs and ovarian, cervical, or endometrial cancer later in life. Most researchers now believe that it is not the drugs that increase the risk of cancer, but rather the underlying condition that makes these women infertile. For example, women who are infertile because they have endometriosis have an increased risk of ovarian cancer. It is even possible that IVF reduces their risk since full-term pregnancy may reduce the risk of cancer.

While much is not known, the risks to health do not appear to be greater than other health risks from medical procedures. We allow people to make their own decisions about whether the benefits outweigh the risks, so long as their decisions are fully informed and voluntary.

What are the health risks to offspring?

The risks to offspring born of ART were initially unknown. Articles in the media talked about "test tube babies" and the potential for creating monsters, but these fears were complete speculation. They were somewhat allayed when the first IVF baby, Louise Brown, was normal. The Browns had another IVF daughter, Natalie, who, in 1999, became the first human born after conception by IVF to subsequently give birth without IVF. Like her sister, Louise also did not need IVF to conceive, and she has given birth to two sons.

Early studies showed no higher rate of birth defects for IVF babies than for naturally conceived babies, so long as they were singletons. Some later studies did find a correlation between IVF and birth defects, including cerebral palsy (CP). It was not known, however, whether the increased risk of CP was due to the IVF per se or to the underlying infertility.

Most fertility specialists believe that the risks of physical harm to offspring from ART, whether from the technology itself or to underlying infertility, are small and well within the acceptable range of risk, especially since the only way of avoiding the disabling conditions is to avoid creating the child altogether. Moreover, it would seem that the same standards of harm prevention should apply equally to the lucky fertile and the unlucky infertile. If we do not require fertile people who risk passing on disabling conditions to avoid reproducing, should infertile people be treated any differently?

A clearer source of cognitive and physical problems stems from multiple births, which increase the risk of prematurity, itself associated with neonatal morbidity and mortality. Multiple births can result from giving women fertility drugs that cause them to release more eggs. Multiple births can also result from the practice of transferring multiple embryos. In the early days of IVF, doctors often transferred three to five embryos in the attempt to get a viable pregnancy. This resulted in a spate of multiple births, the most notorious of which was Nadya Suleman (the woman dubbed "Octomom" in the media) who gave birth to octuplets in 2009, after her doctor had transferred twelve embryos into her uterus. The problem of "super-multiples"—that is, triplets and more—received attention in both the press and the profession. Combined with the increasing success of single-embryo transfer, fertility experts no longer routinely transfer two or more embryos. Many clinics now have a mandatory single-embryo-transfer policy for good-prognosis patients. The resulting decrease in multiple births has improved outcomes in children of ART.

Are the offspring at risk of psychological harm?

Normally, only two people are involved in the procreation of a child: the mother and the father. ART creates the possibility of multiple people playing a role. These potential players include the rearing mother and father, an egg donor, a sperm donor, and a gestational carrier. In addition, in a process known as *egg cell nuclear transfer*, the egg can be divided into two components: the nucleus carrying the DNA and the surrounding cytoplasm which contains the mitochondria. This could be used in cases where a woman has mitochondrial disease. Her nucleus and the cytoplasm from another woman can be used, bringing the number of potential individuals involved to six.

When a child's parents separate, the questions of who will raise the child and who will have visitation rights often involve the courts. These questions are even thornier when multiple people are involved. For example, traditionally, the law has regarded the mother as the one who gives birth to the child. This suggests that the gestational carrier be regarded as "the real mother." But there is also an argument for regarding the woman who provides the egg as the real mother, since some of her genetic traits will be inherited by the child. Or perhaps neither gestational nor genetic connection is the salient factor, but rather motherhood is best determined by intention: that is, who intended to raise the child. Different courts have come to different conclusions. Many legal commentators have persuasively argued that there needs to be uniformity on the issues of child support, custody, and visitation that arise from ART. Others maintain that, quite apart from these legal issues, having so many individuals playing a procreative role could potentially create problems of identity for the child or confusion about kinship relations.

ART is not unique in having more than two potential parents. Divorce and remarriage create blended families, too, with questions about custody and visitation. The problem is not the numbers involved in creating children, but rather uncertainty about who subsequently counts as a parent and what role, if any, the nonrearing biological contributors, such as gamete donors and gestational carriers, should play in the child's life. In the United States, state law governs these matters, which can complicate things when people seek a surrogate or adopt out-of-state. Model state laws could reduce complications and provide more certainty.

As for the psychological effects on children of having multiple potential parents, Alta Charo suggests that we might break out of the strait-jacketed legal approach of insisting that children can have only one mother and one father. It isn't necessarily a burden for children to have multiple people playing different roles in their upbringing. As she suggests, "you can never have too many parents to love you."[5]

The arguments in favor of individuals making their own choices regarding treatments for infertility are strong, so long as they are provided with complete and accurate information about any risks and the likelihood of success. Another issue is whether payment should be the responsibility of individuals or the society in general.

Who should pay?

Fifteen states in the United States have laws requiring insurers to *cover* infertility treatment, and two states have laws that require insurance companies to *offer* coverage for infertility treatment. Some state programs explicitly exclude coverage for IVF, although, even in these states, private insurance companies may provide more generous benefits. When infertility treatments are covered by insurance, the individual user may pay nothing or only a little, but *someone* is paying for it. The question of cost does not disappear simply because the treatment is covered by insurance.

Whether ART should be covered, either by private insurance or as part of a national or state health plan, depends on how one views the inability to have children. One approach, exemplified by the United States, regards having children as something that many people want, but it is not an entitlement. On this view, ART should be available to people as they can afford it, but neither the state nor private health plans have an obligation to pay for it.

A very different view regards having children as a fundamental human right, and something to which all members of a society are, or should be, entitled. These sorts of rights are called *positive rights*. They typically include things like a basic right to food, shelter, and primary and secondary education. By contrast, *negative rights* are rights not to be interfered with. They include things like a right to freedom of speech and religion, a right to travel freely, or to decide where to live and work. Respecting negative rights does not impose financial burdens on a country (or other financing entity), but positive rights do. For this reason, positive rights are dependent on a country's financial situation. Only relatively wealthy countries can have an obligation to provide its citizens with fertility treatment, even if having children is regarded as a human right.

A third approach does not claim that access to fertility treatment is a human right, but rather bases the obligation for nations and health plans to provide ART on the grounds that infertility is a disease. If the state provides healthcare for other diseases, it ought to provide fertility treatment, too. (About disease as a criterion for coverage, see also Chapter 11.)

Some countries, such as France, Germany, and Belgium, offer complete financial coverage for infertility, while others offer coverage with limits on fertility treatment. For example, Israel covers ART but only until the birth of two children. How much a country or subscribers to a health plan are willing to spend on this kind of medical treatment depends both on the country's and people's resources and how they prioritize the treatment of infertility. After all, even if having children is profoundly important to many people, the inability to procreate is not life-threatening. This suggests that less should be spent on

infertility than on fatal diseases. Another factor in prioritiza-
tion is the country's birth rate. A country with a low birth rate
is likely to be "pro-natalist," covering fertility treatment and
other incentives to its citizens to have children.

Is using ART to create nontraditional families ethically acceptable?

Sperm donation is not limited to heterosexual infertile
couples. It can also be used by lesbians or gay men who
want to have a child. Their inability to procreate is not due
to infertility since they could procreate if they had opposite-
sex partners. It is their sexual orientation that inhibits them
from procreating, not a medical problem. A lesbian couple
may use sperm donation and artificial insemination for the
woman who will gestate the fetus. If two gay men wish to
have a child, they will need a gestational carrier, who may or
may not provide the egg. These practices allow the existence
of new types of families, ones beyond the traditional heterosexual nuclear family.

Some critics claim that using ART to create such families
constitutes an attack on the traditional nuclear family. This
claim is hard to understand since enabling new kinds of
families does not prevent traditional nuclear families from
being created. It simply allows for the creation of nontradi-
tional families. The objection must be that there is something
wrong with such families.

Attitudes toward homosexuality have changed dramatically
over the past twenty-five years. In 2015, the US Supreme Court
struck down all state bans against same-sex marriage. In 2017,
the Court effectively legalized same-sex adoption in all fifty
states. Nevertheless, twelve states permit state-licensed child
welfare agencies to refuse to place children in foster care or into
adoption with same-sex couples. In 2021, the Supreme Court
held that the refusal of Philadelphia to contract with a Catholic
foster care agency unless the agency agreed to consider as foster

parents individuals in same-sex marriages, in violation of its religious beliefs, violated the First Amendment.[6]

Balancing freedom of religion against nondiscrimination is a thorny issue. Is there any other reason why same-sex couples should not be able to adopt or have children? For example, is there evidence that having gay parents harms children? Three decades of research on the impact on children of having gay or lesbian parents reveals that the children fare as well as other children, and there is no evidence that sexual orientation impairs parenting ability. If the welfare of the children is not a factor, it is hard to see why LGBTQ people should be denied the right to exercise procreative liberty and realize their dreams of becoming parents.

Does paying gamete donors or gestational carriers commodify reproduction?

People are paid to provide sperm or eggs or to gestate a fetus because few people would perform these services without compensation. While some have objected even to unpaid sperm donation,[7] the primary objection has been to payment for gametes, embryos, or gestational carriers on the grounds that this commodifies and commercializes reproduction and the human body.[8]

As in all other branches of medicine, those engaged in reproductive medicine expect financial compensation. No one suggests that paying the doctors or fertility clinics and their staff commercializes or commodifies reproduction. It is only when the payment is made to providers of gametes or gestational carriers that charges of commercialization and commodification are made. Why? A possible answer is that paying people for their body parts is commodification but compensating professionals for their services is not. This is sometimes supported by the claim that some things should not be for sale.[9] Even if we grant this claim, the question remains: Precisely what things should not be for sale, and why?

The clearest example of something that should not be for sale is human beings. Slavery is morally wrong, even if the enslaved person were to agree to it. In *On Liberty*, John Stuart Mill, one of the greatest defenders of individual liberty, explains why society should not allow it. Someone who sells himself into slavery uses his freedom to deny his freedom, which is contrary to the very purpose of freedom.

Slavery has always been associated with great cruelty, but slavery would be wrong even if slaves were not beaten or branded or raped or separated from their spouses and children. As Kant might have put it, the basic wrongness of slavery is that it treats human beings as if they were mere things, with only monetary value, deprived of the dignity and autonomy that all persons possess (see Chapter 1).

Another clear example of something that should not be sold is votes. Voting is an essential part of democracy. It is the basic way that those who are governed have a say in the rules that they must obey. Allowing the sale of votes contravenes the very idea of democracy.

Clearly, then, people and votes may not be treated as mere commodities. Beyond these examples, things become less clear and more controversial. What about baby selling? Most people object to the notion of a market in babies, but money does change hands in adoption. Indeed, as noted above, it costs about as much to adopt a baby as to undergo IVF. Is it obvious that it is acceptable for adoptive parents to pay adoption agencies and lawyers, but unacceptable for them to compensate the child's parents? Some have even advocated for a regulated market in babies to make up for the adoptable baby shortage.[10]

Another controversial example is prostitution. Some think it obvious that prostitution is immoral and for the same reason that slavery is wrong: it involves selling one's body. Of course, sex workers do not literally sell their bodies. It is more accurate to say that they rent them for sexual purposes. If women are forced into prostitution and cannot leave, that is a form of slavery. If the money goes to pimps who control the sex workers, the scheme begins to look a lot like slavery. However, some women may choose to engage in sex work. Attitudes about voluntary sex work differ, even among feminists. Some feminists oppose prostitution because they think it harms and exploits women and reinforces the idea of women as sex objects, while other feminists support the right of women to choose to do sex work.

Another controversial example is the sale of human body parts. It hardly seems that selling all body parts is immoral. Most people do not have moral objections to selling hair, for example. Some oppose compensation for blood donation, while others do not regard selling blood as wrong if it can be done safely for seller and recipient. The argument about selling blood turns on the likely effects of compensation: Which provides a greater and better blood supply, an altruistic or a compensated system?

There is more consensus on the wrongness of selling human organs, like kidneys from live donors. But is that because it is intrinsically wrong to sell organs, or is the concern the potential exploitation of those who are in dire poverty? Some have argued, given the dearth of kidneys and their ability to save lives, that a regulated market in kidneys should be allowed so long as those who provide the kidneys are compensated fairly and their safety ensured.[11]

Unlike kidneys, hair and blood are renewable, but so is sperm. If it is permissible for people to sell their hair and their blood, why not their sperm? And while eggs are not renewable, women are born with far more eggs than they can use. Should they be prohibited from selling their excess eggs if they are compensated fairly and their health protected?

This brief discussion reveals that more is needed for the commodification argument against paying gamete donors and surrogates to be persuasive. We need to ask, why are gametes and gestation the kinds of things that may not be sold? Simply to say that it is wrong to pay providers of gametes and gestational carriers because that commodifies reproduction is to beg that important question.

Some argue that the reason it is wrong to pay people for their gametes or for acting as gestational carriers is that this is exploitative. Interestingly, the exploitation objection is rarely made to sperm donation. This may be because the process of retrieving sperm is a lot less onerous than retrieving eggs. Or it may be because sperm donors are typically paid relatively small amounts. In any event, the claim is usually that offering payment exploits egg donors, and it is to this claim that we now turn.

Does payment exploit egg donors?

Some have said that it is exploitative to dangle large sums of money in front of young women in exchange for their eggs because it entices them to participate. They may fail to consider sufficiently the risks to their own health and well-being, either because they are not being adequately informed of the risks or because the lure of payment leads them to discount the risks.

Sometimes clinics do conceal or downplay the risks to women to get them to donate eggs, a clear violation of medical ethics. As Dr. Marc Sauer, a prominent fertility doctor in New York, has put it, "The challenge lies in ensuring that all medical groups practice with the same rigorous attention to informed consent necessary for recruiting donors and truly educating women to the risks of participation."[12]

Another form of exploitation is psychological manipulation. Donors can be manipulated to make repeat donations by being made to think they are unusually fertile, producing exceptional amounts of high-quality eggs. The reality is that these women are not super fertile; they have been hyperstimulated. By making them feel special, they can be induced to donate repeatedly. These kinds of exploitative practices should be, and have been, condemned by reputable fertility doctors. If potential egg donors are properly educated about the risks, is offering payment still exploitative?

Perhaps. If potential donors are desperately poor, offering even a modest amount of money can exploit their desperation. This is unlikely in the United States, where donors are usually middle- or upper-middle class, often college students or young professionals. Those seeking donors want women who are "like them," who resemble the prospective rearing mother, physically, intellectually, and temperamentally. They do not want women who are impoverished, addicted to drugs, or in bad health.

If the price for donating eggs is too high, the offer might be exploitative by clouding judgment. In 2000, in response to concerns that some egg donors were being offered excessively large sums of money,[13] the American Society for Reproductive Medicine (ASRM) issued a guideline for compensating egg donors: sums of $5,000 or more require justification, and sums above $10,000 are not appropriate. The guideline did not have the force of law, but ASRM and the Society for Assisted Reproductive Technology (SART) required that its members follow the guidelines. Nevertheless, some high-end fertility clinics and egg donor agencies ignored the guidelines, paying more for eggs from especially attractive donors: actresses, models, Asians, Jews, and Ivy League students with high SATs.

The ASRM guidelines were challenged in a federal lawsuit by a group of women who called it "price-fixing," pointing out that there's no limit on the amount paid for sperm. ASRM settled the suit in 2016, removing the language that required justification for fees higher than $5,000 and essentially banned compensation over $10,000. The current guidelines simply say that the financial compensation of women donating oocytes, for infertility therapy or research, is justified on ethical grounds, but compensation should be structured to acknowledge the time, inconvenience, and discomfort associated with screening, ovarian stimulation, and retrieval.[14]

This approach recognizes that compensation is necessary for there to be an adequate supply of eggs for all who want them. Uncompensated or, as it is sometimes called, *altruistic egg donation* simply cannot meet the demand. While egg donors are typically also motivated by the opportunity to help someone have a child, often because they know someone who has struggled with infertility, few women would be willing to go through the onerous process of egg donation for a stranger without compensation. Moreover, fairness requires that egg donors be adequately compensated for their time, discomfort, and risk. If compensation is structured in this way, as recommended by ASRM, it is hard to see how commercial egg donation exploits donors.

Does payment exploit gestational carriers?

Far more is demanded of gestational carriers than of egg donors. For one thing, the process is longer. It takes thirty-six to thirty-seven days to be an egg donor, as opposed to fourteen to more than twenty months to be a gestational carrier, depending on how quickly the women is matched with intended parents, how well she responds to IVF medications, and time for embryo creation and transfer. In addition to length of time, pregnancy imposes far greater physical discomfort and risks than egg retrieval. Perhaps the greatest difference between being an egg donor and being a gestational carrier is that, at the end of the process, the egg donor has fewer eggs, but the gestational carrier gives up the child she carried for nine months. If she was implanted with an embryo created from another woman's egg, the surrogate will not be genetically related to the fetus, but she will have a biological connection: gestation. If her own egg is used, she will be both genetically and gestationally related to the child.

Noncompensated surrogate arrangements are very rare and typically limited to family members or close friends. Most gestational carriers, like most egg donors, have dual motives: to help a couple have a child and to earn money. Gestational carriers in the United States earn between $30,000 and $60,000, depending on geographical location, and even more for multiple births.

How do gestational carriers feel about giving up the babies? There aren't many studies on the question, although one can find many anecdotal reports. According to one study of only ten women, some of the women felt sad and disappointed from the loss of contact with the children they bore, but most did not regret the role they played, thinking they did something wonderful in helping a couple have a baby. At the same time, "a few were angry and bitter because they felt they had been exploited or abandoned by the children's families."[15] The feelings of exploitation do not seem connected to how much they were paid, but rather to whether they felt respected and appreciated both during gestation and after the babies were born.

The possibility of exploitation looms especially large in the case of international surrogacy; the contracting couples typically come from wealthy countries, while the surrogates usually come from developing countries. In the past, couples in the United States or the United Kingdom could contract with a gestational carrier in India or Thailand for about a third of what it would cost in their own country.

Gestational carriers in the United States are not impoverished. Mostly lower-middle or working class, they view surrogacy as a relatively easy way to afford "extras." By contrast, in a developing country, surrogacy may be the only way out of desperate poverty and thus a choice that a poor woman feels that she cannot refuse. Some philosophers regard offering people choices they realistically cannot refuse as the epitome of exploitation and thus morally impermissible. Others think that it is objectionably paternalistic to deprive people of choices that they reasonably believe will make their lives better, even if these are not choices they would make under better conditions.

Both domestic and international surrogacy can lead to disputes about custody. The 2014 case of Baby Gammy received a great deal of press attention. David and Wendy Farnell, an Australian couple, contracted with a Thai woman, Pattaramon Chanbua, to serve as a gestational surrogate. Embryos were created using donor eggs and David's sperm. Ms. Chanbua was discovered to be carrying twins, a boy and a girl. The boy, originally known as "Baby Gammy," was discovered to have Down syndrome. Ms. Chanbua decided to keep the boy, alleging that the Farnells asked her to abort the fetus with Down syndrome. There was a huge public outcry, with abuse heaped on the Australian couple for rejecting a child with Down syndrome, and tremendous sympathy for Ms. Chanbua.

However, an Australian court ruled in 2016 that the Farnells did not in fact ask Ms. Chanbua to abort the boy, and they did not abandon him. Chief Judge Stephen Thackray said that it was clear that, at some time during the pregnancy, Ms. Chanua had fallen in love with the twins and decided she was going to keep the boy. When civil unrest broke out in Thailand, the couple was advised by Australian embassy staff to leave the country. When Ms. Chanbua refused to give up baby Gammy, who was still in the hospital, the couple left with Gammy's twin, Pipah, and returned to Australia. Ms. Chanbua sought to have Pipah returned to her, but the judge said that taking her from the only parents she'd ever known would not be in her best interest. The judge went on to say that the case highlights the problems with commercial surrogacy. "Quite apart from the separation of the twins, this case serves to highlight the dilemmas that arise when the reproductive capacities of women are turned into saleable commodities, with all the usual fallout when contracts go wrong."[16]

As a result of the Baby Gammy case, Thailand no longer permits foreigners to travel to Thailand for commercial surrogate arrangements, although they are legal for heterosexual married Thai couples. India, once a popular country for individuals seeking surrogates, has also banned commercial surrogacy, as of 2015, for foreign intended parents. Ukraine, a popular international surrogacy destination, is one of the few countries that permits surrogacy for foreign intended parents, although this has been seriously disrupted by Russia's attack on Ukraine in 2022.

Is the use of ART for medical sex selection ethical?

IVF combined with PGT enables prospective parents to discard embryos determined to have chromosomal abnormalities that can cause genetic diseases or developmental disorders. It is often recommended for women older than thirty-five who have a higher chance of having eggs with chromosomal defects, women who have a history of miscarriage, and couples who are carriers for a genetic disease. In such cases, PGT can lower the risk of miscarriage and increase the chances of having a successful IVF cycle at first embryo transfer.

Because PGT reveals not only abnormalities in the embryo, but also its sex, the procedure raises the possibility of being used for sex selection. Discarding embryos of a particular sex may be required in the case of genetic diseases that are sex-linked. For example, Duchenne muscular dystrophy (DMD) usually affects only boys. If the particular mutation that causes DMD is known or can be found out, it might be possible simply to discard only male embryos with that mutation. However, if the particular mutation is not known, the only way to avoid DMD in the resulting child is to discard all the male embryos, whether or not affected.

Some have argued that discarding embryos to prevent a disabling condition in the child is, if not ethically impermissible, at least ethically problematic. We took up that issue in Chapter 8. Here, in this chapter, we will assume the dominant view, that sex selection to avoid serious genetic disease is ethically warranted. Nonmedical sex selection, used not to avoid genetic disease or to improve the chances of a successful pregnancy, but to enable the prospective parents to choose the sex of their child, is ethically much more controversial.

What arguments support the use of ART for nonmedical sex selection?

The main arguments in favor of using ART for nonmedical sex selection are patient autonomy and procreative liberty. Respect for patient autonomy requires medical professionals to respect the decisions and choices that patients make, recognizing that the patient's values may differ from their own. That is not to say that medical professionals are required to do anything that patients request, but rather that the reasons for refusing must be strong ones. The fact that they do not agree with a patient's decision is not, by itself, a sufficient reason to override it.

In *Children of Choice: Freedom and the New Reproductive Technologies*,[17] John Robertson argued that procreative liberty is justifiably restricted only when its exercise would result in tangible harm to specific individuals. His view is not universally accepted. Some countries ban practices that are viewed with disfavor by the majority, even if they cannot be shown to be harmful to individuals. Or they accept a wider view of harmfulness that includes practices that do not represent the country's values. Thus, questions about the legitimate use of ART, like many questions in bioethics, turn on the deeper political question of when individual liberty is justifiably restricted. Currently most ART clinics in the United States offer nonmedical sex selection, which no US state has made illegal. In many other countries, however, including Canada, Australia, and the United Kingdom, nonmedical sex selection is illegal. Should it be?

What are the arguments against nonmedical sex selection?

One argument, expressed in 2007 by the American College of Obstetrics and Gynecology (ACOG) is that nonmedical sex selection can be "motivated by and reinforce the devalu-ation of women."[18] That statement has been withdrawn, and ACOG has not replaced it. In countries like India and China, sex selection, usually by abortion after an ultrasound, is not uncommon, despite the fact that both countries now ban the administering of prenatal tests to determine the sex of a fetus. Sex selection in these countries is part of the explanation for millions of "missing women."[19] In addition, nonmedical sex selection may result in significant gender imbalance, as it has in India and China, with resulting concerns about social insta-bility stemming from men unable to find marriageable women.

The preference for boys, however, is hardly universal. Gallup polls taken in the United States between 1997 and 2018 showed only a slight preference for a boy when couples were asked whether they would prefer to have a boy or a girl if they could only have one child.[20] Other surveys that asked about preferences if the couple were to have more than one child did not show a preference for males over females. Thus, while sex selection may reinforce the devaluation of women in countries where male children are more highly valued than female chil-dren, it seems unlikely that it would have this effect in countries where both sexes are valued. And even in countries that do value males much more highly than females, it is far from clear that banning sex selection would help the status of women. It could even make things worse, as it might lead to a return to older practices of infanticide or neglect of female babies. Depriving girls of food and medical attention in India and China is another reason why there are so many "missing" women.

A second argument is that allowing parents to decide the sex of their future child will reaffirm prejudices about gender. It is alleged that nonmedical sex selection essentially involves gender prejudice because if people did not have such prejudices, they would not care about whether their child was a boy or a girl. Moreover, they are likely to impose rigid gender roles on the child, limiting their options and violating the child's "right to an open future."

However, having a preference about the sex of one's child is not necessarily sexist. It could stem from a belief that being a mother or a father to a daughter is different from being a mother or a father to a son. Not better, just different. Some regard viewing gender as relevant to the experience of parenting as wrong-headed. They maintain it should make no difference to you whether your child is a boy or a girl, and only those with sexist attitudes would think otherwise. This seems to us breathtakingly simplistic, ignoring the role that gender plays in both personality and relationships with others.

In 1999, the Ethics Committee of ASRM issued a report saying that the use of IVF with PGD solely for sex selection purposes should be discouraged because of risks of gender bias and social harm. In 2001, the committee concluded that clinics should be permitted to offer preconception sex selection to couples seeking gender variety, also known as "family balancing." Why, though, should nonmedical sex selection be limited to those seeking family balancing? If wanting the experience of parenting a child of a particular sex is a legitimate reason for sex selection, why should it be permitted only to those who want more than one child?

A third argument emphasizes respect for embryos. It maintains that while it is permissible to discard embryos if they are unlikely to go to term or if the resulting child is likely to have a serious disease or disabling condition, to discard embryos based on a preference for one sex over the other fails to show proper respect for embryos. However, IVF often results in more embryos than can be safely implanted. If only one embryo will be transferred, then a choice has to be made between healthy, viable embryos. How should this choice be made? Many couples have no preference about the sex of their child. They might ask the doctor to choose "the best embryo," that is, the one most likely to result in a "take-home baby." But there may not be a "best" embryo. If a couple has a preference regarding the sex of the child, why would basing the choice on their preference display a lack of proper respect for embryos?

ASRM does not take a position on the ethics of nonmedical sex selection, saying that it remains ethically controversial. It holds that practitioners are under no obligation either to provide or refuse to provide nonmedical sex selection. Clinics are encouraged to develop policies on the provision of nonmedical sex selection and to discuss these policies with patients at the time of informed consent for PGT.[21]

Concluding thoughts

ART has been around for more than forty years. As with many new technologies, it has raised many concerns, most of which have not materialized. People have not rushed to substitute IVF for sexual intercourse in creating their families. Although it is estimated that eight million babies have been born worldwide from IVF, fewer than two percent of all births in the United States result from IVF. Denmark leads the world in the use of ART, and, even there, the percentage of IVF is estimated to be about ten percent.

Many of the original concerns about the health risks for pregnant women and offspring have been assuaged, although this is something that should continue to be studied. As the technologies have improved, success rates have gone up. At the same time, it is vital that fertility specialists be frank with potential patients about their chances of having a child and the risk of childlessness if procreation is delayed. Concerns about adverse psychological effects on offspring have not been borne out; children created by IVF do as well as children created through sexual intercourse.

Fears about the wealthy using the poor as sources for gametes or embryos or as gestational carriers have not materialized, largely because impoverished people are not regarded as desirable candidates. Most egg donors receive between $5,000 and $10,000 per retrieval cycle in developed countries. This seems fair compensation for a lengthy and onerous process. Gestational carriers in developed countries can earn anywhere between $30,000 and $100,000, depending on various factors, including location. Again, given the time, risks, and burdens of pregnancy, this does not seem inordinately high.

Nevertheless, some of the options in ART can create new problems. For example, an embryo created by one couple was mistakenly transferred into the womb of the woman in another couple. As a result, the woman gave birth to twins, one of which was genetically related to the other couple.[22] Such cases, while shocking, are extremely rare. A more common problem is that sperm donation can result in large numbers of children who have half siblings. If the children do not know they are related, they may form romantic relationships or even marry. The problem can be addressed by limiting the number of donations from a given sperm donor[23] and by being transparent about the origins of children created through gamete donation.

Today, many parents know the sex of their child prior to birth, including many who do not use ART to conceive. The ability to know and even choose the sex of one's child in most of the world has not led to the gender imbalance experienced in India and China. In societies that favor males, ART may facilitate gender imbalance, but it does not cause it. Nor are restrictions on ART likely to eliminate or lessen discrimination against and oppression of women. The evils of sex discrimination and the devaluing and oppression of women must be tackled directly. Until they are, the preference for male children that continues to exist in some cultures and countries will not diminish.

10

WHAT IS REQUIRED FOR A HEALTHCARE SYSTEM TO BE JUST?

What questions of justice arise in comparing healthcare systems?

Distributive justice concerns how the goods and resources of life are distributed among the people they affect. Questions about distributive justice abound in healthcare. Who, for example, should be admitted to intensive care during a pandemic when not all who need it can be accommodated? Who should get scarce organs for transplant when not all can be saved? In insurance, should healthier subscribers share in the higher costs of care for those who are less healthy? Must access to affordable basic healthcare be guaranteed for everyone?

Some of these questions are about justice *within* a healthcare system—priorities for receiving intensive care in a pandemic, for example. Others, the focus of this chapter, are about *the systems themselves.* One of the most central is whether healthcare should be provided by a single national health service, by various providers but insured through public "single-payer" insurance, or insured by many insurance plans ("multipayer" insurance).

Examples of countries that have single-payer insurance are Canada, Taiwan, and (with some modification) France. Great Britain exemplifies countries with a national health service. Countries with multipayer systems include, on the highly regulated end, Germany, Netherlands, and Switzerland, and with a less regulated variety, the United States. Some segments of US healthcare, however, are single-payer (Medicare for senior citizens and Medicaid for those younger than sixty-five and with low incomes), and military veterans receive care from a mini-national health service, the Veterans Administration. China's system is a mix of public and private medical institutions and insurance programs; ninety-five percent of the population is covered by public basic insurance, but that insurance covers only slightly more than half of total medical expenditures.[1]

To assess healthcare systems, this chapter will employ three important theories of distributive justice—utilitarian, egalitarian (based in Kantian ethics), and libertarian. Their notions of justice differ, and they lean toward different conclusions about what structural type of system achieves justice best. Healthcare systems are often seen as falling on a spectrum from those characterized by more equity and justice, but which employ more collective coercion, to those that achieve less equity but allow more individual liberty. Much debate in health policy then tends to be a battleground between the political left, willing to compromise liberty to achieve equity, and the political right, willing to sacrifice equity and universal coverage to avoid encroaching on liberty.

The paradigm of the former is a unitary public system, either *single-payer insurance* for care provided by various private and public facilities, or a public *national health service* that directly delivers care to an entire population. Egalitarians tend to see justice as requiring a unitary public system in one of these two forms. Both provide universal access to a basic minimum of care.

On the opposite, liberty-emphasizing end of the spectrum is a *competitive, multipayer insurance market*. It appeals to consumers' liberty to choose among different insurance plans. In the pure form of this paradigm, individuals remain free to skip health insurance entirely, and insurers have no constraints in bidding for any group of subscribers with whatever premiums they believe adequate to cover that group's care. Consumer and insurer liberty are paramount.

As we explore the three different conceptions of justice and the realities of health insurance, we will see that liberty and equity do not so neatly line up with their commonly associated partners this way (liberty with completely "free-market" multipayer private insurance, and equity with single-payer insurance or national health service). The tensions between equity and liberty are real, but the stereotypical associations break down when the basic values of liberty and equity are better understood and the realities of how health insurance works are accounted for. That arguably opens the door for libertarians to embrace compulsory, universal coverage for a basic minimum of care and for egalitarians to support properly structured systems of competitive private insurance. The practical upshot: some form of universal access to basic care is required for a system to be just.

We make no attempt to determine which philosophical theory of justice—utilitarian, egalitarian, or libertarian—is most defensible. Rather, our intent is to clarify the implications of each for choice of a healthcare system and account for other relevant aspects of distributive justice.

How do utilitarian views of justice apply to healthcare systems?

In utilitarianism, the goal is to maximize the aggregate well-being of all individuals affected (see Chapter 1). A just distribution of benefits and harms is then the distribution that maximizes well-being in a society. Sometimes it will be relatively egalitarian, as with the basic food and water necessary for everyone's health and well-being. Also, at the very core of utilitarianism is a fundamentally egalitarian element: each person's benefits and harms must be counted equally—in proportion, of course, to their respective amounts. With some goods, however, quite unequal distributions may be justified.

Allowing some people to earn and keep much more than others manage to, for example, may provide incentives to produce that end up boosting overall well-being in a society.

In healthcare, many examples of universal provision can be cited as maximizing well-being. Good basic dental care for everyone, including public health dental prevention such as fluoridated drinking water, may create more total well-being for a given investment than less efficient acute dental care, though the latter may seem more urgent and humane. Universal provision of basic primary care may avoid so much use of hospital emergency rooms, resulting in better health and lower ultimate cost, that it is an essential part of any defensible healthcare system. We might ordinarily think of such distributions as "efficient" and not "just," but for a utilitarian they are both, for an ultimately just distribution is one that maximizes utility.

A utilitarian sense of justice has a number of strengths in assessing a healthcare system. One is that it readily accommodates "spin-off effects." At first glance a system that provides affordable basic healthcare to everyone, for example, may not seem efficient, given how much it can cost, but, beyond its direct health benefits, the solidarity and sense of individual security such a system creates may mean that it actually maximizes overall well-being compared to any system less successful in achieving equal access. Another is that a utilitarian sense of justice readily acknowledges that healthcare should have no special claim on resources without comparing what those resources could produce if they were invested elsewhere (in education, for example). In certain ways, yes, health and healthcare are "special" goods, but in a utilitarian view of efficiency and justice, they should never be insulated from tradeoffs with other things that may contribute more to people's well-being.

On the other hand, this very fluidity between healthcare and other sectors of the economy may constitute one of the greatest challenges to utilitarian reasoning: How can we make reasonably good calculations of well-being across such a wide field of comparison? How does one compare, for example, the value of an extra likely year of life from exemplary healthcare with the benefits of better education for a whole lifetime? If we cannot, how can we ever gain a reasonable sense of how much of a nation's gross domestic product (GDP) should be spent on healthcare? And if we cannot feasibly determine that, how can we ever know what level of basic healthcare constitutes the just minimum to which everyone should have access?

What does an egalitarian view of justice require?

In egalitarian views of justice, in contrast to a utilitarian view, a just distribution does not depend on whether it increases the aggregate well-being of a population. Essential goods should be distributed relatively equally even if that does not maximize well-being overall. Healthcare, especially with its effect on life itself, demands basic equality in provision. Equal *health* for all is of course not possible, and even equal *healthcare* is not the proper goal, for some people need much more than others. But egalitarian justice does require *equal healthcare for equal healthcare needs*.

To see how this translates into a choice of healthcare system, we must consider the role of insurance. For most people, affordable healthcare requires insurance, spreading out the cost of an individual's care across a pool of people, some of whom will need much more care than others. Justice in healthcare then requires a just system of insurance. But insurance comes in a huge variety of forms. How much insurance, for how wide a scope of all the things in healthcare that it could cover?

Several prominent refinements of egalitarian justice have been developed to address these questions. They both constitute a "moderately egalitarian" view of justice. By focusing on equality of *opportunity*, they make room for limited kinds of inequality.

Richard Arneson, for example, incorporates individual choice and responsibility into the heart of distributive justice.

> People should not be worse off than others through no fault or voluntary choice of their own. Situations where people are much worse off than others because of their own sufficiently blameworthy actions or choices may be tolerated [as not unjust], as painful or distasteful as those situations may be.[2]

Or more briefly,

> It is unjust for people to be worse off than others due to outcomes that it would not have been reasonable to expect them to avoid.

Applied specifically to healthcare, this view of justice demands financial sharing: The financial burdens of medical misfortune ought to be shared by well and ill alike, unless those burdens are created by the unreasonable choices for which people should be legitimately held responsible. The practical effect? Health insurance must be provided for large enough groups (in insurance lingo, large enough "pools") to level out most of the huge expense differences in insuring different people. The largest pool, of course, would be the whole society.

American philosopher Norman Daniels develops the egalitarian approach somewhat differently, drawing on the larger theory of justice as fairness espoused by late-twentieth-century philosopher John Rawls. Daniels captures the core of Rawls' view in his own notion of *fair equality of opportunity* (FEO) that applies directly healthcare: Disease and disability "constitute a fundamental restriction on . . . the normal range [of opportunity to] which the individual's particular skills and talents would ordinarily have made available to him."[3]

The special nature of healthcare is then apparent: other goods also contribute to human well-being, but healthcare contributes something especially fundamental—it helps to preserve and restore equality of opportunity. The right to basic healthcare is needed to protect that opportunity for everyone. It is not contingent on whether the investment of resources necessary to assure universal access to basic care contributes more to general well-being than other investments would. Fair equality of opportunity for each and every person must come first.

Neither of these moderate egalitarian views claims that all healthcare should be distributed equally according to medical need. Do patients have a right to a half-million-dollar treatment, for example, whose chance of success is only twenty percent, and then only for a statistically likely additional half year of life? Or to routine mammography for women in their forties for breast cancer detection, when the additional effectiveness of such routine use is fewer than two lives saved for every 10,000 extra mammograms performed?[4] Perhaps not. And if not, such measures arguably comprise a "second tier" of care that may, within the limits permitted by justice, be omitted from universally accessible "basic care." Some will choose to purchase that care directly or buy insurance for it, but it would not need to be included in the basic minimum. (The extent of care that should be included in a "basic" or "decent" minimum is pursued in Chapter 11.)

At this point the moderate egalitarian emphasis on fair equality of opportunity runs into a major challenge: Is it really helpful in determining what is included in the basic minimum of care to which everyone has a right? Since the focus is on opportunity, one is led to ask, *opportunity for what*? Realistic opportunity for a better education, for example, may, because of the resources required, compete with healthcare that lies at the edge of the package of "basic" care that should be accessible to everyone. A particular cancer treatment may provide some the opportunity to live another five years, while investing the same resources in higher levels and quality of education could open up a very different and rich set of opportunities in people's lives. What should the society do as a matter of policy—fund (or subsidize) the expensive cancer treatment or provide much better access to education? Does "equality of opportunity" really tell us anything?

Moderate egalitarian principles of justice reside in the general moral view referred to in Chapter 1 as Kantian ethics. Fairness and respect for each and every individual person are at Kantian ethics' core. In healthcare, justice is not simply a matter of promoting the well-being of a society, but of respecting individual rights, including the right to basic healthcare.

What does libertarian justice imply for choice of a healthcare system?

Neither equity nor maximum well-being, but liberty, is the core value in the libertarian conception of justice. Some have thought that there is thus no such thing as a libertarian theory of *justice*; for libertarians, it is thought, justice doesn't matter, only liberty does. But libertarians very much do have a sense of justice. It does not focus on any equal distribution of well-being, for they regard that as a futile and wrong-headed goal. Even if such a distribution could be achieved, it would always get disrupted by people's choices—some highly beneficial, and some damaging, but in any case, their choices. What justice requires is the equal protection of "liberty rights"—rights not to be interfered with.[5]

Liberty rights are sometimes referred to as "negative" rights, in contrast with "positive" rights that guarantee their holders something that must be provided by others. The right to travel is a negative right because you're free to travel where you like, but you're not owed a bus ticket. The right to primary and secondary education, on the other hand, is a positive right because it's not just a right to go to school if you can afford it, but a right that the state provide schools, teachers, books, etc. Generally, positive rights are not supported in libertarian justice because, to be realized, they require some compulsory contributions that intrude on others' allegedly legitimate liberties. If a person strongly prefers, for example, that much of what she contributes through taxes and premiums to support healthcare be devoted instead to education, professional development, and private discretionary choices, including philanthropic contributions, then those taxes and premiums restrict liberty. (In the United States, healthcare costs constitute roughly eighteen percent of GDP, though in most high-income countries it is only eight to twelve percent.) For some, minimal insurance covering only the most basic and catastrophic care will be a reasonable choice, given how much less expensive it is than the coverage for all "necessary medical care" typical in universal coverage systems.

In the pure libertarian view, insurance should be an open market, leaving subscribers who are likely to stay well ("low-risk" subscribers, in insurance lingo) at liberty to buy insurance from insurers willing to insure them at a cost far less than those more likely to need care. "Free market insurance" is an appropriate term—subscribers and insurers are each free to come together at an agreed price. Unless the low-risk subscribers have somehow caused the less fortunate prospects of the others, the disparity is no injustice. They are not obligated in the name of justice to share in the extra expense of insuring those who need more care. In libertarian thinking, compassionate aid, while it may be laudatory, should be voluntary.

Objections to this view are strong and intuitive. Especially strong is the moral call to assist those who, through no fault of their own, have fallen into debilitating or life-threatening illness that can ruin their lives. Is it not a matter of basic humanity for fortunate persons to respond compassionately to such need? Why are people obligated to help others only when they are in some way responsible for the others' plight, as libertarians claim? When individual need is great, compassion pulls people so strongly toward assistance that it feels like obligation. And maybe, morally, it is.

Even if libertarians have a cogent reply to this point, we shall see that their defense of "free market insurance" gets badly disrupted by some basic features of health insurance markets. These features also disrupt common utilitarian and egalitarian views of justice in healthcare and pull them, too, out of their traditional positions.

How do "market failure" and "cost-shifting" affect health insurance?

Markets for health insurance exemplify what economists call "market failure." [6] By this they mean that an open market of buyers and suppliers inevitably fails to supply the good being marketed to those who most want and need it. Why is this?

In a voluntary insurance market, competing insurers will offer lower premiums for those who are less expensive to insure. In competition with each other, they will keep lowering that cost for the youngest and healthiest to the point where they can still profit on this segment of the population. And many of the youngest and healthiest, if insurance is fully "free-market" and they are free to go without insurance, will refuse to buy unless its price for them drops to something very low. Insurers may offer insurance at that low a price if they can restrict those eligible for it to people very unlikely to incur costly care.

The mirror image of this also occurs on the high-cost end of the market. If insurers do not have to cover everyone, they will offer insurance to high-risk subscribers only at rates actuarially adequate to cover those persons' medical costs. Without healthier subscribers in the same pool to help achieve lower premiums, the cost of insurance for those needing a lot of care will sky-rocket to far more than what they can afford. Affordable insurance for those who most need it will simply dry up. To be sure, insurers will be quick to offer more affordable prices if they can exclude coverage of new subscribers' preexisting conditions or if they can cancel the insurance of anyone who becomes unacceptably expensive, but such features leave subscribers exposed to the very risks that insurance is designed to blunt. The market failure is real.

A society may be tempted by an attractive but misleading remedy: prohibit insurers from dividing their subscribers into high- and low-risk pools, from being able to cancel a subscriber's insurance, and from excluding preexisting conditions from coverage. That is, require insurers to offer insurance at the same "community-rated" premium to everyone. Will this work? Not at all. It will only increase the ranks of the uninsured. To many in the healthier and generally younger segments, the resulting community-rated premium will seem not worth paying, so they won't insure. Then premiums for those who remain must increase even more. An insurance "death spiral" ensues.

The obvious response to this problem is not to allow people to pick their time to get insured, postponing insurance until they think they need it. People need to pay into insurance all along. To prevent market failure, not only must insurers be barred from using preexisting condition exclusions, cancelations, and widely different risk-rated premiums, but *people must be required to have insurance.* They cannot be allowed to pick their time to get insured.

A second important phenomenon, "cost-shifting," also disrupts healthcare markets. In a society that does not provide universal insurance or require everyone to be insured, many uninsured people will arrive at hospital emergency rooms unable to pay. If hospitals are particularly compassionate and not under competitive pressure to offer the best prices to insurance companies to get the business of their subscribers, they can afford to serve uninsured patients with "uncompensated care" and then shift the cost of that care onto other, paying, usually insured patients by charging them more. Under competitive pressure, however, no individual hospital can recoup the cost by charging other paying patients enough unless its competitors also serve uninsured patients. If not required to, many will not.

Exactly this set of forces played out in the 1980s among hospitals in the United States, with its large proportion of voluntary insurance. Collectively, citizens then had a choice: (a) watch hospital after hospital turn away patients who arrive at emergency rooms unable to pay, or (b) level the playing field and require all hospitals to serve patients with "uncompensated care," the costs of which the hospitals shift onto their other patients. The first choice was unpalatable and unpopular, so, through political channels, they chose the latter. In 1985, the US Congress passed legislation, reaffirmed in 1998, requiring all hospitals to accept nonpaying patients for emergency care.[7] Flaws in the market were addressed by legislative mandate. This has seldom happened in other developed countries because the United States is virtually alone in having a private insurance market system that does not require everyone to be insured.

Such market failures must be acknowledged before the moral advantages of structurally different healthcare systems can be assessed. Any competitive, multipayer health insurance system will need to be constrained to correct for market failure. The viable private insurance market alternative to single-payer insurance or a national health service is not unconstrained "free-market" insurance, but an insurance market sufficiently regulated to avoid market failure.

What is unfair "free-riding"?

A second basic problem for voluntary insurance markets is unfair "free-riding." Before we look at its impact on health insurance in particular, it is important to understand the fundamental role the problem of free-riding plays in justifying and limiting state power in general. Free-riding and the "public goods" it involves provide an important justification of the state in both conservative and liberal political philosophies.

The justification begins by observing that many of the most important benefits that the state provides accrue inevitably to everyone—what economists and other scholars call "public" or "non-exclusive" goods. Public safety, national defense, and widespread education are examples. Once the enterprises needed to produce these goods are in place, it is impossible to exclude a person who chooses not to contribute to them from many of their benefits. The state (or whoever the relevant collective entity is) may therefore extract from beneficiaries their fair share of the taxes and obedience needed to produce these goods. Call this what it is: coercion.

When the full principle expressing the need to prevent free-riding is spelled out, such coercion is justified even from a liberty-emphasizing perspective: *A person should pay her share of the costs of a collective enterprise that produces benefits from which she cannot be excluded, unless she would actually prefer to lose all the benefits of the enterprise rather than pay her fair share of its costs.*[8]

Note the strong condition in the principle to respect people as free and responsible persons when a community requires them to contribute: *if* people would have to pay to avoid being excluded from the benefits, they would prefer to pay rather than lose the benefits.

Suppose, for example, that in a particular jurisdiction (state, county, province, etc.), hospitals are required to provide emergency care for everyone who arrives in the hospital regardless of whether they are insured or otherwise have the ability to pay (option "b" in the previous section). At the same time, people are not required to have health insurance. Many people who believe they are highly unlikely to need the care that insurance would cover then "go bare" without insurance (usually relatively young people). But, of course, when an accident or unexpected disease strikes them, they nonetheless get emergency care without paying much of its cost. They typically know this in advance, which may have been one of the reasons they decided not to insure. But they are not excluded from the benefits, for which they largely do not pay. They free-ride on the policy that seems the right one for the community to have—no one dying on hospital doorsteps for lack of care.

What is the fair share that they should be expected to pay? It would be the affordable part of their insurance premium had they (and others like them) insured. Making them pay that should be called what it is: mandatory insurance. In a multipayer private insurance market system it goes by the "insurance mandate" label, or just by "single-payer" in single-payer systems.

It is important to realize the powerful, unifying role across ideological lines that making people pay their fair share of a collective enterprise to avoid free-riding plays in justifying state power. The prevention of unfair free-riding is itself fundamentally a pro-individualist, responsibility-emphasizing principle, compatible with libertarian senses of justice.[9] In holding people responsible for the costs of the collective enterprises from which they benefit, the principle keeps collective solutions to human needs restrained, tying their justification to the benefits people get and their ability to pay a share of its costs.

To what extent does free-riding affect arguments about insurance?

It is apparent from the example used above that the prevention of free-riding generates an argument for mandatory or universal insurance. In a voluntary market system, however, some who can reasonably afford insurance will still reject it. Some such "rejecters" believe they are less likely to need insurance, or perhaps they are philosophically libertarian and reject egalitarian principles for insurance. Preventing unfair free-riding is, though, part of their moral outlook, providing the justification for their preferred, minimal state.

The extent of the benefits that uninsured people get when most people in their society are insured—"public good" benefits from which they cannot be excluded—can easily be overlooked. They are relieved of some heavy obligations to help that they would almost certainly feel were their friends, neighbors, and relatives not insured. They avoid the sadness and loss from the deaths and chronic conditions that many would suffer were it not for care that insurance makes accessible. The cost-shifting of emergency room and other hospital services that results when people without insurance still have to be cared for is dramatically lower when most are insured. Employment and reliability at work are enhanced by the better health that often results from accessible care, bolstering the economic health of the society. Widespread insurance—especially universal or near-universal insurance—creates many "public" goods.

The flip side of the benefits from which those who reject insurance cannot be excluded is the costs they impose on others. An uninsured person presents others with torturous decisions about whether to bail her out if she becomes ill beyond her means. If they bail her out, they bear a financial cost; if they do not, a moral and emotional cost. Such free-rider considerations may explain a great deal of the predominant attitude toward insurance in countries such as Germany and the Netherlands, where all non-indigent, low- and middle-income citizens are expected and required to get insurance.[10] People who fail to are subject to social disapproval, which can in turn form the political basis of requiring people to be insured. This reflects not so much paternalistic disdain for those who fail to care for themselves but moral condemnation for free-riding on others and neglecting their social responsibilities.

In the case of health insurance, the most feasible way—perhaps the only way—to prevent substantial free-riding is to require everyone to be insured for basic care. Since the need to prevent unfair free-riding is part of libertarian and "classical liberal" as well as utilitarian and egalitarian political philosophy, the prevention of free-riding argument for universal insurance can constitute real common ground amid all the other disagreements people of different persuasions have about healthcare systems.

Why is insurance dangerous, and how can that danger be addressed?

Insurance is critical to making healthcare accessible. Medical expenses come unexpectedly, often in high degrees and for care that is urgent. Only people with great and immediately accessible wealth will have no need for insurance. When we speak of a "healthcare system," therefore, we see it as involving either insurance or its near equivalent, an agency that provides care directly for an entire population.

Insurance, however, is dangerous. It readily creates overuse of care and escalating expense. Health economists and policy scholars have long recognized this, although the public often does not. The phenomenon might be called the *insurance effect*: *Once a patient is insured, neither patient nor provider have much incentive to pay attention to whether the prospective value of the care is worth its cost. As long as the care is somewhat beneficial, insured patients will want it, even when its statistically likely benefits may not be worth its total cost. Moreover, since insurance pays the providers of care, they, too, have little incentive to discipline the use of care and often a clear incentive not to.*

The problem is only aggravated when providers are compensated "fee-for-service" (FFS): doctors by procedures and hospitals by both procedures and "bed-days." The drug Avastin for metastatic breast cancer, for example, may show barely any net effectiveness in clinical trials in comparison with other treatments, and the cost of a year of life gained on average from it may be extremely high. Yet, especially when it is perceived as "last chance" therapy, many insured patients will want it, and plenty of providers will be willing to prescribe it. Give providers an incentive to do more procedures and they will recommend and do more procedures; give hospitals an incentive to fill beds and build more of them, and they will do that. To be sure, they will not, if they are remotely ethical, advise and do procedures that are on balance harmful, but when the benefit–harm balance seems to be at all positive, though only barely so, providers and hospitals readily and understandably lean toward prescribing the care.

Most insurance systems, in response to this problem, develop means of controlling cost and the volume of services. Instead of being paid FFS, for example, hospitals can be paid by the "diagnostic-related group" into which patients fall. Or physicians can be compensated by an amount per patient per year ("capitation"), or they can be salaried. All methods of compensation have their weaknesses and strengths. Capitation, for example, may commendably emphasize the preventive care and early diagnosis that reduces later hospitalizations, but it can also lead to undertreatment in late stages. If, by contrast, FFS is attractive because it avoids capitation's incentive to undertreat at times, FFS's unattractive side—the strong incentive to overtreat—might be disciplined by significant patient cost-sharing (preferably, graduated with patient income) or by strict rules on clinicians to follow "practice guidelines."

Another, very different response to the insurance effect than trying to reduce the volume of services within covered categories is to tighten those categories themselves. "All medically necessary care" is common language in health insurance contracts, but "medical necessity" is a highly elastic notion. Some cases are beyond dispute—an appendectomy for a ruptured appendix, for example, or chemotherapy that has an established record of saving patients. In other cases, "medical necessity" gets read as covering any procedure that addresses the patient's condition, regardless of how effective it is.

Within this broad challenge of how to discipline costs is a task close to the heart of justice: establishing the scope of what is included within the "basic" ("decent") minimum of care for which everyone should be insured. Every system that tries to guarantee affordable access to basic care has an operational definition of that minimum. It cannot be all care, delivered to everyone in the highest quality and the most patient-accommodating way, for there will always be care above the reasonable guaranteed minimum that some, even many, will want. *Any system, to have a claim on being just, will need to control costs*, for, to the extent that it does not, resources will be less available to meet all the other needs of a just society. Moreover, research on the "social determinants" of health points to income, education, employment, food, and control over one's work environment as more strongly associated with longevity and health than are health insurance and healthcare.[11] This provides all the more reason for controlling healthcare costs in order to be able to better address these social determinants.

We will return to the setting of priorities for what goes into the basic minimum of care in the next chapter on justice *within* a healthcare system, Chapter 11.

What role does "public health" play in a just system?

A healthcare system is comprised of individual treatments for those already ill, individual care to prevent illness from developing, and so-called *public health programs* aimed at protecting and improving the health of an entire population. Most of this chapter's discussion so far has concerned a system's structure for providing individual treatment and prevention. Insurance, whether public or private, and whether single-payer or diverse multipayer, is focused on delivering care for individuals. In public health, by contrast, the focus is on a nation or community. Vaccines are of course administered to individuals, but vaccination is aimed not just at protecting the immediate individuals being vaccinated but at controlling contagion throughout a community. Safe water and other community hygiene measures are similarly aimed. Some specialties in medical science itself—epidemiology, infectious disease, and global health among them—focus on what happens in populations.

In the past century, public health measures have almost certainly had greater effect than individual treatment medicine. From 1920 to 2020, average life expectancy at birth in high-income countries increased from roughly forty years to slightly over eighty, and in low- and middle-income countries from thirty-five to seventy. The greatest shares of this remarkable rise in longevity have come from public health measures: sewage collection and treatment, clean water, milk pasteurization, vaccination, auto safety (seat belts, especially), and adequate food supplies. Developments and inventions critical to these include not only vaccines, but also methods of pasteurization and chlorination, sewer systems and the toilet, and artificial fertilizers. The lives saved by vaccines, toilets and sewers, and artificial fertilizers are in the billions, in the hundreds of millions for chlorination and pasteurization, and the millions for refrigeration and seat belts. No medicines or medical procedures get into the billions level. Antibiotics and blood transfusions have saved hundreds of millions, but no other improvements in treatment have saved more than millions.[12]

Still, public health's contribution often gets relatively little attention, though weaknesses in public health can be glaring when they surface. The COVID-19 (SARS-CoV-2) pandemic in the early 2020s revealed the critical importance of good public health. Contact tracing, for example, is woefully weak without a strong public health infrastructure, including good epidemiological data. Though understandable, it is hardly excusable that, until crises hit, public health tends to be taken for granted. After all, precisely when it is done well, it remains invisible (see Chapter 11, treatment and prevention). Any healthcare system will need to be diligent in attending to public health if it is to be effective.

The significance is not only public health's effect on total health in a society, but also on justice. Health systems struggle mightily to achieve equitable access to individual treatment and prevention for disadvantaged segments of their populations. Public health measures, too, can be marred by inequitable distribution, but, in their very nature, aimed as they are at whole communities and populations, they are likely to generate more equally distributed benefits across a population. No healthcare system is likely to come out well in an assessment for justice without a strong public health component.

Global health justice, too, depends on strong public health, including the availability of vaccines. At the time of this writing, COVID-19 vaccines have not been nearly as available in many low-income countries as they have been in virtually all high- and high-middle-income ones. The "three-for-me, none-for-you" situation where affluent nations have high rates of third booster shots while many nations cannot afford even many initial shots is a travesty of injustice in global health.[13] Many remedies for this are available, but the most overlooked may be loosening the patent rights over the vaccine formulas held by the large companies that developed them (see Chapter 12). Reducing patent rights globally or, more feasibly, granting early temporary licenses for quality-certified production in lower income countries (India and South Africa, among others) could alleviate a good share of the problem. Globally assisted investment in the affected countries' health systems for administering vaccination is also critical.

In any case, the failure of high-income countries to assist is self-defeating. Witness the Omicron variant that was able to develop so easily in the fertile ground of low-income countries' unvaccinated populations. "Vaccine equity is not charity," observed Benjamin Schreiber, deputy chief of UNICEF's global immunization program, "it is an epidemiological necessity."[14]

(Another major issue of justice for healthcare systems is, of course, inequities from structural racism and race-related disadvantage. See Chapter 2, where those issues are addressed in the context of the provider–patient relationship.)

Can common ground be found in debates about healthcare systems?

The different philosophical views of distributive justice presented in this chapter all speak to the basic structure of a healthcare system. For utilitarians, a social structure is just when it maximizes the aggregate overall well-being of everyone affected. Because well-being includes elements such as individual security and reassurance, beyond the direct health benefits of healthcare, utilitarians can be especially strong in their support for a system that guarantees universal access to basic care.

Moderate egalitarian theories of justice directly insist on universal access to a reasonable level of basic care. They do not, however, support a strict "medical egalitarianism" in which the care that anyone gets has to be provided to everyone who needs the same. Moderate egalitarians tolerate different "tiers" of healthcare, allowing those who have the means to "buy up" to additional, allegedly higher quality care to do so. What makes healthcare "special" compared to other goods, and a large part of what morally demands that healthcare to be universally accessible, is the contribution that healthcare makes to overall opportunity in life. Because "opportunity" has various different dimensions, however, egalitarians will always face the difficult challenge of determining what is a just level for the basic healthcare that is universally accessible. Resources may be better spent on less care and less insurance and more on education, for example. This is especially the case once insurance is recognized as "dangerous" in creating incentives to use care regardless of high cost and minimal benefit.

In libertarianism, "free" markets are favored even if they do not lead to maximal overall well-being or fair equality of opportunity for they represent the liberty of consumers and suppliers. Unfettered markets for health insurance, however, are afflicted by "market failure." Insurance companies compete for the subscribers least expensive to insure, would-be subscribers look for the least expensive insurance, and they find each other. Those who remain become more expensive to insure. A "death spiral" for insurance can quickly result: many people who need insurance and want it the most will not be able to find it at an affordable price.

Unfair free-riding also poses a challenge to voluntary market systems. Those who choose not to insure, thinking they are unlikely to need expensive care, still end up in emergency rooms and expensive hospitals, with the cost of their care shifted onto the hospital's other patients who can pay because they are insured. If those who do not insure can still receive much of the emergency and urgent care they need, and they also gain the other benefits of living in a widely insured population, they become "free-riders" not paying their fair share. The solution? Require everyone to be insured for basic care. The principle driving this conclusion, the prevention of unfair free-riding, is important even in libertarian political philosophy. Libertarians can thus, on the basis of their very own principles, support universal insurance for basic care. To be sure, to them as well as to others, it will be important that excessive costs fueled by insurance are controlled, whether by competition or other means.

This constitutes considerable common ground in debates about the best structure for a healthcare system. Libertarians: multipayer insurance, but with universally accessible basic care, not an unfettered insurance market. Egalitarians: universal access to basic care, but not without controlling the costs that insurance itself exacerbates. Utilitarians: efficiency in producing maximum benefit at minimal cost, but not without considering the "special" role that healthcare plays in providing security and opportunity. And for all three, good public health programs.

Concluding thoughts

Many people, when they think about justice in healthcare, tend to focus on particular questions about allocating scarce resources (e.g., whom to save when not all can be saved) or on specific practices that perpetuate injustice for underserved and disadvantaged populations. It is equally important to consider how justice applies to the very *structure* of a healthcare *system*. Amidst the political debates about what structure would be best for a given society, we must not lose sight of what justice demands. As different as contending philosophical views of justice are, when they are applied carefully to healthcare system structure with an understanding of some basic facts about health insurance, they yield a surprising amount of common ground: everyone should be insured for basic care, the cost of insured healthcare must be disciplined, and the public health sector of the system must be strong.

11

HOW CAN SCARCE RESOURCES BE ALLOCATED JUSTLY?

In this chapter, we address dilemmas about the just allocation of scarce resources *within* healthcare systems. They abound. Some are specific, immediate, and focused on individuals, such as who should have priority for transplant organs in short supply. Others are wider in their reach, such as how much should be included in a basic minimum of care accessible to everyone.

While all resources are scarce in the sense of being finite, the dilemmas raised by contexts of immediate scarcity of care for individuals are some of the most gripping and difficult. In this chapter, we begin with those, in two contexts: organs for transplant and emergency treatments in a pandemic like COVID-19. Among the issues highlighted by pandemics, though not confined to them, are whether the past behavior of patients should affect their priority for care, and whether priorities should be adjusted for structural inequities of health. Another issue emerges from these: What is the relative priority of preventive measures compared to acute "rescue" care for people already ill? Then we move to another overarching issue: What should the basic minimum of accessible care include? (A basic minimum was important in the preceding chapter in assessing what kind of healthcare system to have. In this chapter, the question is not whether to have a system that guarantees a universal minimum, but how to determine what care that minimum should include.) We will explain and assess an influential method used in many countries to help decide that, cost-effectiveness analysis (CEA). We conclude with a specific controversy emerging from the use of CEA, whether years of life at the end of life—life in the face of death—should be accorded extra value (an "end-of-life premium").

Who should have priority for life-saving organ transplants?

Organ transplantation almost always takes place in the context of organ shortage. In the United States, for example, while nearly 40,000 vital organ transplants are done annually, the supply of organs available at any point in time is typically at least 100,000 short of patient need. Waiting lists are long. How should they work? Who should be at the front of them?

To get on the waiting list, a person's organ failure should have begun. Otherwise, people who may never need to be on the list would take up places. Though they need to be in organ failure, however, candidates must also have a reasonable prospect of success. If failure is already too advanced or other life-threatening conditions are present, the person may not. To give an organ to patients without a reasonable chance of success, instead of to those with much better prognosis, would amount to "wasting" organs.

But how dominant should a patient's positive prognosis be in establishing priorities among those on the waiting list? If everyone on the list is in need, and all have a chance of successful transplant, who should go to the front of the line?

One method for deciding is a point system. Everyone gets points for several different relevant factors, including:

- time on the waitlist ("first come, first served")
- urgency (how close the person is to death if she does not receive an organ)
- prognosis (chance of success with a transplant)

- rectification of previous unfairness (mistaken delay in getting on the list, for example)

Note that the second and third factors tend to pull against each other: the greater the urgency, the further along in organ failure and the lower the odds of successful transplant. Yet both are relevant, so the question becomes one of relative importance.[1]

Balancing these different factors and determining their appropriate relative weight in a point system is difficult. And perhaps another consideration not in this point system should affect distribution: Should everyone on the list retain some chance of getting an organ, even when they get near the end of their wait and their prognosis is not so good and their priority within the point system low? If every individual is to be respected, shouldn't everyone still have a chance of getting a life-saving organ even when their likelihood of success has dropped? Preserving that chance would constitute "maintaining hope" for everyone. It could be achieved by periodically conducting a lottery for everyone on the list, with winners receiving an organ from the small number reserved for the lottery winners. Such a procedure would end up saving fewer lives since the average rate of success would be lower compared to allocating all organs by the regular point system with its weight for prognosis, but is it what each individual deserves as they move through the list?

Is there any way to discern how much importance such a maintenance-of-hope factor should have? Perhaps. Suppose that, at the point of entering the waiting list, people were asked about this and that they were willing to sacrifice some of their overall likelihood of surviving and wished to have the lottery that preserves some hope for everyone. It's not hard to imagine that they would, for they can all imagine what it will be like to get further into their time on the list and have virtually no hope of any longer of getting an organ without that lottery. There is some empirical evidence, in fact, that people are willing to do just that.[2] In utilitarian terms—actually saving the most lives—this makes no sense. But if people going on the waiting list endorse such a policy, out of respect for their preference it may be the right thing to do.

This is but one instance of the complex considerations that allocation decisions for specific kinds of treatment can involve. Not only are several different and often competing ethical theories at work, but good application of any of them is dependent on multiple empirical facts, some of which may be difficult to know at the time. A just allocation of specific treatments may remain indeterminate, but even brief ethical analysis may clarify the reasons why.[3]

In a pandemic, who should get care first?

In some situations of immediate and stubborn scarcity, prioritizing who gets treatment is referred to as *triage*. Not all can be saved, and decisions must be made quickly. From military contexts especially, two triage principles have emerged as paramount: save critical healthcare workers first and devote few if any life-saving efforts to those who cannot be saved. These principles have obvious utilitarian justification, and they likely raise little objection from other views of justice either. The two principles are not limited to battlefield emergencies. In the COVID-19 pandemic of 2020–2022, scarce treatment, including vaccines, frequently went to healthcare workers first so that their ranks for saving others would not be depleted.

Embedded in all the other considerations about who should have priority for care is a larger conflict: saving the most *lives* versus saving the most *years of life*. The difference can be substantial. Which would be better—save 1,000 people near the very end of their lives, who will then on average live only two years, or save one-fourth as many younger people (250), each of whom will live on average another forty years? The former saves four times as many lives, but the latter five times as many years of life (10,000 versus 2,000). A strong case can be made for either.

For saving the most *lives*:

- Imminent potential death is a powerful reference point. The value to people of whatever time they have left is surprisingly equal among people with different length prospects (see second-last section of this chapter). Who can say to an older person that his very life has less value?
- An individual ninety-year-old faces a four times greater threat to life than a forty-year-old. Those under greater threat should get help first.

For saving the most *years of life*:

- Even many older persons will say that the young should be saved first, both because they have the most to lose and because older people have already had more of life.
- Why do we value life? For most people, without thinking about it, it is for *the time in life* that one can have. That should pull us toward saving the most time in life.

A utilitarian framework of maximizing the value of whatever survival can be achieved will lean toward saving the most years of life. Those with other moral perspectives may support that as well. In Kantian ethics the focus is on fairness between individual persons. What is most fair when a twenty-year-old and a ninety-year-old cannot both have top priority for being saved? Seldom, if ever, has a twenty-year-old already had the same opportunity in life that a ninety-year-old has had. If equality of opportunity is the heart of egalitarian justice in healthcare (see Chapter 10), and if life itself is the absolute prerequisite of all opportunity, then as a matter of fairness and equality the younger person should be saved before the older. (We would have to be careful, of course, that in such thinking we were not guilty of "agism," harboring prejudices against an old person's life as less worth living.)

In recent decades two such fair opportunity-oriented views have been particularly prominent: the "prudent life span" approach of American philosopher Norman Daniels and the "fair innings" view of British economist Alan Williams.[4] For both, priority for young before old is not discrimination against the elderly, and it does not show them less respect; it is a matter of fairness in life. A variant of their view was expressed in more personal terms by Larry Churchill during the COVID-19 pandemic.

> As I near 75 my overall sense is one of deep gratitude. I have been offered many opportunities and enjoyed much happiness. . . . I have been favored . . . by excellent health benefits. . . . At some point I should be prepared to . . . [exercise] restraint, especially when the consequences of not doing so are evident all around me. Part of the moral meaning of aging lies in a sense of reciprocity across generations. As the pandemic rages on, . . . my claim on scarce and expensive services will cost others their lives. This is a bargain I am unwilling to make. My death from Covid-19 . . . would be sad, but not tragic. Yet the death of children and young adults is a tragedy. I have had many turns at bat; they have had very few.[5]

In a pandemic, though, it may be natural for people to focus on saving lives, not years of life. The context is emergency, with decisions urgently demanded for the here and now. The years and decades in the longer range ahead fade into the future. In the actual COVID-19 pandemic, moreover, the love of families for their elderly relatives more vulnerable to severe illness and death was amply revealed in how horrified many were by all the deaths in nursing homes. And another aspect can mitigate the argument that the young should generally be favored on grounds of fair opportunity: many older persons have been severely restricted in their opportunities by systemic or other kinds of unjust discrimination.

Should past behavior affect priority for care?

In the ethical culture of healthcare, the general practice has been to treat patients equally according to their current medical needs, regardless of any of their previous health-damaging behavior. A person may have created her liver failure by excessive alcohol use, for example, but as long as her prognosis is not too poor, she can still get on the waiting list for a transplant. Or a smoker may have damaged his lungs to the point of repeatedly needing acute care, but he is given the same care as someone whose lung failure is in no way the result of unwise decisions. A truly striking example of this conviction occurred when a suicide bomber in Israel, after killing and injuring people around him, arrived at the hospital with his victims and was treated with the very same care and commitment they were.[6]

Certain ways of holding people responsible for their health are accepted—higher premiums for health insurance, for example, or taxes on cigarettes. And sometimes the damaging behavior may medically disqualify a person from treatment; excessive drinking may have already greatly reduced the chance of surviving with a transplant or the likelihood that this behavior will continue after transplantation may doom its prospect of success. But, in general, providers take their patients "as they are."

Should that still be the practice, though, when the damaging behavior directly endangers others who then get squeezed out of needed care? This can happen in any emergency situation where a shortage of life-saving resources is exacerbated by some people's behavior, causing others not to get needed treatment. At times during the

COVID-19 pandemic that did happen. After vaccines were readily available, hospitals were still overwhelmed with more patients than their ICU beds could handle. Nearly all the COVID patients needing the ICU were unvaccinated, most having refused vaccination when it was readily available. Other patients with entirely different conditions also needed intensive care, but hospitals' ICUs could not take everyone. Would it be wrong for a hospital in these circumstances to give unvaccinated patients lower priority for the ICU?

Arguably, this kind of case is different from the typical one where patients are and ought to be treated equally despite poor choices. Here the refusal to vaccinate puts *others* at risk. Why should such a person have the same priority for urgent care as others whose choices have not put anyone else at risk?

As compelling as this point is, it seems treacherous to assign those who refuse to vaccinate lower priority. How clear is the line between those whose damaging choices have put others at risk and those who have merely made bad choices? Moreover, not being vaccinated might reflect living in a cultural or community mind-set where vaccines are regarded as ineffective or dangerous, or are even not as readily available. How truly voluntary are their choices? How easy was it for them, in their actual context, to understand the effectiveness of vaccines in keeping virtually everyone who gets vaccinated out of the hospital?

Assigning lower priority to COVID victims who refuse vaccination cannot be definitively justified. But treating everyone the same has the result that some who did not vaccinate—and so are partly responsible for their own plight—get life-saving care, while others who did the responsible thing and were vaccinated are squeezed out of an essential ICU bed or ventilator. That may be even harder to justify. The matter remains a hard ethical dilemma.

Should priorities be adjusted for structural inequities of health?

A quite different priority issue is presented by the possibility of compensating for structural disparities in health that result from wider inequities in the social determinants of health (housing, education, wealth, income, employment). Many of these are connected with race and ethnicity (see Chapter 2). In the aggregate, when compared to their White counterparts, racial and ethnic minority residents of the United States experience higher rates of illness and death across a wide range of health conditions, including diabetes, hypertension, obesity, asthma, and heart disease. As a result, the life expectancy of Black Americans is four years lower than that of Whites. The burden of COVID-19, too, is disproportionate. Adjusting for age, mortality rates from COVID-19 infection are more than three times higher for Black and Latino populations.[7]

The focus of the priority questions raised by such structural inequities is a demographic group, not particular individuals and their behavior, as it was in the previous section. Should members of the group be compensated for unjust inequities in health by gaining some priority for admission to ICUs or by some priority to receive vaccines when supply is limited?

For *truly collective public health* measures, they arguably should. Justice may not only permit but require priority for measures aimed at preventing and ameliorating hypertension or type 2 diabetes in disadvantaged populations, for example. To be sure, other populations may then miss out on some public health programs that might have benefitted them instead, but that will not put them at an unjust health disadvantage; they are already better off from structural inequalities.

For *individual acute care*, on the other hand—the scarce ICU bed, for example—the argument for compensating for structural inequities on the basis of disadvantaged group membership is weaker. The non-minority individual who does not get the care because members of the disadvantaged group are accorded priority may suffer greatly as a result (by dying, perhaps). As individuals, unlike the patients who have refused to vaccinate and were therefore given lower priority, *they have not done anything to increase others' risk.*

This point may not be sufficient to close the argument, but it does pull us back toward the general practice of treating all patients equally by medical need. Compensation to help rectify structural inequities is more defensible in collective public health measures than it is in individual acute care.

What priority, if any, should treatment have over prevention?

Fairly and effectively allocating scarce resources in a pandemic raises a larger question pervasive in setting priorities within healthcare: What is the proper balance of preventive measures and acute treatment? The proverbial saying that "an ounce of prevention is worth a pound of cure," is alleged to have originated with Benjamin Franklin in Philadelphia in 1735.[8] He was speaking of fire prevention, but his comment applies to healthcare, too. Even if fully curative treatments for a condition are available and they are no more expensive than preventive measures for the benefits they produce, prevention avoids the burdens people experience when they fall ill. Support for emphasizing prevention long predates Franklin. The Hippocratic Oath that many physicians take when entering practice includes a pledge to "prevent disease whenever I can, for prevention is preferable to cure."[9]

Despite this, in actual practice, prevention still seems so often to take a back seat to treatment. After many experiences of seeing persons right before us under threat and needing treatment, are we really going to say that preventive measures are equally or more important? The strong moral pull of "rescue" lies behind the priority that many societies give to acute care and curative treatment. In high- and high/middle-income countries, expenditures on prevention are overwhelmed by spending on treatment. In the United States, prevention accounts for less than eight percent of total healthcare spending, and the same disparity characterizes high- and upper-middle-income countries internationally: preventive measures constitute well less than twenty percent of primary care expenditure and less than eight percent of overall healthcare spending.[10]

Can such dominance of treatment over prevention be ethically justified? A life saved by prevention, after all, is surely just as valuable to the person whose life it is as a life saved by treatment. Any priority for treatment seems foolish and short-sighted. Nonetheless, at least two plausible defenses are made for it.

Identified versus statistical lives. While treatment and acute care save identifiable individual lives, the lives preventive measures save are only "statistical." Certain elements of diet and lifestyle are known to reduce the incidence of advanced diabetes, for example, but we do not know who will actually benefit from those measures. Ethical relationships demand something more of us when those at risk, as in acute care settings, are specific individuals.

The distinction, though it is roughly accurate, is overdrawn. In much prevention, just as in treatment, the *recipients* of care are identifiable. To be sure, prevention's *beneficiaries* are seldom known at the time care is provided since it is applied to a larger number of people than those who actually benefit. But the same is often true of treatment. Though a treatment may appear to have been successful, the improvement may have come about without it. Our knowledge of who actually benefits can be clouded.

Risk exposure. People needing treatment are generally at higher risk of harm when presenting themselves for treatment than are people who might get preventive measures. This higher "base-line risk" for individuals needing treatment means that they are individually *worse off* than those who could be helped by prevention. Candidates for treatment are *already in trouble*. The force of this point was poignantly expressed by a Norwegian Health Director in commenting that any reordering of priorities from cure to prevention would amount to "taking from the sick and . . .[giving] to the healthy."[11]

These points about statistical versus identifiable lives and differences in risk exposure can be incorporated in a more refined question about priority: *Should we provide less efficient treatment to identifiable individuals who are at higher risk for relatively immediate harms before we provide more efficient preventive care to equally identifiable individuals at lower risk for more distant harms?*

Even refined in this way, the skeptical *ethical* question still stands: Why should treatment have priority over prevention when the lives ultimately saved by prevention have no less value than the lives saved by treatment? At the same time, it is readily understandable why, *psychologically*, prevention gets less attention and investment. As Geoffrey Rose memorably commented, often "a preventive measure that brings large effects to the community offers little to each participating individual."[12] In reducing salt in processed foods to lower blood pressure, or reducing trans-fats to lower cholesterol and reduce cardiovascular disease, the benefits to the individual are distant. The individual who eventually benefits from prevention gets lost in a statistical aggregate. This may not constitute a good moral justification for giving prevention a back seat, but it certainly explains why we would give treatment greater attention.

This comparative invisibility of the benefits that flow from prevention is most pronounced in public health. Amid the COVID-19 pandemic, Leana Wen, American physician and former Baltimore (Maryland) City Health Commissioner, noted that *when public health works, it's invisible.* "If you prevent children from getting lead poisoning, there's no face of someone with lead poisoning because you've prevented it from happening. As a result, public health becomes the first item on the chopping block. . . . [With COVID-19, at least in the United States, we have] a stark example of what happens when there's chronic neglect of . . . public health."[13] If the more successful public health measures are, the more invisible are their effects, no wonder the public's motivation to support public health wanes.

Still, this tendency is unfortunate. How unfortunate it is can be seen not only when a pandemic comes upon us but by looking back at the astonishing increase in average life expectancy in the past century-plus. During that time it doubled—yes, doubled! Life expectancy in high-income countries rose from forty years in 1880 to eighty years by 2010. Globally, life expectancy rose equally fast, from thirty-five years to more than seventy in 2019. Much of this striking extra life in little more than a century was due to public health efforts. Six of the eight innovations that saved the most lives in this period were preventive defenses against infectious diseases—various public sanitation measures and vaccines. The lion's share of the advance was due to collective public health.[14]

It is troubling, to say the least, that with all this additional life due to it, public health still gets the short end of funding and attention in the healthcare systems of many high-income countries. Fair equality of opportunity for a person can be destroyed as much by lack of preventive care as by lack of treatment. When preventive measures can deliver the same or even better health benefits and avoid some of the higher costs of treatment, prevention is indeed better than cure. This is especially true in low-income countries. They may be wise in using their resources first to provide preventive services to avoid diabetes, for example, before covering an acute treatment like kidney dialysis.

What should be included in the basic minimum available to everyone?

Like the comparative importance of prevention compared to treatment, another overarching allocation question in any healthcare system is what should be included in the basic minimum of care that should be accessible to everyone. The matter is sometimes approached initially by determining which *categories* of care ought to be included. That quickly, however, runs into problems. Primary and preventive care must be included, along with emergency care. But then post-emergency acute care must be included, too, to avoid a revolving cycle of emergency room readmission. In fact, almost no entire medical category of care can be left out. Even cosmetic surgery should not be excluded as some reconstructive cosmetic surgery is as vital for people's well-being as other physical reconstructions. Whole categories such as long-term care or mental health care are sometimes omitted, but when they are, strong pressure to include them soon develops, for they, too, can be equally important to a person's well-being. Whole category exclusions become defensible only on budgetary, not ethical, grounds.

Will "disease" work any better as a criterion for what to include, so that only services to prevent or treat disease are covered? It will not. Maternity care is standard coverage, for example, but pregnancy is not a disease. Basic maternity care is effective in responding to medical complications, and, even when not strictly necessary for that, it is important for assurance. Contraceptive services may be covered, but the pregnancy they prevent is not a disease. Avoiding pregnancy may nonetheless be extremely important for equality of opportunity, as well as generally for how well people's lives go. Their lives generally do go better if they can become parents when they want to and are ready for that awesome responsibility.

If neither whole categories nor disease work, we need a more fine-grained method. An attractive method that many healthcare systems use is CEA (see p. 202). Regardless of how much of a nation's economic resources should be devoted to healthcare, any treatments or services provided should generate more human benefit for the resources they require than any of the excluded services and treatments would. If the covered items are not comparatively cost-effective, they should be replaced by some that are, for they would provide greater health benefit for the same cost, or equal benefit for less.

To utilitarians, the moral attraction of CEA is fairly obvious, but it has taken vigorous criticism for being cold-hearted in overemphasizing cost and efficiency. Against this, the late health economist Alan Williams strongly defended CEA: "*Not* to seek to become more efficient [in producing health benefits] is what is unethical. . . . Inefficiency means needlessly worsening the health of the people that doctors are there to serve. . . . Someone who acts without regard to costs is not 'ethical,' but 'fanatical.'"[15]

Even if this claim on behalf of CEA is right, however, CEA is hardly a simple method for allocating healthcare resources. The cost side may seem simple, but even that can be difficult to measure. The real cost of a treatment or service will need to be "net cost," taking into account the savings from avoiding other expenses down the line that the use of a given treatment/service will create. The effectiveness (benefit) side is even more challenging. One will need a common unit of health-related benefit if the cost-effectiveness of a treatment/service that extends life is to be compared with the cost-effectiveness of another measure that improves quality of life without extending it. To get this common unit of benefit for use in CEA, health economists have created the concept of a *quality-adjusted life year* (QALY). It sounds like a "wonky" notion, but the essential idea is fairly simple.

What is a "quality-adjusted life year"?

The first thing to notice is that it is not a *natural* unit of value, but a *constructed* one designed to put life extension and quality-of-life improvement onto the same scale. It accomplishes that aim by discerning the tradeoffs between life itself and quality-of-life improvement that people are willing to make. To get evaluations of different conditions (referred to as *health-state ratings*), people's preferences are typically elicited with either *time tradeoff* (TTO) or *standard gamble* (SG) questions. TTO questions ask respondents what portion of an anticipated remaining life in a certain compromised health condition—paraplegia, for example—they would be willing to sacrifice to regain full health. SG questions ask what risk of death people would be willing to take in getting a treatment to regain full health. These are clearly tradeoff questions.[16]

Let's pursue the paraplegia example. Suppose that, on average, people imagining themselves with the condition of paraplegia are willing to trade twenty percent of their life expectancy to gain a cure. If they are, they would be rating their health-related quality of life at eighty percent of what it would be with full limb function—a 0.8 rating, or a twenty percent "quality adjustment." Then extending the life of persons with paraplegia by ten years would be a gain of eight QALYs (10 × 0.8), and restoring them to full limb function for ten years would be a gain of two QALYs (10 years × the 0.2 gain in quality of life). If we know the life extension and quality-of-life improvements likely to result from a treatment, and if we know the quality adjustment for the initial and resulting conditions, we can estimate the statistically likely number of QALYs the treatment produces. And if we also know the treatment's cost, we can then compute its *cost per QALY*. We can then compare that with the cost per QALY of other measures to discern which are the most efficient in producing health benefit.

Comparing the cost/QALY of different treatments can produce surprising results. In a famous 1985 study, health economist Alan Williams compared renal dialysis, which extends life, with hip replacements that increase quality of life. His conclusion? Reduce the number of life-saving dialysis beds in Great Britain's National Health Service and shift the resources saved to doing more hip replacements. For the money spent, renal dialysis saved fewer QALYs. If funds were shifted to doing more hip replacements, fewer lives would be saved, but more QALYs would be produced.[17] Controversial? Certainly: but the power of the QALY's incorporation of both life-saving and quality improvement into a common unit of health benefit was revealed.

Ethical questions about the methodology arise immediately. Among them: Whose preferences should be used for the quality adjustment? A standard story in the study of how people evaluate health conditions is that actual patients, particularly those with chronic illness and disability, rate their quality of life more highly than "hypothetical patients" do—people who only imagine themselves with the conditions they rate. Most of the difference is attributable to actual patients' adaptation to their condition.[18] Sometimes the difference is great enough to affect the priorities that come out of CEA. Persons who are only imagining themselves with paraplegia, for example, are often willing to trade twenty percent of their life expectancy to gain a cure (a 0.80 rating), while those who actually have the condition are willing to trade only five percent (a 0.95 rating). Using hypothetical patient ratings means that eight QALYs are saved by a treatment that extends the life of a person with paraplegia ten years (0.8 × 10). Using actual patient ratings, the benefit generated is nine and a half QALYs (0.95 × 10).

There are plausible arguments on both sides of this issue of whom to ask, but the case for using the ratings of actual patients is stronger. Health state valuation is an attempt to get at the relative values of the real conditions people experience, and it is only actual patients who directly experience those conditions. That is the real health and life at stake. Shouldn't that be what is evaluated in whatever method we use to set priorities?

In addition to "internal" questions like this about how to run CEA using QALYs, however, there are more troublesome questions about whether the whole methodology is morally sound.

Is it ethical to use QALYs to allocate healthcare resources?

If we stand back from all the procedural detail, the intuitive case for using cost/QALY in prioritizing decisions is not hard to grasp: the health gains and losses for everyone in a healthcare system should count equally. It is the same essential claim made by utilitarians in defending their view of morality and justice more generally: equal benefits and equal harms should count equally for everyone.

But don't QALYs discriminate against the disabled and chronically ill? When years of life saved get quality-adjusted, those in conditions rated less than full health do not count for as much in any competition for lifesaving resources, so lifesaving measures for people with paraplegia, for example, are seen as having less value. That is correct, but only half the story. Right within the way QALYs work is a counterbalancing effect. Relative to a 0.95 rating for paraplegia, for example, expressions about paraplegia that generate a 0.80 rating do indeed disadvantage persons with paraplegia in competing for *life-saving* resources, but the lower rating gives them an advantage in competing for *quality improvement* measures: the gain from 0.8 to 1.0 is greater than from 0.95 to 1.0. The value of saving their lives diminishes with lower ratings, but the value of care that improves their quality of life back toward full health increases.[19] But then how can the use of QALYs be said to constitute any *overall* disadvantage to the disabled and chronically ill? And if it doesn't, how can it constitute discrimination against them?

This is an attractive response in defense of QALYs, but it is not convincing. QALYs face a more basic moral problem right at their core as a common unit of health benefit for both life itself and quality of life. For treatments and services that reduce pain and suffering and improve quality of life, valuations of different health states from actual patients work reasonably well in revealing the relative value of different quality-of-life improvements, but the value of added years of life is more problematic.

Here's why. The value of *life itself*—being alive at all for a given time, not the quality of life during that time—is life's value compared to not being alive—that is, the value of life compared to death. With death, however, a person loses everything of experienced value. Compared to that, any life short of one in the most difficult and despairing conditions (one that would make life "not worth living") can assume enormous value to the person whose life it is. *Something*, when it's all one can get, is worth a very great deal compared to *nothing*. This alone tends to equalize the value to each individual person of life extensions in widely varying health conditions.

When we also recognize the phenomenon of adaptation, we can see how compelling the claim is that, for different people across a wide range of health states, from poor to very high, life itself has equal value. We already know that health state ratings by persons with a condition like paraplegia are higher than the ratings expressed by people who only imagine themselves with paraplegia (see previous section). The difference is even greater for someone who, asked to rate the impairing condition, is unwilling to trade *any* of their life expectancy to gain a cure. Such "no-traders" insist that, even with paraplegia, life compared to death has, for them, full 1.0 value.[20]

Even if they were willing to trade some time in life to get a cure, a moment's reflection reveals that *life itself has as much value for them as it has for those who survive unimpaired*. In saying she would be willing to sacrifice one year of twenty if she could regain full limb function for the rest of her life, a person with paraplegia has not at all said that her life itself (i.e., compared to death) has any less value *for her* than the life itself of the person without paraplegia has *for that person*.[21]

But if the equal value of life is stubborn, the conviction that quality improvement has significant value is also. Even the "no-traders" who insist that, despite paraplegia, life compared to death has full 1.0 value, see real value in regaining full limb function. In the way it has been constructed, though, the essential structure of the QALY implies that *if* their life extension has full 1.0 value, then regaining limb function has *no value*. But of course it does have value! For them, life itself is as valuable as it is to anyone else, *and* restored limb function has real value. The very structure of the QALY as a unit of health benefit cannot accommodate the *real* values of *both* life extension and quality-of-life improvement to disabled and chronically ill persons. The QALY, then, is not an ethically acceptable unit of health benefit.

Can CEA, if not the QALY, be revised to get around this problem? Some have tried.[22] Cost analysis could be done using different sorts of health benefit, comparing the cost per year of life among different life-extending treatments and services and then, separately, the cost per increment of quality-of-life improvement as well, with no attempt to put the two on the same scale of value. One would still have to compare saving lives with improving quality of life, but one would make those hard decisions directly, not through a numerical calculation of QALYs. Such "CEA without QALYs" might still be highly relevant based on the conviction that we should not be spending resources on doing things that create less benefit while passing up other measures that generate more. CEA is ethically alive and kicking, though the QALY would seem to be on life support.

Do "reference point" effects justify extra value at the end of life?

Another point of challenge to cost-effectiveness analysis is its typical assumption that a year of life saved has equal value whether it is a year at the end of life or one of many years saved earlier. The mathematics of CEA are greatly simplified by this assumption, but it is highly questionable. At least one agency that features CEA and QALYs in its work, the United Kingdom's National Institute for Health and Care Excellence (NICE), has departed from this assumption and now employs an "end-of-life premium" in recommending priorities to the National Health Service (NHS). Additional value is accorded to the short spans of life often at stake at the end of life. Saving a person for an additional month at the end of a terminal illness, as long as the quality of that life still makes life worth living, is accorded more value than one-twelfth of a year, or a last year more than one-tenth of a ten-year life extension produced by treatment.[23]

Such an end-of-life premium has a sound basis in how people see the value of their own lives. The general phenomenon is known as *reference point effects*. They are present, for example, in the previously noted adaptation to chronic illness: life has higher value for people actually living with disabling or chronic conditions than people think would be the case without having had to live with them. With the condition as a new reference point for living their lives as well as they can, their subjective quality of life is often remarkably high. Similarly, when someone can gain at most only another year from a treatment, that added year can have much greater *per-year* value than they would see in living any one of an additional ten years they might gain in some other scenario. If the value of a last year that people experience really does increase in this way, then the priorities established by NICE for the NHS should reflect that. An end-of-life premium is not favoritism toward people near death; it is only acknowledging additional life's real value to the people involved.

Incorporating such reference point effects makes CEA a more sensitive and ethically acceptable tool in setting priorities. Even with such refinement, however, it will not be capable of assessing some treatments. Assisted reproductive technologies, for example (see Chapter 9) allow people who otherwise couldn't have children to have them. How can the value of being parents, and the value of the lives of children who would otherwise not come into existence, be compared with the more typical health improvements and extensions of existing lives that CEA assesses? Even at its best, CEA is only one consideration in judging what should be covered by insurance.

CEA needs to be used as one important consideration, not by any means the only one, in determining what should be included in what care gets covered and provided through insurance, public or private. To ignore it, however, would indeed be negligently failing to get the most value, and most likely also the fairest and most equitable value, out of our investments in healthcare.

Concluding thoughts

Dilemmas about how to achieve an ethically just distribution of scarce resources occur frequently in healthcare. Ethical reasoning about just allocation within healthcare can be guided by the same normative frameworks for distributive justice that contend with each other generally. Utilitarian and egalitarian considerations, especially, repeatedly leap to the forefront in allocation decisions in healthcare. Factual inquiry is also crucial, and, as we have seen in some of the discussions in this chapter, the facts about actual effects to precisely whom, caused by what, can be exceedingly complex in allocation dilemmas. Sometimes they get us to a reasonably clear and firm conclusion. Sometimes they do not. And when they do not, it is better to know that they don't—and why—than to plow ahead unaware.

12

WHAT IS A JUSTIFIED PRICE FOR PHARMACEUTICAL DRUGS?

What is an ethically justified price?

Even in many wealthy countries like the United States, people regard prescription drugs as overpriced. In most low- and many medium-income countries, very few brand-name, patent protected drugs are affordable. As a portion of the entire cost of healthcare, drugs are a sizable item. In the United States in the past decade, for example, they have made up roughly twenty percent of total expenditures, with brand-name drugs accounting for more than seventy percent of that.[1] It is little wonder that pharmaceutical drug prices are vigorously debated.

What are the causes of these prices? Patent protection is a big factor, allowing pharmaceutical companies to delay the introduction of less expensive generic competitors to their brand-name drugs. So are the various practices of authorizing agencies like the US Food and Drug Administration (FDA) and the European Medicines Agency (EMA), some of which make it nearly impossible to know the comparative effectiveness of different drugs for the same condition (discussed below). Dubious practices by pharmaceutical companies also contribute: fraudulent marketing, ghost-authoring of medical journal articles about trial results, the influence on the FDA and EMA of Pharmaceutical Research and Manufacturers of America companies (PhRMA, or "Big Pharma"), and more.[2]

Many strategies for lowering prices have been proposed and some adopted. They include price negotiation by large buyers, such as government insurance agencies; expanded use of generic versions of brand-name drugs; shorter periods of patent protection; greater use of comparative effectiveness trials; and shorter trials.

All of these considerations about pricing are relevant, but our focus in this chapter is different. It is not on the political issues, on what currently influences drug prices, or on what measures could actually reduce the price of drugs but rather on this ethical question: What would be *a justified price*, and *how could that be determined*? Discerning such a price will involve both economic elements and considerations of value. Economic ones because, obviously, the costs incurred in developing a drug and bringing it to market need to be taken into consideration in determining a fair price. And considerations of value because a drug must provide sufficient value to its recipients if its price is worth paying.

The chapter will begin with a consideration commonly used by drug companies to justify price: namely, the costs of research and development (R&D). Then we will evaluate the role of market competition in setting prices, noting the effect on such competition of several characteristics of drug markets: patent protection, government authorization, insurance as the medium through which most drugs are purchased, the frequent desperation of buyers, and the reasonable belief that life is priceless. Moreover, just as any justification of price will need to consider what costs of development are relevant, so it will also require reasonable estimates of how effective the drug is. Thus, the next section deals with various barriers to discerning effectiveness. Then we explore the attractive and very sensible sounding concept of "value-based pricing," after which we consider some reforms that could make this way to discern justified price feasible. In a final section, we explore the serious challenges for drug pricing from the perspective of global justice, especially in a pandemic.

A warning for the reader: the subject of this chapter requires what may seem to be some rather "wonky" discussions and concepts, but bear with us. Drug pricing is, indeed, a complex subject, involving notions common in economics and drug policy but frequently not familiar to the general reader. We devote a whole chapter to the topic not only because of its ethical dimensions, but also because of its everyday importance to virtually everyone.

What costs of research and development justify price?

In one sense of "cost," a drug's cost is what patients and insurers pay for it. That is the sense used, for example, when the "cost of drugs" is used to refer to a portion of the overall expense of healthcare. We will usually refer to this sense of cost—what various parties pay to purchase drugs—as their "price." The aim of this chapter is to determine what that price would need to be to be justified. To do that one needs to account for cost in a different sense: the cost to the manufacturer of developing and producing the drug. If developers and manufacturers are to stay in business, cost in this sense will need to be covered by the sales revenue a drug brings in. A pharmaceutical company does not need to make up its costs separately for each and every one of its drugs, but it does need to make up what it spends on developing and producing all of its drugs.

Typically with pharmaceuticals, the costs of R&D for a new drug far outweigh the costs of subsequent production, and they are controversial and complex. Recouping the cost of producing a drug after it has been developed is seldom controversial; we will pay little attention to it. Marketing costs are more controversial because of the arguably improper ways drugs are often marketed to consumers and providers, but for reasons of space we will not attend to marketing costs either.

Compared to most industries, the costs of R&D for pharmaceuticals are high. Estimates for the *average* cost of developing *a single new drug* range widely, from $100 million, to $800 million, to as high as nearly $4 billion.[3] Numerous factors contribute to this wide disparity, including whether the savings from tax deductions that companies take for their R&D are included (they are in the lower estimates). Separate from the already complex matter of what the actual costs of R&D are is the issue on which we focus here: What portion of these costs should count in justifying a drug's price?

One segment of R&D which there might be ample reason to exclude are the costs incurred in developing "me-too" drugs—drugs whose purpose, use, and effectiveness in treating a given condition are the same as drugs already on the market. The initial drug for a given condition is a "first-in-class" drug. Subsequent ones for the same condition(s) are known as "next-in-class." After one or two next-in-class drugs have been developed, creating helpful competition, a next-in-class drug is spoken of as "me-too."

Companies have a strong incentive to develop such drugs when the patient population for drugs in that class is very large. Anticholesterol statins, antihypertension drugs, and antidepressants are good examples. When the market for such drugs is tens or hundreds of millions of users, capturing even a modest fraction with a new me-too drug can be hugely profitable. The value to patients of developing such drugs, though, is virtually nothing. Even when the new drug for the same condition is chemically different (a "new molecular entity"), it may add little of value to the array of effective options. Nonetheless, companies include the cost of developing such drugs, including the expensive attempts that fail, in justifying their prices.

Me-too drugs have made up a hefty portion of new drugs developed by Big Pharma, as much perhaps as eighty percent. As few as twenty percent of drugs newly approved by an authorizing agency like the FDA are new molecular entities, and fewer yet may provide improvements over older drugs.[4]

Bolstering the incentive for me-too drug development—vital to it, in fact—are certain long-standing policies of authorizing agencies. The FDA and the EMA, for example, allow that, for effectiveness trials, the new drug need only be compared to a placebo in the same way the original drugs in that class were shown to be effective, not compared to current, best-available treatments. Companies then know that if they develop a new drug for the same condition for which an effective drug already exists, it can be approved on the basis merely of being more effective than a placebo. The new drugs can often then gain patent protection as well.

To be sure, having a few equivalent drugs from different companies creates competition that can push down price. It does not take many to do that, however. Market competition is supposedly a good way to set prices because it stimulates the production of more useful products that serve people's needs and desires, but further me-too drugs are of little if any value to patients even when, with sufficient marketing, their sales volume is considerable. As a general rule, the R&D expenses that pharmaceutical companies incur in creating me-too drugs should not count in justifying price.

An utterly different situation is presented by the development costs of treatments for rare, so-called *orphan diseases*. Affecting very small populations (typically, less than 1 in 2000, or 0.05 percent of a population), the R&D costs for such drugs may be as great as those for drugs with much larger patient markets, but they cannot be spread across nearly as many patients. Biogen, for example, priced Spinraza, the first drug for a very rare genetic motor neuron disease, type 1 spinal muscular atrophy (SMA), at $750,000 for the first year of individual treatment and $375,000 for each year thereafter. Untreated infants with SMA are often unable to lift their heads, most ultimately require ventilation, and few live past age two.

With Spinraza, muscular strength and coordination is greatly improved, and these children's lives could end up extending well into adulthood or beyond.[5]

The per-patient costs of developing a drug like Spinraza, and its resultant price, may seem exorbitant, but an ethical case can be made for these costs and their inclusion in the drug's price. Perhaps Biogen could spread Spinraza's development costs out into the prices of all its other drugs, or society might pitch in and provide subsidies for its development, but these solutions present their own difficulties. In any case, no one should claim that society is showing some kind of unethical favoritism toward children with SMA if it is willing to pay so much more for their drug than for treating more common diseases. There is no *unfair* favoritism here. People with rare severe diseases are already worse off just by having them. If we let the high per-patient cost of the only effective medications for their condition discourage even developing—much less providing—such treatments, people with rare diseases will be even worse off. In any egalitarian ethical framework for just distribution (see Chapter 10), those who are worse off through no fault of their own should get support. Paying more for orphan disease treatment is thus not unfair. The extremely high per-patient R&D costs for these drugs may indeed justify their price.

The contrast between these two assessments of the proper role of R&D costs in justifying drug prices could not be greater. For me-too drugs that contribute little if any real value, R&D costs justify little if anything. For rare disease drugs, they justify a lot.

Is market competition a good determinant of drug price?

Competitive markets are defended as generally providing goods at an optimal price sufficient to lure producers to provide an adequate supply of good quality but low enough to make the item worth its price to knowledgeable buyers. Medical care, however, does not fit the competitive model well. Patients may not be all that independently knowledgeable, having to depend on their providers, who typically have a financial stake in the matter, for judgments about what is good care. Patients are often caught in pressured and urgent situations in which they cannot shop around for the best options at the best price. Insurance is needed to spread the high and immediate costs of unpredictable events over a longer period of time and pool of subscribers, but, once in place, it removes the incentive for either patient or provider to discipline what is provided and spent (see Chapter 10, the danger in insurance). Many patients' desperation for anything—*anything*—that can help makes assessment and comparison of whether a new drug actually helps difficult. And the conviction that "life is priceless," which in a certain sense it surely is, gives medical providers and drug companies tremendous leverage in setting prices higher than may be necessary to recoup their legitimate costs with reasonable profit.

These well-known limitations on medical markets are amplified with pharmaceuticals. Patents, as intellectual property rights, provide companies strong incentives to invest in R&D, but they may insulate companies too much from competition. Even after drug patents expire (normally fifteen to twenty years), the methods of a drug's production may remain opaque. Obscure financial arrangements and perverse incentives may be difficult to root out—for example, sitting on a modification that would allow a lower dose or less frequent use of a drug.[6]

Patents, at least when properly limited, can be viewed as allowing pharmaceutical markets to function well. They give drug developers sufficient safety from others jumping in to mimic their product to allow them to recoup the often large costs of R&D. Without them, it is commonly thought, companies would have insufficient incentive to invest in developing new and valuable drugs. These investments are almost always gambles that many times fail to produce. Without the temporary protection against competition provided by patents on the drugs that are successfully developed, pharmaceutical companies simply will not produce many innovative drugs.

The devil, though, is in the details. The length of patents and the requirements for getting them can determine whether they create needlessly large profits and excessive prices or whether they provide only the protection that especially small pharmaceutical companies need in trying to break into a market or pursue drugs that major companies take little interest in. Internationally, patents are particularly contentious, often making life-saving drugs unaffordable in low- and middle-income countries (LMICs) during the patent protection periods when the medicines are utterly vital, as with vaccines during a pandemic. Some international trade agreements have selectively reduced patent protections to enable LMIC companies to manufacture at generic drug cost, but such reductions have been palpably inadequate in the COVID-19 (SARS-CoV-2) pandemic, to take just one example.[7]

If patents are necessary to create sufficient development incentives, the question still remains how much of the profit from that development private pharmaceutical companies should get. Almost all pharmaceutical R&D builds on years of expensive foundational research funded and conducted by universities, institutes, and public agencies (the National Institutes of Health [NIH] in the United States, for example). Final profits from sales could be allocated proportionally by the relative amount of public versus private company investment.

Fair and productive competition in pharmaceutical markets is dependent also on purchasers and users being able to discern how effective various drugs are. But here is another big problem: the real effectiveness of many drugs is hardly transparent and frequently not really discernible at all.

What makes it difficult to discern the true effectiveness of a drug?

Significant barriers to discerning a drug's true effectiveness are built into the structure of most current trials and authorizations and the lenient requirements for disclosing the information gained in them. Two such elements are the use of surrogate endpoints and placebo-control trials (PCTs).

Surrogate endpoints

Many randomized controlled trials (RCTs) used to obtain approval for cancer drugs, for example, are based on "progression-free survival" without convincing evidence of actual extended life. To be sure, much slower tumor growth during the time span of a trial can be a promising sign of significant remission, but we do not actually know whether the stalled tumor growth for that period ultimately results in longer life or that it reduces the most painful aspects for patients in their final stage. For trials of statin drugs, the surrogate endpoint of lower LDL (bad) blood cholesterol in often used. In the absence of reliable evidence of actually preventing heart disease and death, this has led to considerable criticism of pharmaceutical companies' claims about their effectiveness. The PCSK9 inhibitors Repatha and Praluent, for example, have been shown to greatly lower LDL in many statin-resistant patients, but longer survival has not been shown.[8]

To be sure, there is something to be said for using surrogate endpoints. For treatments of conditions whose route to eventual heart attack, stroke, or death can be very long, surrogate endpoints may be appropriate; otherwise, promising drugs for these conditions would often not be authorized for decades. When drugs are approved on the basis of surrogate endpoints, however, approval should generally be temporary, with follow-up trials required.

Placebo-control trials

An equally if not more significant limitation on what we know about many drugs' effectiveness is that many next-in-class drugs are approved on the basis only of the same placebo comparison used in the trials that got the earlier first-in-class drug its approval (see earlier discussion). Suppose a new statin, for example, is developed for the same conditions addressed by some existing statins. If all that is required for approval is that the drug be more effective than a placebo, the drug may be no better, or even worse, than the existing therapies. The FDA and EMA standards for approving drugs for effectiveness typically require only demonstration of effectiveness with a PCT, not an *active-control trial* (ACT) that compares the new drug to an existing drug for the same conditions whose active therapeutic ingredient has been shown effective compared to a placebo.[9]

What a physician should know in prescribing the new drug is whether it is more effective than, or at least as effective as, the older drug. If drug companies are not required to conduct ACTs, and if, as is likely, no one else goes to the time and expense of conducting such a trial after agency approval, the drug will end up being used without anyone knowing its relative effectiveness. An extremely important ethical issue is at stake here. To serve the interests of their patients, providers should prescribe the likely most effective treatment, but with sole reliance on placebo controls in drug trials, they simply cannot know what the most effective treatment is. Drug approval policy directly clashes with basic doctor–patient medical ethics.

The resulting ongoing informational deficiency for physicians and patients that results from this reliance on PCTs for next-in-class drugs, as bad as it is, is not their only ethically objectionable aspect. Even enrolling trial participants in such

PCTs violates the obligation of healthcare providers to serve the best interests of their patients. Absent some unusual special circumstance, how can it be ethical to enroll patients in an RCT with a placebo-control arm *if it is already known that an existing therapy is better than a placebo*? (see Chapter 4).

Any plausible ethical defense of PCTs in these circumstances would have to rely on the informed consent of patients to be part of such a trial. But for that they ought to be informed not just that they might be in the trial's placebo arm, but that, if they were, they would be getting *what is already known to be inferior* (the placebo).

Other information deficiencies from clinical trials may also prohibit providers and healthcare plans from knowing the drawbacks and benefits of different therapies. Companies may bury negative data in trials that were abandoned (trials for different dosages and conditions other than the existing approval involved, for example). Not all trials of agency-approved drugs are made available to the public upon approval nor is the full analysis of the agency. And once a number of drugs for prevalent conditions are approved and widely used, there is little incentive to do large and long trials to discern marginal differences between them, trials that could show results that in a large population would amount to truly significant differences. Possibly, for example, one of the two most widely used statins in the United States and United Kingdom, atorvastatin or simvastatin, is statistically slightly more effective or has somewhat fewer downsides than the other, but without such a trial we will never know.[10]

Almost all of these informational deficiencies lead to inflated estimates of drugs' effectiveness, bolstering specious arguments for prices higher than are warranted.

Should "value-based pricing" be used to determine price?

Basing a drug's price on its value is intuitively attractive. What could be more appropriate than paying for a drug what it is worth—its value—to the people it will affect? Sometimes, of course, a drug should cost much less than what it is worth. Aspirin is a prime example. No longer patent-protected and easy to manufacture at high quality, market competition is an appropriate pricing process for aspirin even though market pricing, as we have seen, has serious deficiencies for drugs generally. While drugs like aspirin should be extremely inexpensive, however, drugs that cannot be viably sold for such low prices should be priced to reflect only what they are worth. Why should society or individuals pay more than what is commensurate with a drug's value? If it isn't worth in human value what it costs, the money should be spent on other things that are.

Determining the "worth" of a medication, though, is hardly easy. Several basic elements are essential to know. (1) The drug's health *effects*, including both positive gains and any risks of harm. (2) The health *benefit* that those effects constitute, especially compared with other, quite different health benefits. For example, what is the amount of health benefit in gaining decades of enhanced mobility and reduced pain from an arthritis drug, compared to the five-year average of extended life achieved by a cancer drug? Finally, (3) the *monetary value* of those health benefits. As much as people may recoil at "putting a price on life," this is required if value is going to be translated into price. Since "money" is a universal medium of exchange, health benefits' "monetary value" is simply a way of expressing those benefits' value relative to the other things that people and societies can use the money to buy.

The first of these elements—effects on health—has been discussed in the previous section. The second—relative health benefit—is often measured in amounts like the quality-adjusted life year (QALY), constructed to incorporate the very different quality-of-life improvement and life extension aspects of healthcare into a common unit of benefit (see Chapter 11). The third element—monetary value—will require that the unit of health benefit being used (a QALY, say) be assigned a standard monetary value or a range of such value. That value constitutes a limit on what cost/QALY is worth paying, so that drugs which cost more than this for the QALYs they produce are not priceworthy. Initially, for example, the first PCSK9 inhibitors to control cholesterol were priced at $274,000–302,000/QALY, rendering them outside the $50,000–150,000/QALY limit often regarded in the United States as worth paying. Cutting these drugs' price in half would bring them within that priceworthy range. Having a value-based pricing standard would bring pressure on companies to do that.[11]

Such a structure for value-based pricing is commonly referred to as *health technology assessment* (HTA). In the United Kingdom, HTA is done by the National Institute for Health Care Excellence (NICE), and in the United States most prominently by the private Institute for Clinical and Economic Review (ICER). ICER and NICE have assessed hundreds of treatments, including many pharmaceutical drugs, first discerning their likely benefits in terms of QALYs and then using monetary value (dollars or pounds) per QALY to determine which are worth paying for. In countries with emerging or established use of HTA, $/QALY values can be used to negotiate drug prices down to the level at which they become worth their price. HTA is hardly confined to the United States and Europe and is now increasingly significant in Asia.[12]

The second and third elements used in this kind of value-based pricing—QALYs for the units of health benefit produced and dollars (or other monetary unit) per QALY—pose all the same ethical issues raised in Chapter 11 about the use of QALYs in the ethical allocation of resources. The most difficult is the tension between the equal value of life in conditions good and bad, and the essential framework of the QALY in which quality-of-life improvements are put on the same scale of benefit as life extension. This framework (as noted in Chapter 11) makes the value of saving a life in compromising conditions less than the value of saving a life in full health for the same period of time. Some of the more sophisticated articulations of value-based pricing forthrightly acknowledge this highly questionable character of QALYs but still employ them. Neumann, Cohen, and Ollendorf, for example, entitle one of their sections "QALYs: The Worst Way to Measure Health, Except for All the Others."[13] If we badly need a value-based method for pricing drugs, and if there is no feasible way to do it except by relying substantially (though not exclusively) on QALYs, then QALYs may be a necessary measurement tool in setting ethical drug prices.

The "not exclusively" qualification is important. The simple number of QALYs achieved by a drug should be supplemented by several other considerations: *end-of-life premium* and other *reference point effects* (see Chapter 11), extra consideration for orphan diseases (earlier this chapter), and preserving hope at the end of life with "last-chance" therapies.[14]

Conceptually, value-based pricing provides the most intuitively attractive ethical framework for drug pricing. Market competition has a limited role, too (witness the aspirin example), as does the degree of patent protection needed to recoup justified, not wasteful and merely profit-seeking, R&D investments. The greatest challenge to actually discerning sound value-based prices may lie in what we don't know about the actual effects of drugs on health. Excessive use of surrogate outcomes and the failure to use best-available-therapy comparisons in effectiveness trials mar the data usually available, and the integrity of value-based pricing can be no better than the facts about effectiveness that it uses. Moreover, even when the therapeutic effects are reasonably clear, disagreements about how to estimate the value of those improvements can muddy the process. Even so, many judgments about the relative value of health benefits are not controversial. Ten years of extra life in a better-than-death condition are better than two years, for example.

Despite its challenges, value-based pricing is still the most ethically defensible method for drug pricing. The challenge for the future is to get it recognized as such and to eliminate or reform some of the practices that disrupt our ability to discern real effectiveness.

What reforms are needed in markets and regulation?

Requiring active-control trials instead of only placebo controls and getting real-health not just surrogate outcomes would make value-based pricing considerably more attractive than it currently is to governments as well as private insurance companies. These changes would also greatly reduce the incentive for for-profit Big Pharma companies to run up R&D expenses trying to develop me-too drugs. Such reforms would still be entirely within the current framework of pharmaceutical development dominated by private for-profit companies.

Very different nonprofit alternatives for pharmaceutical R&D have not received nearly as much attention. That is unfortunate. Arguably, nonprofit frameworks may engage in more efficient development and more readily achieve justified prices. R&D by for-profit companies is already a combination of private and public investments (the NIH in the United States, for example), but R&D can also be conducted solely by nonprofit institutions. A singular, outstanding example is the Mario Negri Institute (MNI), founded in the 1960s by two young Italian scientists and funded initially by a wealthy Italian jeweler for whom the Institute is named. In the five decades since, the Institute's research has produced more than 12,000 articles in peer-reviewed journals, nearly twenty percent of which are rated high-impact.[15]

The Institute is a real-world answer to those who are sympathetic to the hardest hitting criticisms of large pharmaceutical companies but who may be skeptical that anyone other than for-profit companies can pursue vigorous and productive drug development. The Institute takes out no patents on what it develops and makes all of its studies and trial data public. It uses best-available-therapy comparison rather than placebo-control trials whenever an effective drug in the same class already exists, and it insists on real benefit outcomes, not surrogate endpoints. It never uses ghost writers to publish its results, and it emphasizes bench-to-bedside integration after a drug is developed to discern what combinations of drug, patient, dosage, and other treatment are ultimately the most clinically useful.[16]

Getting to truly justified drug prices may be more likely with a process like that used by the Mario Negri Institute than with for-profit pharmaceutical companies working through agencies like the US FDA and EMA. Even if that is the case, however, will many potentially effective drugs be missed without the lure of profit behind development? This is an empirical question, the answer to which depends on highly complex, comprehensive, and often difficult to procure information.

Rather than make an overarching judgment about whether a for-profit/patent system or a nonprofit/open information one will produce the best drugs at justified prices, it may be more realistic to focus on reforming the current bad incentives in for-profit, patent-based structures in addition to expanding the best nonprofit development. The reforms might include

- Development and agency approval should involve greater reliance on best-available-therapy comparison trials and less use of surrogate endpoints.
- If trials show a drug to be only equally effective, not superior to other drugs in its class, it should be so labeled. To provide market competition with a more important and constructive role, efficacy information (including negative trial results) should be made transparent.[17]
- Long-term trials (at least careful and transparent tracking) should be required as follow-up to initial approval.
- A drug patent's length could vary by the degree of benefit and innovation, as determined by HTA.
- Value-based assessment by the likes of NICE and ICER should be more widely used by government and private

payers, as long as the ethical quandaries about value of life and fair impact in special circumstances (orphan diseases, for example) are given proper attention.

Is patent protection compatible with global justice?

Even if such reforms were highly successful in achieving more justified prices in relatively high-income countries, huge challenges globally would remain. Incentives in the current dominant for-profit structure result in much less attention on developing drugs for diseases prevalent in the developing world compared to illnesses more common in high-income countries. For decades the distribution of research and health technology has followed a well-known 90/10 ratio: ninety percent of the funding of health research and access to medicines, including drug development, is invested in treating the wealthiest ten percent of the world's population. With R&D in particular, much more research is devoted to the cancers, psychological disorders, and cardiovascular diseases common in high-income countries than to the infectious diseases and challenges to maternal health prevalent in low- and middle-income ones. If pharmaceutical companies can sell the drugs for diseases prevalent in wealthy countries at much higher prices than they can the drugs needed in lower-income countries, then of course they will concentrate on the former.[18]

To address this imbalance a variety of pricing and reward arrangements have been conceived, but their achievements are small compared to the immensity of the challenge. A nonprofit structure for pharmaceutical R&D investment in which very few drugs were patented might accomplish more but only if it had adequate funding.[19]

Alternatively, significant reduction in global health inequities could be achieved by relaxing patent protection to allow the production of the most badly needed drugs for countries that cannot remotely afford patent-protected prices. In a pandemic like COVID-19, the effect of unmodified patent protection is graphic. By February 2022, a year after the first vaccines were made available, vaccinations rates for one dose or more were only eleven percent overall in low-income countries, but seventy-eight percent in high- and upper-middle-income ones. Some of this is due to the leverage of countries with greater ability to pay; in an expression of their "vaccine nationalism," rich countries buy up the vast majority of the supply for themselves. If production in other countries (India, for example) were allowed, manufacturers there could produce and sell the vaccines for a small fraction of the patent-protected price. Otherwise, lower-income countries will continue to have far fewer vaccines to administer, and many thousands of people, at the very least, will die as a result.[20]

Two large companies, Pfizer and Merck, responded to this maldistribution early in 2022 with what may appear to be a laudatory step, but one that is inadequate at best and arguably hypocritical. With considerable fanfare they announced they would allow their new COVID-19 *treatments* to be made and sold at much lower prices in ninety-five poorer countries, home to half the world's population. Yet Pfizer continued to refuse permission for affordable versions of its highly effective *vaccine* to be produced. If vaccines were more accessible and more people were vaccinated, fewer people would get sick and need treatment. Fortunately, Moderna decided in March 2022 not to enforce the patent on its COVID-19 vaccine.[21]

The case for relaxing patent protection for vaccines in a pandemic is overwhelming. Given the likely hundreds of thousands, even millions of lives not saved under the current restrictions, the utilitarian case for substantially limiting vaccine patent rights is overwhelming. The only possible utilitarian argument for not doing so would be that incentives to develop vaccines—and develop them quickly—would be so weakened by relaxing patent protection that effective vaccines would either not be developed at all or developed more slowly, costing even more lives to be lost. For the production and sale of the initial rounds of vaccine in high-income countries, this may be a plausible argument, but is it so for the production of vaccines for poorer countries *after the vaccines are well established*? Plenty of development incentive remains from the early profits to be made in wealthier countries.

In disputes about intellectual property rights like patents, the relevant considerations are not only utilitarian elements, but also fairness and rights. Generally, patent holders are the rightful owners of their inventions and should be able to restrict others' use, just as writers and composers should retain copyright over the materials they create; open use of their property takes unfair advantage of their creative effort. In the real situation of something like the vaccines for COVID-19, however, such arguments are dubious. Through agencies like the US NIH, the public invested heavily for years in the RNA and mRNA technologies used by pharmaceutical companies to develop the vaccines, people volunteered for the trials, and public infrastructure enabled their distribution. It is not unfair to pharmaceutical companies to allow other manufacturers to produce the drugs. Global justice demands it.[22]

Concluding thoughts

Drug pricing and the incentives that prices create involve complex economic considerations, and the barriers and prices and other pharmaceutical policies create have huge implications for human well-being. The stakes are not merely economic and monetary. They are often ethical: lack of access for many in the world and other arguably unfair and counterproductive effects. Given the impact of drug prices on people's real lives, pharmaceutical pricing warrants ethical attention as much as other topics traditionally more prominent in bioethics.

13

IS IT ETHICAL TO GENETICALLY MODIFY HUMANS?

One of the most exciting prospects in modern medicine is *gene therapy*, the prevention or treatment of genetic disease by modifying or editing genes. We now know that almost all diseases have a genetic component. In some, such as Huntington's disease, an inherited mutation is virtually certain to cause the disease. In others, such as heart disease or many cancers, inherited genetic mutations will increase susceptibility to the disease, but people with those mutations do not necessarily get it. Environmental factors are also important in triggering genetic diseases. People genetically predisposed to developing lung cancer, for example, may never develop the disease if they never smoke.

We start with gene therapy, which, while promising, is still in its infancy. A lot more research is needed before it is proved safe and effective. Of course, questions about safety and effectiveness, including cost-effectiveness, are not unique to gene therapy; all new medical treatments need to be proved safe and effective.

Genetic modification raises further questions because it might not be used exclusively for the prevention or cure of disease. It could, in theory, be used to enhance normal human abilities—to make individuals "better than well." We explain what genetic enhancement is and present arguments that have been made against doing it. Would it be a violation of individual rights? Would it ultimately create a race of superhumans, exacerbating inequality and changing the very nature of humanity? Would it give humanity the power purposely to alter human evolution, and, if so, is this an invitation we should accept? What implications might this have for individuals, now and in the future? How might this affect families and the relations between parents and children? What are the long-term implications for society? Before we can address these ethical issues, we need to know more about the science of gene therapy.

What is gene therapy?

Gene therapy can be of two kinds, somatic cell or germline. Both kinds attempt to inactivate, or knock out, disease-causing genes. The difference between the two lies in the kinds of cells targeted by the therapy.

Somatic cells are all the cells in your body, except for reproductive cells (i.e., sperm and eggs, also known as gametes). Somatic cell gene therapy is performed on born human beings who have certain genetic diseases. One way it works is by inactivating, or knocking out, a gene that is functioning improperly. It can also work by replacing a mutated gene with a healthy copy, or it can introduce a new gene to help fight the disease. Somatic cell gene therapy has had some notable failures,[1] but also some successes. Most recently, two babies received the first gene therapy for Tay-Sachs disease, a lethal disease without a treatment. After two years, both remain seizure-free. More testing is required to learn whether the treatment can fully stop disease progression.[2] Somatic cell gene therapy is experimental and is only used for serious diseases when there is no better alternative.

Germline gene therapy would attempt to prevent disease by modifying genes in the germline; that is, in gametes and embryos. At this time, the consensus is that clinical germline gene therapy, also known as hereditable human genome editing (HHGE), is too dangerous to be done. It is prohibited in the United States, in many European countries, in China, and in many countries around the world. If it could be done safely and effectively, HHGE would prevent the transmission of a genetic disease from the parents to their offspring. However, unlike somatic cell gene therapy, the prevention of genetic disease would not be limited to the person who developed from the modified gametes or embryo, but would also prevent the genetic disease in all of that individual's descendants. HHGE thus holds the promise of eradicating some genetic diseases from the face of the earth within a few generations. Its promise is also its peril, however, since any unforeseen and harmful side effects would also be inherited, and it remains to be seen whether these could be reversed.

The role of bioethics in the development of any consensus on these issues is, first of all, to convey to the public the facts of genetic modification in understandable, nonspecialized language. Philosophical bioethics has another important role: namely, presenting and evaluating the arguments that have been raised against gene editing to distinguish those that need to be seriously considered from those that are spurious.

What is CRISPR?

Gene therapy took a huge leap forward with the discovery of a new gene editing technology, known as clustered regularly interspaced short palindromic repeats (CRISPR). Jennifer Doudna and Emmanuelle Charpentier were awarded the Nobel Prize in Chemistry in 2020 for describing how the technology functions and showing how it could be used as a tool for genome editing. Theoretically, CRISPR could be used in either somatic cell or germline gene therapy.

CRISPR is based on a mechanism in nature that bacteria have evolved to protect themselves against viruses. It acts like tiny molecular scissors that scientists can use to selectively cut out and replace genes. This is especially promising for the treatment of diseases caused by a mutation in a single gene, since only one gene would have to be edited. Some well-known monogenic disorders are Huntington's disease, Tay-Sachs disease, sickle cell disease, and cystic fibrosis. However, CRISPR technology is not limited to the treatment or prevention of genetic disease. It has revolutionized the creation of vaccines, including vaccines against COVID-19. Its potential uses include medical diagnosis, agriculture, and the creation of cleaner fuels. As often happens in science, a discovery may lead to uses not envisioned at the outset.

CRISPR is currently being tested in numerous clinical trials for patients with sickle cell anemia. In the future, CRISPR might be used to prevent or treat some forms of blindness, breast and ovarian cancer, and early-onset Alzheimer's. In 2016, a team at Sichuan University became the first in the world to use CRISPR in a Phase 1 clinical trial to treat a patient with aggressive lung cancer. Phase 1 trials are intended to prove only safety and feasibility, which was shown in this trial. More studies will be needed to determine if CRISPR can be used in an effective treatment for aggressive lung cancer.

Even in single-gene disorders, gene editing is extremely difficult to do as it requires targeting the mutation at exactly the right location on the gene. There is also the risk of unintended harmful side effects. The technical challenges are great, and the risks are real. Nevertheless, CRISPR-based treatments for genetic disorders have the potential to be used in thousands of conditions caused by specific inherited mutations.

In 2017, a team in Portland, Oregon, announced they used CRISPR to edit a human embryo. Led by Shoukhrat Mitalipov, they applied CRISPR to fifty embryos at the single-cell stage to splice out a mutation in a single gene, $MYBPC3$. That mutation is the cause of a deadly disease, hypertrophic cardiomyopathy, affecting an estimated 1 in 500 people worldwide, that results in the abnormal thickening of heart tissue. "Most of those afflicted show no symptoms until their heart unexpectedly stops. There is no way to prevent or cure hypertrophic cardiomyopathy, and it generally remains undetected in those carrying the mutant gene until they suddenly drop dead."[3]

None of the edited embryos in the Oregon trial was allowed to develop for more than a few days, and they were never intended for implantation. Some critics had doubts as to whether the team actually managed to correct the genetic defect, and therefore whether the therapy would have prevented the disease in a child, had the embryo been implanted and gone to term. And, even if the team was successful in editing the embryos, much more research will be needed before the treatment is clinically approved.

What safety concerns does CRISPR raise?

The main safety concern in both kinds of gene therapy is unintended harmful side effects. Such effects may occur because the mechanisms used in CRISPR do not always work perfectly. The treatment could cause unwanted changes at or near the target site or elsewhere in the individual's genome, which could lead to cancer or other problems that might be worse than the disease that was being targeted.

In addition, replacing a mutated gene with a different gene can end up making the patient worse off because variants that decrease the risk of some diseases may increase the risk of others. For example, a common genetic variant decreases a person's risk of developing Parkinson's disease but increases the risk of developing schizophrenia. We just don't know what influence this variant has on many other diseases, or what might result from its interaction with other genes and with the environment. Such concerns are heightened in HHGE because the unwanted changes would be inherited by all the individual's descendants.

In 2017, the National Academy of Sciences and the National Academy of Medicine issued a new report about germline editing.[4] The study committee said that such research could not be ethically done at present but might be in the future.

It recommended stringent criteria that would need to be met in order to allow clinical trials for genome editing of the human germline. They include (1) an absence of reasonable alternatives; (2) restriction to editing genes that cause or strongly predispose to serious disease or condition; (3) credible data on risks and potential health benefits; (4) rigorous oversight during clinical trials; (5) comprehensive plans for long-term, multigenerational follow-up; (6) continued reassessment of health and societal benefits and risks, with ongoing input from the public; and (7) reliable oversight mechanisms to prevent extension to uses other than preventing a serious disease or condition. The co-chair of the study committee, Alta Charo, said that there are some cases of hereditable gene editing that are "really compelling, where people don't have good alternatives and yet want to have children who are genetically related and are healthy. So, we're not talking about 'designer babies'; we're talking about healthy babies."[5]

Guidelines are clearly important in deciding whether germline gene editing is ethical. However, the existence of guidelines cannot prevent rogue scientists who would be ignorant of or simply ignore existing guidelines and protocols.

Who was He Jiankui, and what did he do?

He Jiankui, a Chinese biophysics researcher, used the gene-editing techniques he learned as a postdoctoral student at Stanford University in California to start a gene-sequencing company, Direct Genomics. Motivated by personal ambition, combined with patriotic fervor and a genuine desire to help people, He Jiankui and his team used CRISPR on twenty-two embryos in order to confer immunity to HIV infection.

He Jiankui did not come up with the idea of using germline modification to prevent the transmission of HIV. Scientists working with sex workers in Kenya had discovered that a small number of the women had not contracted AIDS despite repeated exposure because they naturally had a variant form of the CCR5 gene that encodes a protein to which the virus cannot attach.[6] He Jiankui's idea was to replace the normal CCR5 gene in embryos with the variant that creates HIV resistance.

His team found twenty-two couples who wanted children in which the men were HIV-positive. The women were not. By September 2017, eight couples had been enrolled. Two of the edited embryos were implanted in a woman who gave birth in November 2018 to twins, given the pseudonyms "Lulu" and "Nana."

What was unethical about what He Jiankui did?

He Jiankui's idea—introducing a mutation that would protect the children of infected men from HIV—was not a crazy idea. HIV is a serious disease, although it is not a genetic disease. It is transmitted through bodily fluids, most commonly during sexual activity or the sharing of needles. While it can also be transmitted from an infected woman to the fetus during pregnancy, the women in Dr. He's trial were not seropositive. It is possible, though rare, for an HIV-infected man to transmit HIV through his sperm to his child, even if the child's mother is not infected. The use of experimental procedures in medicine is ethical only if there are no existing measures to treat or prevent the disease. Was that true in this case?

It was not. HIV transmission from infected men to their offspring is typically prevented by sperm washing. He Jiankui dismissed this possibility on the ground that China's HIV-positive parents were banned from fertility clinics and therefore they didn't have this option. That does complicate the ethical situation. At the same time, given that the transmission from infected father to embryo is unlikely, and the risks to the future children unknown, genetically modifying embryos was not justified. Moreover, it is doubtful that the couples enrolled in the trial had any idea of the potential risks; they were therefore unable to give genuinely informed consent, a serious ethical lapse.

Other ethical breaches were shocking. For example, the document of the ethics committee of a Shenzhen hospital allegedly approving the trial turned out to have been forged. The embryologist hired by He Jiankui to edit the embryos kept the trial secret from his own hospital and from the fertility doctor who would implant the embryos. When the hospital asked for the father's blood sample, the team submitted a sample from a different man, one who was HIV-negative.

He Jiankui ignored the warnings of Western colleagues that implanting edited embryos flouted existing legal and ethical norms. He seemed genuinely surprised at the reaction to his experiment, expecting to be treated as a hero in China for helping to achieve its goal of becoming a force in genetic science. In fact, he was fired by his university, sentenced to three years in prison for "illegal medical practice," and fined 3 million yuan (US$430,000).[7]

In 2019, the US National Academy of Medicine, the National Academy of Science, and the British Royal Society established the International Commission on the Clinical Use of Human Germline Genome Editing. In 2020, the Commission issued its Report, recommending caution in future uses of HHGE. Specifically, it recommended that initial uses of HHGE should be limited to certain circumstances: serious monogenic diseases that cause severe morbidity or premature death, in which parents have no option for having a genetically related child without the disease or the expected proportion of unaffected embryos would be less than twenty-five percent, and the parents have had one unsuccessful trial of preimplantation genetic diagnosis (PGD). An International Scientific Advisory Panel should assess scientific safety and efficacy and an international mechanism for addressing concerns about deviations from these standards should be created.[8]

There are several lessons from this cautionary tale. One is the importance of global guidelines for HHGE. Whether these guidelines should include a permanent ban or just a moratorium on genetically modifying embryos is an ongoing controversy in bioethics. However, as the example of He Jiankui shows, there must also be mechanisms for ensuring that the guidelines are followed.

The importance of transparency in research is also crucial. If He Jiankui had been open and honest about what he was doing, he likely would have been stopped by the Chinese government.[9] His failure to be transparent is indicative of the enormous pressures on researchers to be innovative, to beat the competition. Benjamin Hurlbut, a bioethicist at Arizona State University, says about He Jiankui, "Of course, he made his own choices. But he was a product of his environment." Hurlbut went on to say that calling Dr. He a "rogue scientist" seems to excuse the rest of science from having played a role. "That's just not true."[10]

Can genetic modification of embryos to prevent disease be justified?

Most couples at risk of transmitting a genetic disease to their offspring do not need to modify their embryos. They have an alternative: pre-implantation genetic testing (PGT) and embryo discard. Given the risks posed by germline gene therapy, one might ask what's the advantage of modifying human embryos to prevent genetic disease when that outcome can be avoided by in-vitro fertilization (IVF) and PGT.

One reason is that not all patients can produce unaffected embryos for transfer. Such cases may occur when both members are homozygous for a recessive condition, like sickle cell disease or cystic fibrosis, or one member is homozygous for a dominant condition, like Huntington's disease. However, because such cases are rare, some bioethicists to say the research is not worth its risks.

> [It] can be argued that trying to satisfy the desire of a few couples for genetically healthy and genetically related

children does not in itself warrant the time (energy), talent (skills), and treasure (finances) needed to develop heritable human genome editing for this purpose. Not to put too fine a point on it, why should scientists, governments, philanthropists, and other investors direct resources to address the desire for genetically healthy and genetically related children using genome-editing technology when, in almost all cases, there are safer, simpler, and cheaper ways of achieving this goal and building loving families?[11]

There is a wider use for HHGE, however, than those very few couples who cannot produce unaffected embryos. Even when a couple can produce unaffected embryos for implantation, successful HHGE of the affected embryos would increase the number of viable embryos available for transplantation, thus increasing the chances for a successful pregnancy. The question still remains, though, whether this need is great enough to justify the cost and risks of developing HHGE.

Another rationale in favor of developing HHGE is that it is preferable to cure rather than discard embryos. This is particularly so for those who regard human embryos as having the same moral status as born babies. At the same time, there is no guarantee that any instance of gene editing of embryos will be successful. There will still be a need for follow-up prenatal testing, the results of which might be the choice to abort. Even if gene therapy is preferable to embryo discard—and that is an open question—it is unlikely to completely avoid the need for abortion.

What about enhancement?

Susceptibility to disease is not the only trait affected by one's genes. Virtually every trait we have, whether physical, mental, or emotional, has a genetic component. One of the objections that has been made to techniques like CRISPR is that it could be used by parents to design their children, to get offspring who are smarter, more attractive, and generally better than they would be without gene editing. Is HHGE ethically acceptable only if the aim is to treat or prevent disease?

Before proceeding to the ethical arguments opposing HHGE for non-disease traits, a word of caution about what it could actually achieve is warranted. Many people are under the impression that prospective parents could simply hand a clinician a list of desirable traits, physical and psychological, to get a child "to spec." This is based on a misunderstanding of how gene editing techniques work and what they can accomplish.

As we saw earlier, gene editing is most likely to be effective in the case of monogenic diseases, a single mutation on a single gene that can be knocked out or replaced. It is unlikely to be effective for most diseases, which involve multiple genes interacting with each other as well as the environment. If this is true for multifactorial diseases, it's even more true for non-disease traits, such as intelligence, attractiveness, having artistic talent, or being good at sports. To think that such traits can be implanted in embryos by genetically modifying them is deeply wrong, betraying both a simplistic understanding of genetic inheritance and a failure to consider all the environmental influences that shape human beings.

At the same time, even if parents will never be able completely to determine their children's traits, genetic modification of embryos might one day make it possible to influence, to some degree, non-disease traits in offspring. Perhaps one day parents may have the ability to provide their offspring with a "genetic edge" for desirable traits, comparable to the genetic edge often naturally provided children by parents who have those desirable traits.

Assuming that concerns about safety and efficacy can be resolved, would the use of HHGE for such enhancement purposes be wrong?

Does enhancement threaten authenticity?

Sometimes it's alleged that a person who has been genetically modified would have a less authentic personality than other people. That is, their traits would not be genuinely theirs. In a series that was briefly aired on US television some years ago, a genetically modified character says, "I sometimes wonder whether I'm really cheerful or if I was just modified to be cheerful?" This makes no sense. If cheerfulness is (partly) the result of one's genes, *how* you got the gene, naturally or via HHGE, shouldn't make any difference.

Consider this real-life example. Numerous studies found that people who have one or two copies of the short allele of the 5-HTT gene are more susceptible to becoming depressed after a stressful event, whereas those who have one or two copies of the long allele are more resilient to depression. Suppose that it were possible to modify an embryo so that it had two copies of the long allele instead of the short allele. The resulting child would presumably be more resistant to depression after a stressful event—just like a child who inherited the long allele from her parents. It makes no more sense for the genetically modified person to worry if she's genuinely more resistant to depression than it would for the child who naturally inherited the long allele to wonder if she is.

Does enhancement violate autonomy?

This objection maintains that genetically modifying an embryo to increase the chances that a child will have, or not have, certain traits is wrong because this would violate the child's autonomy.

For example, suppose the parents select genes to give their children a genetic edge for athletic ability. According to this argument, this is wrong because they are imposing on the child their desire that the child become an athlete. Maybe if they hadn't selected for genes associated with athleticism, the child would have wanted to become a poet or a mathematician. The parents are imposing their values, their particular conception of what's worth doing, on the child even before the child is born.

However, this suggests that people who were not genetically modified as embryos make free choices about the genes they inherit and the resulting influence on their interests and talents. But of course no one selects their own genes. We all just play the hand we get.

Consider the offspring of people with exceptional talents, such as Jaden and Jaz, the children of former tennis stars, Steffi Graf and Andre Agassiz. As a youngster, Jaden loved baseball while Jaz was into hip hop dance. The athleticism of the children was undoubtedly partly a result of their genetic inheritance. Would it make any sense for Jaden and Jaz to claim that their autonomy was therefore infringed? Of course not. If Andre and Steffi had forced their kids to be tennis players, it might be objected that they were violating their children's autonomy. In fact, they were careful not to push their children into any particular activity but to let them find their own interests.

If autonomy is not infringed when we get the genes we have through chance—the genetic lottery—autonomy is not infringed when genes are the result of parental choice so long as parents do not force their children into particular activities. It's the style of parenting that risks violating autonomy, not whether genes are inherited or deliberately modified.

Might enhancement be damaging to parent–child relationships?

It might be argued that even if the child's autonomy is not violated, genetic enhancement poses a threat to the parent–child relationship. Michael Sandel[12] argues that enabling parents to choose or influence traits would contribute to an unfortunate trend, one that he labels "hyper-parenting." Hyper-parents don't merely want to guide their children but to control everything about them. They wouldn't stop at giving their offspring a genetic edge for athleticism, say. They would push their children to be super athletes. They would be willing to pay big bucks to achieve that goal, and they would be disappointed if the genetic modification were unsuccessful. As a result, the children would likely feel that they didn't measure up. It would be a mistake, according to Sandel, to develop technologies that encourage and exacerbate the tendency toward hyper-parenting.

Most of us would agree that hyper-parenting is an unfortunate trend. Parents should not want to control everything about their children. Part of being a good parent is to recognize that one's children are not just extensions of oneself and to accept them for who they are. It is tragic when parental love is conditioned on a child's being a certain kind of person or when children feel that the price of being true to themselves is the loss of parental acceptance.

At the same time, good parents *do* try to shape their children in certain ways. Someone who said, "I never try to influence my children. I just love them for who they are," would be a terrible parent. People and cultures can vary on what this means, but someone who was indifferent to whether a child was considerate or rude, kind or cruel, or selfish or generous would be a defective parent.

Someone might respond that of course parents should try to shape their children's characters in accordance with their values so long as those values are permissible ones. Although parents are given a great deal of leeway in how they raise their children, there are limits. Parents who subject their children to diets that may cause illness or death are likely to have their children taken away from them, as are parents who subject their children to physical or emotional abuse. But so long as parental values remain within acceptable limits, which are likely to vary from culture to culture and from age to age, parents may attempt to shape their children's characters. Indeed, that is what parents are supposed to do.

Presumably, then, the hyper-parenting objection to HHGE is not to the attempt to *shape* our children, so long as such shaping doesn't cross over into exerting total control over every aspect of the child's life. The objection is rather to using a particular method, HHGE, to achieve that goal. But why should the method matter?

Perhaps the objection stems from the recognition that we just don't know what the long-term effects of germline gene editing will be, and harmful errors could be inherited by future generations. That's a legitimate safety concern, as we have maintained throughout.

Opposition to genetic means of shaping could stem from a very different source: namely, a belief that genes are deterministic in a way that no other influences are, such as environmental influences. Someone might think that it's fine to try to inculcate in children desirable traits, such as responsibility or intellectual curiosity, if this is done through education or parental influence, but it would be wrong to use HHGE for the exact same purpose even if HHGE were shown to be effective and safe; HHGE would determine the child's make-up in a way that environmental forces, including education, do not. Thus, HHGE would restrict the child's choices in a way that education does not. Let's assess this.

Are genes more deterministic than environmental influences?

The claim that genes are deterministic, whereas environmental measures are not, is simply false. For one thing, environmental influences can make permanent changes in a young child's body and mind. Children who are severely malnourished may become permanently cognitively disabled. The same is true of some children born with fetal alcohol syndrome. Child abuse and trauma may cause permanent psychological harm. Nor does genetic inheritance completely determine a person's traits. A good environment can modify harmful genetic influences, and a bad environment can increase the likelihood that harmful genes are expressed. The effect of genes cannot be separated from environmental factors like education, health-care, nutrition, and many others.

Moreover, consider the effect that literacy or the development of agriculture, both environmental influences, have had on humanity. These influences have permanently changed human nature. Moreover, education, which is clearly environmental, actually changes the connections in the brain, leading the Swiss physician and bioethicist Alex Mauron to refer to education as "neuronal phenotype manipulation."

If the objection to HHGE is based on the false claim that genetic changes are immutable in a way that environmental influences are not, it must be rejected. However, it could be argued that Sandel's objection is not based on this sort of mistake. Rather, he thinks that developing technologies that allow parents to influence traits prenatally would exacerbate the trend toward hyper-parenting. Would it? Surely, this would depend on the motives for using HHGE.

For example, suppose neuroscientists discovered that a particular genetic mutation is associated with a lack of self-confidence. A lack of self-confidence is not a disease, but it can be crippling in extreme cases. Imagine a couple who both have this genetic mutation. Their resulting lack of self-confidence has made their lives much less good than the life they hope their child will have. They plan to consult psychiatrists and educators to provide the best environment for their child to be able to cope with the condition, but if HHGE were proved to be safe and effective, they would also be interested in using it to knock out the deleterious gene. Their motive for using genetic modification wouldn't be to exert control over the child but to improve the child's well-being. It's hard to see why that is objectionable.

If the trend to hyper-parenting is what's worrying, that's what we should focus on, rather than fetishizing the technology. Moreover, we should not reject wholesale a technology that could have good uses because it might have bad uses, unless it would be impossible to prevent bad uses and the bad-ness of those uses clearly outweighed the good that could be achieved. Of course, as with any research, there can be impor-tant questions about its value and whether resources might be better spent elsewhere. If we do decide that the potential benefits of human genome editing are worth the risks, we must seek to minimize the risks. Nevertheless, concerns about hyper-parenting do not justify a preemptive, permanent ban on HHGE for non-disease traits, much less such a ban on re-search into preventing genetic disease simply because it might lead to enhancement.

Is gene therapy worth the cost?

One source of opposition to the development of gene therapy, either somatic or germline, is that it is not a good use of lim-ited funds. Françoise Baylis, for example, argues that while research into gene therapy will be funded by taxpayers—ordinary people—it will be used almost exclusively by rich people because it is so expensive. She acknowledges the possi-bility that initially high costs will go down, as happened in the case of the cost of sequencing the human genome. "But if the cost of gene transfer therapies for inherited genetic disorders is any indication, genome editing therapies will likely be very expensive and not widely accessible."[13]

Precisely the same objection, however, was made about IVF, and yet today IVF is used by ordinary people, in part because the cost has gone down and in part because it is covered in many places by insurance. The same could happen with gene therapies.

The problem of how fairly to determine the cost of a treat-ment, and therefore accessibility, is a fundamental problem in healthcare (see Chapters 11 and 12). Gene therapies pose a special problem. The pricing model typically used by phar-maceutical companies is based on the expectation that patients will need repeated doses. By contrast, gene therapy is likely to require only a single intervention. Pharmaceutical companies have argued that putting a high price tag on gene therapy is the only way that they can recoup the huge costs for research and development, as well as clinical trials. Thus, it may seem that gene therapy will inevitably be priced out of the reach of ordinary people. However, to decide to forego a pharmaceutical intervention because it is too expensive fails to take account of the savings that could be achieved within a healthcare system by curing or mitigating chronic conditions that would otherwise require more costly lifelong medical interventions.[14]

The important thing to remember is that pricing is not a fixed feature beyond human control. Instead of simply rejecting a potentially beneficial therapy because it would cost too much, we should figure out ways to make it affordable. This will require collaboration between numerous stakeholders: insurers, hospitals, drug companies, government, and taxpayers. The aim should be to ensure that an accessible and affordable healthcare system is developed for all medical treatments deemed to be necessary and justifiable. Our claim is not that this is easy, but rather that this is where the focus should be.

Is genetic enhancement incompatible with social justice?

The social justice objection is not merely that such interventions are likely to be expensive, at least at first, and open only to wealthy people. The claim is also that allowing genetic interventions for enhancement would perpetuate the advantages the wealthy already enjoy and hand down to their children, thus exacerbating inequality.

Unlike the arguments from authenticity, autonomy, or even hyper-parenting, concerns about inequality must be taken very seriously. Inequality has skyrocketed in America, even before the coronavirus pandemic, which has made things much worse. Over the past three decades, the wealth of the top ten percent of US households has risen by almost ten percentage points, while wealth controlled by the bottom fifty percent has been cut nearly in half. White Americans hold nearly eighty-five percent of the nation's wealth, compared with just over four percent for Black households. The COVID-19 pandemic has both revealed and increased this inequality. Although people can differ about how much inequality is tolerable, it seems clear that societies in which some people are fabulously wealthy and others can barely survive are neither just nor sustainable. We should be working to reduce inequality, not increase it.

However, any advantages that might be provided by genome editing will be insignificant compared to the advantages already enjoyed by the wealthy, such as better housing, better neighborhoods, better schools, and better healthcare. This is partly because of the difficulties outlined above in using gene editing to get desirable traits. Why spend thousands of dollars in the hope of passing on better genes when you can get the same social advantages by sending your children to elite schools and sending them abroad? Inequality is caused by fundamental structural problems in society. It is these problems that demand our attention. Bans on HHGE may well be warranted, but not because HHGE is likely to make a significant difference in inequality.

A further point has been made by Allen Buchanan.[15] It is not a foregone conclusion how a technology will be used or made available. That is a social decision. If it turns out that HHGE is effective in increasing intelligence, for example, it could be made available to families that wanted it. The technology would not have to be used to increase inequality; it could be used to decrease it. We don't have to let access be decided by the market. We could insist that a technology that would even the playing field be available to the least advantaged. If we fail to do this, the problem is not the technology, but the ways we've chosen to use it.

Should we alter human evolution?

Some have argued that what is wrong with HHGE is that, for the first time, human beings have the chance deliberately to change the human genome. "Eventually, we could guide human evolution. Does this mean that we should?"[16]

One reason for thinking that we should not is that any deliberate attempt to change the human genome is "playing God." This objection is not unique to genetic interventions, but can be used against human overreaching in several areas, for example, assisted reproduction. The problem with the "playing God" objection is that it is too broad. It would make all attempts to prevent or cure disease immoral, a conclusion that few people could accept. Intervention into natural processes is not, by itself, objectionable. What is objectionable is taking undue risks or making changes we will later come to regret, but this sort of objection comes under safety considerations. It's being reckless or unwise that is objectionable, not "playing God."

Another rationale for opposing HHGE stems from regarding the human genome as having an inherent normative value. This is suggested by Article 1 of United Nations Educational, Scientific and Cultural Organization (UNESCO)'s Universal Declaration on the Human Genome and Human Rights, which claims that the "human genome underlies the fundamental unity of all members of the human family, as well as the recognition of their inherent dignity and diversity." The human genome is, on this view, the "heritage of humanity," although this is qualified as being "in a symbolic sense."[17] But what exactly does all of this mean? The UNESCO Declaration is vague, but here is a plausible interpretation:

> Philosophically speaking, if the "naturally" evolved human genome represents the basis, or at least an important part of human nature, then any systematic manipulation of the human germline must be regarded as a severe intervention into human nature that fundamentally differs from most somatic gene therapies and other already implemented interventions, such as IVF or PGD. It could therefore be inferred that we have a duty to preserve the integrity of the human germline, even if

germline manipulation is, eventually, considered sufficiently safe.[18]

Steven Pinker categorically rejects such views.

Germline editing should be treated like any other medical procedure, weighing benefits against harms. It should not be banned out of a nebulous terror about tampering with a sacrosanct entity called "the human germline"—a concept which is biological nonsense.[19]

Why does Pinker say that the concept "the human germline" is "biological nonsense"? First, as Henry Greely points out, there *is* no one human germline genome. "Every living person has a 'germline genome,' and each one is different."[20] Second, the worry about tampering with the human genome—that is, all the germline genomes of all living humans—is misplaced because the human genome is being continually shaped and changed by evolutionary forces, including countless human activities. Each of us changes the human genome when we do something as prosaic as choose one mate rather than another, affecting who gets born. It is simply impossible to avoid tampering with the human genome. "[E]very major medical advance—antibiotics, vaccines, sterile surgical and obstetric techniques—influences who lives to reproduce and who doesn't, and so, indirectly alters the genome. Certainly wars, pandemics, and education do so too."[21]

Still, even if we unavoidably change the human genome through human activities, ought we change the human genome *directly and deliberately* and, ultimately, guide human evolution?

This question raises two issues. First, do we, as a species, have the wisdom to direct human evolution? As a caution against scientific hubris, this is something that should, of course, be considered. However, it is not an in-principle argument against directing human evolution but rather a plea for caution in light of unforeseen dangers.

Second, is there a right to inherit a genome that has not been deliberately modified? All existing human beings have inherited a genome that has "naturally" evolved; that is, a genome that has not been deliberately modified. Does this naturally evolved genome have normative significance? The argument for this claim might go something like this. The genome of our species, which is the result of many millions of years of evolution, is an intimate part of who we are and the core of our biology. All human beings have a special moral status, which endows them with human rights and human dignity, simply in virtue of being human. Therefore, what makes us human—that is, the human genome—also has special moral significance.

But is it *our DNA* that has moral significance? As we saw in Chapter 7, some have argued that moral status should not be based on something as arbitrary as species membership but rather on having the characteristics of persons. However, even if the human genome has moral significance because it is the basis of our all being members of the human family of man, that in itself says absolutely nothing about the morality of modifying the human genome. It might if genetic editing created an entirely new human genome, but that is not what techniques like CRISPR do. Nadia Primc writes,

> The deletion of a gene associated with severe genetic diseases, as well as its replacement with a "healthy" variant, does not disrupt the genetic connection with the rest of the human family, as the vast majority of the genome will remain intact. Perhaps a different conclusion will be drawn for the possibility of genetic enhancement, as this could introduce very distinct genotypical and phenotypical traits. However, as long as manipulation of the human germline is restricted to the prevention of severe

genetic diseases, and if this is realized through the de-
letion or replacement of particular genes or part of the
DNA with "healthy" human variants, there will be . . . no
abrupt disruption to human lineage.[22]

Does this mean that the only ethically acceptable use of genetic modification is the prevention of disease? Or might it be
permissible—assuming, once again, safety and efficacy—that
HHGE could be used not to prevent disease but to improve
the human species?

This was suggested nearly forty years ago by Jonathan
Glover in the first philosophical treatment of human gene
editing.[23] Glover suggests that it would require almost
willful blindness to think that the human species could not
be improved. In particular, he notes our species' limited capacity for imaginative sympathy and altruism, which explains,
at least in part, our persistent failure to eliminate war. Other
unpleasant, but all-too-human, characteristics include greed
and aggression. Might we one day be able to reduce the prevalence of these characteristics in our species? And if we could,
should we?

What if the changes were not limited to improving existing
capacities for sympathy and altruism, but were more radical,
like providing humans with gills for living under water? What
if the enhanced humans were so much more intelligent than
existing humans as to constitute a new race of superhumans?
What if the superhumans became our overlords and made us
their slaves?

Because these possibilities are completely speculative, and
indeed in the realm of science fiction, it is extremely difficult, if
not impossible, to know how seriously to take them. Moreover,
given the technical difficulties of engineering desirable non-
disease traits, it seems unlikely that HHGE ever would be
able to create humans with fewer flaws. Why, then, should research dollars be devoted to it? At least for now, it is eminently

sensible to restrict HHGE research to attempts to prevent or cure serious genetic disease.

Concluding thoughts

The most serious arguments against gene editing are based on safety and efficacy. These are issues that must be resolved before gene editing can move from the laboratory to the clinic. This is true of both somatic cell and germline gene editing, although the risks in germline modification are clearly greater.

Arguments based on misconceptions about how genes work in the production of traits and what gene editing technology can accomplish should be rejected. It will never be possible to hand a clinician a list of traits and design a child according to that list.

Nevertheless, as we learn more about the contribution of genes to non-disease traits, it may one day be possible to give children a "genetic edge" to acquire or avoid desirable traits. Moreover, regardless of how likely HHGE will be in successfully providing offspring with a genetic edge, their parents might believe that it works, and companies might exploit this for profit. Such social concerns, and ways of avoiding harmful outcomes, should certainly be considered, along with safety and efficacy, as we decide what technologies to invest in and which ones should be permitted.

An important question in assessing technology is, as always, to ask if the potential benefits are worth the risks. Given the risks of HHGE, it is hard even to justify it for the prevention of serious genetic disease, much less for purposes of enhancement. Surely the critics are right that there are better uses for research dollars. But these are matters of safety, risk assessment, and cost-benefit analysis and not in-principle objections to hereditable human genome editing.

NOTES

Chapter 1

1. Julia Annas, "Virtue Ethics," in *The Oxford Handbook of Ethical Theory*, ed. David Copp (New York, NY: Oxford University Press, 2006), 515–536. Mark Timmons, "Natural Law" and "Virtue Ethics," in his *Moral Theory: An Introduction* (Lanham, MD: Roman and Littlefield Publishers, 2013), 71–109 and 269–303.
2. Bonnie Steinbock, "Molly and Adam Nash: Using Preimplantation Genetic Diagnosis to Save a Sibling," in *Ethical Issues in Modern Medicine: Contemporary Readings in Bioethics, 8th ed.*, ed. Bonnie Steinbock, Alex John London, and John D. Arras (New York, NY: McGraw Hill, 2012), 628–629.
3. Timmons, 2013 (note 1), 71–110. See also Mark Murphy, "The Natural Law Tradition in Ethics," *The Stanford Encyclopedia of Philosophy* (Summer 2019 edition), ed. Edward N. Zalta, https://plato.stanford.edu/archives/sum2019/entries/natural-law-ethics/.
4. Thomas J. Boyle, "Toward Understanding the Principle of Double Effect," *Ethics* 90 (1980): 527–538. Timmons, 2013 (note 1), 82–89.
5. Tom L. Beauchamp and James F. Childress, *Principles of Biomedical ethics*, 1st and 7th editions (New York, NY: Oxford University Press, 1979 and 2013). Tom L. Beauchamp, "Principlism in Bioethics," in *Bioethical Decision Making and Argumentation*, ed. Pedro Serna Bermudez and Jose Antonio Seoane, International Library of Ethics, Law, and the New Medicine, vol. 70 (New York, NY: Springer Publishing, 2016), 1–16, https://doi.org/10.1007/978-3-319-43419-3_1.

6. John C. Arras, "Principlism: The Borg of Bioethics," in *Methods in Bioethics: The Way We Reason Now*, ed. James Childress and Matthew Adams (New York, NY: Oxford University Press, 2017), 1–26.

7. For a brief description, see Steinbock, London, and Arras, 2012 (note 2), 39–41. For a comprehensive presentation and defense, see Albert Jonsen and Stephen Toulmin, *The Abuse of Casuistry* (Berkeley: University of California Press, 1988).

Chapter 2

1. Richard H. Thaler and Cass R. Sunstein, *Nudge: Improving decisions about health, wealth, and happiness* (New Haven, CT: Yale University Press, 2008).

2. The case of children is more complex than the case of adults who are severely cognitively impaired. In general, minor children do not participate in medical decisions, but have such decisions made for them by parents or guardians. However, it has been argued, and is increasingly being accepted, that parents and physicians should take into consideration the views of older children who possess unusual thoughtfulness and maturity.

3. Onora O'Neill, *Autonomy and Trust in Bioethics* (Cambridge, UK: Cambridge University Press, 2002).

4. Jay Katz, "Informed Consent—A Fairy Tale? Law's Vision," *University of Pittsburgh Law Review* 39, no. 2 (1977): 137–174.

5. Interestingly, the same arguments from equal protection and bodily autonomy that motivated the abortion rights movement were used in subsequent decades to legalize medical assistance in dying (see Chapter 6).

6. However, student protests against the draft undoubtedly played a role in lowering the voting age to 18 in 1971, as it became increasingly difficult to justify denying the vote to men under 21 when these same young men were being asked to fight and die for their country.

7. Eric. J. Cassell, *The Nature of Suffering and the Goals of Medicine* (New York, NY: Oxford University Press, 1982).

8. Ezekiel J. Emanuel and Linda L. Emanuel, "Four Models of the Physician-Patient Relationship," *Journal of the American Medical Association* 267, no. 16 (1992): 2221–26.

9. Bernice S. Elger and Jean-Claude Chevrolet, "Case Study: Beneficence Today or Autonomy (Maybe) Tomorrow?" *Hastings Center Report* 30, no. 1 (January-February, 2000): 18–19.

10. For an insightful analysis of racism and some ways in which clinicians and bioethicists could fight it, see Camisha Russell, "Meeting the Moment: Bioethics in the Time of Black Lives Matter," *The American Journal of Bioethics* 22, no. 3 (2022): 9–21.

11. Centers for Disease Control and Prevention (CDC), *Racism and Health, 2022,* https://www.cdc.gov/healthequity/racism-disp arities/index.html. Accessed Mar. 30, 2022.

12. Allies for Reaching Community Health Equity (ARCHE), "Racism can make you sick." https://healthequity.globalpoli cysolutions.org/resources/stories/racism-can-make-you-sick/, accessed Feb. 21, 2022.

13. Joanne Lewsley, "What are the effects of racism on health and mental health?" *Medical News Today,* July 28, 2020, https://www.medicalnewstoday.com/articles/effects-of-racism, accessed Feb. 20, 2022.

14. Roni Caryn Rabin, "Doctors Are More Likely to Describe Black Patients as Uncooperative, Studies Find," *New York Times,* Feb. 16, 2022, https://www.nytimes.com/2022/02/16/hea lth/black-patients-doctor-notes-diabetes.html, accessed Mar. 21, 2022.

15. Roni Caryn Rabin. 2022. "Maternal Deaths in the U.S. Climbed in 2020," *New York Times*, Feb. 24, 2022, A15, https://www.nyti mes.com/2022/02/23/health/maternal-deaths-pandemic.html, accessed Mar. 21, 2022.

16. Nicole Torres, "Research: Having a Black Doctor Led Black Men to Receive More-Effective Care," *Harvard Business Review*, August 10, 2018, https://hbr.org/2018/08/research-having-a-black-doctor-led-black-men-to-receive-more-effective-care#:~:text=African%20Americans%20make%20up%2013,7%25%20of%20U.S.%20medical%20students.&text=They%20found%20t hat%20black%20men,those%20seen%20by%20nonblack%20doct ors, accessed Mar. 21, 2022.

Chapter 3

1. Epitomized in the United States by the *Quinlan* court decision: *people do not lose their rights when they become incompetent*; those rights just have to be exercised by others. The decision also established that the right to refuse medical treatment held for withdrawing as well as initially withholding treatment. *In re Quinlan,* New Jersey Supreme Court, 70 N.J. 10, 355 A.2d 647 (NJ 1976).

2. Significant elements of the substance of this section are based on the more extensive discussion in Paul T. Menzel, "Change of Mind: An Issue in Advance Directives," in *Ethics at the End of Life: New Issues and Arguments*, ed. John K. Davis (New York, NY: Routledge, 2017), 126–137, and in Menzel, "Stopping Eating and Drinking by Advance Directive for Persons without Decision-making Capacity: Ethical Issues," *Voluntarily Stopping Eating and Drinking: A Compassionate, Widely Available Option for Hastening Death*, ed. in Timothy E. Quill, Paul T. Menzel, Thaddeus M. Pope, and Judith K. Schwarz (New York, NY: Oxford University Press, 2021), 176–203 at 178–182.

3. *Bentley v. Maplewood Seniors Care Society*, British Columbia Supreme Court 2014, BCSC 165. *Bentley v. Maplewood Seniors Care Society*, Court of Appeal for British Columbia 2015, BCCA 91, 5. Thaddeus M. Pope, "Prospective Autonomy and Ulysses Contracts for VSED," one of two sections of Pope and Bernadette J. Richards, "Decision-Making: At the End of Life and the Provision of Pretreatment Advice," *Journal of Bioethical Inquiry* 12 (2015): 389–394, at 1–2. See also Quill et al., eds. (note 2), 206–207, and Katherine Hammond, "Kept Alive—The Enduring Tragedy of Margot Bentley," *Narrative Inquiry in Bioethics* 6, no. 2 (summer 2016): 80–82.

4. Ron Berghmans, "Advance Directives and Dementia," *Annals of the New York Academy of Sciences* 913 (2000): 105–110.

5. Rebecca Dresser and John S. Robertson, "Quality of Life and Non-Treatment Decisions for Incompetent Patients." *Law, Medicine & Health Care* 17, no. 3 (1989): 234–244. For a comprehensive treatment of this challenge that also deals with Dresser's numerous other writings, see L. W. Sumner, *Assisted Death* (Oxford, UK: Oxford University Press, 2011), 102–117, and *Physician-Assisted Death: What Everyone Needs To Know* (New York, NY: Oxford University Press, 2017), 174–180.

6. The Ms. A case is adapted from Norman L. Cantor, "Testing the Limits of Prospective Autonomy: Five Scenarios," in Cantor, *Advance Directives and the Pursuit of Death with Dignity* (Bloomington, IN: Indiana University Press, 1993).

   Ms. Snyder is modified from the case contributed by Dena S. Davis to the chapter by her and Paul T. Menzel, "Stopping Eating and Drinking by Advance Directive: Ethical Issues," in Quill et al., 2021 (note 2), 187–188.

Another case prominent in the literature, not dealt with here, is "Margo," treated extensively by Ronald Dworkin in *Life's Dominion: An Argument About Abortion, Euthanasia and Individual Freedom* (New York: Alfred A. Knopf, 1993), 220–232, and by Agnieszka Jaworska, "Respecting the Margins of Agency: Alzheimer's Patients and the Capacity to Value," *Philosophy and Public Affairs* 28, no. 2 (1999): 105–138.

7. Substantial portions of this and the next section are adapted from Paul T. Menzel and Bonnie Steinbock, "Advance Directives, Dementia, and Physician-Assisted Death," *Journal of Law, Medicine & Ethics* 41, no. 2 (2013): 484–500, at 488–490.

8. David DeGrazia, *Human Identity and Bioethics* (New York: Cambridge University Press, 2005), 159–202.

9. Nancy Rhoden, "The Limits of Legal Objectivity," *North Carolina Law Review* 68 (1990): 845–865, at 860.

10. Among others who have made this point is Norman L. Cantor, "On Avoiding Deep Dementia." *Hastings Center Report* 48, no. 4 (July-August, 2018): 15–24, DOI.org/10.1002/hast.865. A similar point focused on the role of lives, not just being alive, is used to explain why a person can be harmed posthumously: Richard H. Dees, "Primum Non Nocere Mortuis: Bioethics and the Lives of the Dead," *The Journal of Medicine and Philosophy: A Forum for Bioethics and Philosophy of Medicine* 44, no. 6 (2019): 732–755, DOI. org/10.1093/jmp/jhz024.

11. We do not present the noted defense of ADs by philosopher Ronald Dworkin, using a distinction between "experiential" and "critical" interests. See Dworkin 1993 (note 6).

12. Menzel and Steinbock, 2013 (note 7), 495–497, and Paul T. Menzel and M. Colette Chandler-Cramer, "Advance Directives, Dementia, and Withholding Food and Water by Mouth," *Hastings Center Report* 44, no. 3 (May-June, 2014): 23–37, at 28–29, https:// onlinelibrary.wiley.com/doi/abs/10.1002/hast.313.

13. Jessica N. Zitter, *Extreme Measures: Finding a Better Path to the End of Life* (New York, NY: Avery, 2017), Chapter 2.

14. These and related matters were perceptively discussed by Tracey Bush in a presentation for The Completed Life Initiative: Tracey A. Bush and Lonny Shavelson, "Is the Right to Die Being Held Hostage to a Right to Healthcare?" Presentation for The Completed Life Initiative, November 11, 2021, video at https://vimeo.com/647084155. See also Chapter 2.

Chapter 4

1. Bonnie Steinbock, Alex John London, and John D. Arras, eds., *Ethical Issues in Modern Medicine: Contemporary Readings in Bioethics, 8th ed.* (New York, NY: McGraw Hill, 2012), 702–705.

2. Nuremberg Military Tribunals, "Permissible Medical Experiments," *Trials of War Criminals before the Nuremberg Military Tribunals under Control Council Law No. 10: Nuremberg, October 1946–April 1949*, volume 2 (Washington, DC: U.S. Government Printing Office, 1949), 181–182. The numbering and grouping of the principles here have been altered from the tribunal's list, and some have been omitted. All italics are added emphasis.

3. John D. Arras, "The Jewish Chronic Disease Hospital Case," in *Oxford Textbook of Clinical Research Ethics*, ed. Ezekiel J. Emanuel, Christine Grady, Robert A. Crouch, Reidar K. Lie, Franklin G. Miller, and David Wendler (New York, NY: Oxford University Press, 2008), 73–79. Jay Katz, Alexander Morgan Capron, and Eleanor Swift Glass, eds., *Experimentation with Human Beings* (New York, NY: Russell Sage Foundation, 2008), "The Jewish Chronic Disease Hospital Case," 9–65.

4. In practice the *material information standard* will have to address what information is material in a specific circumstance. The dominant answer has been the *reasonable person* standard— the information that is material to a reasonable person, not necessarily to a particular patient, for whom more or less information could be material. See Rebecca Dresser, "The Reasonable Person Standard for Research Disclosure: A Reasonable Addition to the Common Rule," *Law, Medicine & Ethics* 47, no. 2 (2019): 194–202.

5. David J. Rothman and Sheila Rothman, *The Willowbrook Wars* (New York, NY: Harper and Row, 1984), 260–267.

6. Rothman and Rothman, 1984, ibid., 267 (emphasis added).

7. The factual information in this subsection is largely from James H. Jones, "The Tuskegee Syphilis Experiment," in Emanuel et al., eds., 2008 (note 3), 86–96.

8. Steven Johnson, *Extra Life: A Short History of Living Longer* (New York, NY: Riverhead Books-Penguin, 2021), 138–141.

9. Benjamin Freedman, "Equipoise and the Ethics of Clinical Research," *New England Journal of Medicine* 317 (1987): 141–145.

10. UK Collaborative ECMO Trial Group, "UK Collaborative Randomised Trial of Neonatal Extracorporeal Membrane Oxygenation," *The Lancet* 348: 9020 (July 13, 1996): 75–82.

11. Freedman, 1987, ibid., and Benjamin Freedman, "A Response to a Purported Ethical Difficulty with Randomized Clinical Trials Involving Cancer Patients," *Journal of Clinical Ethics* 3, no. 3 (fall 1992)): 231–234.

12. World Medical Association, "Declaration of Helsinki 2000," available at https://www.wma.net/what-we-do/medical-eth ics/declaration-of-helsinki/doh-oct2000/.

13. The FDA's defense of its practice of allowing PCTs is based largely on what scientists call "assay sensitivity," the ability of a study to distinguish between active and inactive treatment effects. See Charles Weijer, "The Ethics of Placebo-Controlled Trials," *Journal of Bone and Mineral Research* 18, no. 6 (2003): 1150–1153. Even if assay sensitivity is a legitimate reason for having a placebo-control arm for next-in-class drug candidates, however, it is no reason for not *also* requiring an active-control arm. See also Chapter 12.

14. Robert A. Crouch and John D. Arras, "AZT Trials and Tribulations," *Hastings Center Report* 28, no. 6 1998): 26–34.

15. David Wendler, "Risk Standards for Pediatric Research: Rethinking the *Grimes* Ruling," *Kennedy Institute of Ethics Journal* 14, no. 2 (2004): 187–198.

16. Lawrence K. Altman, *Who Goes First? The Story of Self-Experimentation in Medicine* (New York, NY: Random House, 1987). Niyaz Ahmed, "23 Years of the Discovery of *Helicobacter pylori*: Is the Debate Over?" *Annals of Clinical Microbiology and Antimicrobials* 4, no. 17 (2005): 1–3.

17. Garth Rapeport, Emma Smith, Anthony Gilbert, Andrew Catchpole, Helen McShane, and Christopher Chiu, "SARS-CoV-2 Human Challenge Studies—Establishing the Model during an Evolving Pandemic," *New England Journal of Medicine* 385 (September 9, 2021): 961–964.

18. Elizabeth Pratt, "We Don't Have Enough Women in Clinical Trials—Why That's a Problem," *Healthline*, October 25, 2020, https://www.healthline.com/health-news/we-dont-have-eno ugh-women-in-clinical-trials-why-thats-a-problem. Numerous similar gender-related issues were raised two decades earlier by the Institute of Medicine (US) Committee on the Ethical and

Legal Issues Relating to the Inclusion of Women in Clinical Studies, *Women and Health Research: Ethical and Legal Issues of Including Women in Clinical Studies: Volume 2: Workshop and Commissioned Papers*, ed. Anna C. Mastroianni, Ruth Faden, and Daniel Federman (Washington, DC: National Academies Press, 1999).

19. Rachel Fabi and Daniel S. Goldberg, "Bioethics, (Funding) Priorities, and the Perpetuation of Injustice," *American Journal of Bioethics* 22, no. 1 (January 2022): 6–13, with accompanying commentaries 14–35.

20. Bobby Saunkeah, Julie A. Beans, Michael T. Peercy, Vanesssa Y. Hiratsuka, and Paul Spicer, "Extending Research Protections to Tribal Communities," *American Journal of Bioethics* 21, no. 10 (October, 2021): 5–12, at 9, with accompanying commentaries 13–37.

Chapter 5

1. Not all countries that have adopted brain death use the whole-brain standard. In the United Kingdom, for example, death occurs at the irreversible cessation of brainstem function. The brainstem controls automatic functions, such as breathing and circulation, but it also includes the reticular activating system, the on/off switch that makes consciousness possible. Thus, irreversible cessation of function in the brainstem entails the irreversible loss of both unassisted respiration and circulation and the capacity for consciousness.

2. Ariane Lewis, Richard J. Bonnie, and Thaddeus Pope, "It's Time to Revise the Uniform Determination of Death Act," *Annals of Internal Medicine* 172, no. 2 (2020): 143–144, at 143.

3. K. C. Vijayan, "Lawyer Declared Brain Dead Wakes Up After Calls to Pull Plug on Her," *The Strait Times*, March 24, 2013.

4. James L. Bernat, "The Whole-Brain Concept of Death Remains Optimum Public Policy," *Journal of Law, Medicine & Ethics* 34, no. 1 (2006): 35–43.

5. Alan Shewmon, "'Brainstem Death,' 'Brain Death' and Death: A Critical Re-evaluation of the Purported Equivalence," *Law and Medicine* 14, no. 2 (1998): 125–45.

6. Ibid., 136. T.K. had a heart attack and died in January 2004, at age 24.

7. Rachel Aviv, "What Does It Mean to Die?" *The New Yorker*, February 5, 2018.

8. Ibid.

9. Ibid.

10. Ibid.

11. Liz Szabo, "Ethicists Criticize Treatment of Teen, Texas Patient," *USA Today*, January 9, 2014. https://www.usatoday.com/story/news/nation/2014/01/09/ethicists-criticize-treatment-brain-dead-patients/4394173/.

12. Stuart J. Youngner, "Defining Death: A Superficial and Fragile Consensus," *Archives Neurology* 49, no. 5 (1992): 570–2, at 571.

13. Shewmon, 1998 (note 5).

14. Robert D. Truog and Franklin G. Miller, "Changing the Conversation About Brain Death," *American Journal of Bioethics* 14, no. 8 (2014): 9.

15. Jeff McMahan, "An Alternative to Brain Death," *Journal of Law, Medicine, and Ethics* 34, no. 1 (2006): 44–48, at 47.

16. Ibid., at 48.

17. David DeGrazia, *Human Identity and Bioethics* (New York, NY: Cambridge University Press, 2005), 149.

18. Amir Halevy and Baruch Brody, "Brain Death: Reconciling Definitions, Criteria, and Tests," *Annals of Internal Medicine* 119 (1993): 519–25, at 523.

19. Ibid., 524.

20. Robert Veatch, "Controversies in Defining Death: A Case for Choice," *Theoretical Medicine and Bioethics* 40, no. 5 (2019): 381–401.

Chapter 6

1. Philippa Foot, "Euthanasia," *Philosophy & Public Affairs* 6, no. 2 (1977): 85–112, at 85.

2. Although contemporary competence is required for physician-assisted dying in most jurisdictions, which would rule out individuals in advanced dementia, in some countries (notably Belgium and the Netherlands) a carefully constructed advance directive can be considered evidence of voluntariness.

3. Jefferson Chase, "Remembering the 'Forgotten Victims' of Nazi 'Euthanasia' Murders." *Deutsche Welle* 2017, https://www.dw.com/en/remembering-the-forgotten-victims-of-nazi-euthanasia-murders/a-37286088, accessed Jan. 8, 2022.

4. *The Economist*, 2015, "24 & Ready to Die," https://www.youtube.com/watch?v=SWWkUzkfJ4M, accessed Jan. 8, 2022.

5. Jessica N. Zitter, *Extreme Measures: Finding a Better Path to the End of Life* (New York, NY: Penguin Random House, 2017).

6. *Compassion in Dying v. Washington*, 1994, 850 F. Supp. 1454.

7. *Washington v. Glucksberg*, 1997, 521 U.S. 702.

8. Samia Hurst and Alex Mauron, "Assisted Suicide and Euthanasia in Switzerland: Allowing a Role for Non-physicians," *BMJ* 326: 7383 (2003): 271–273.

9. Ronald Dworkin, *Life's Dominion* (New York, NY: Vintage/ Penguin Random House, 1994), p. 117.

10. Yale Kamisar, "Some Non-Religious Views against Proposed 'Mercy-Killing' Legislation, Part I," *Human Life Review* 2, no. 2 (1976): 71–114, at 73, originally published under the same title in *Minnesota Law Review* 42, no. 6 (1958): 969–1042.

11. Oregon Health Authority, Public Health Division, "Annual Reports," 2021, https://www.oregon.gov/oha/PH/PROVI DERPARTNERRESOURCES/EVALUATIONRESEARCH/ DEATHWITHDIGNITYACT/Documents/year23.pdf, accessed Jan. 8, 2022.

12. Christopher de Bellaigue, "Death on Demand: Has Euthanasia Gone Too Far?" 2019, https://www.theguardian.com/news/ 2019/jan/18/death-on-demand-has-euthanasia-gone-too-far-netherlands-assisted-dying, accessed Jan. 8, 2022.

13. Government of Canada, "Medical Assistance in Dying," 2021, https://www.canada.ca/en/health-canada/services/medical-assistance-dying.html, accessed Mar. 22, 2022.

14. Amyotrophic Lateral Sclerosis Society of Canada, "10 Facts About Pain and ALS," 2017, https://als.ca/wp-content/uplo ads/2017/02/10-Facts-About-Pain-English.pdf, accessed Mar. 25, 2022.

15. Kamisar, 1976 (note 10), at 73.

16. Lewis Mitchel Cohen, *No Good Deed: A Story of Death, Murder Accusations, and the Debate Over How We Die* (New York: Harper Collins, 2010).

17. Paul T. Menzel and Bonnie Steinbock, "Advance Directives, Dementia, and Physician-Assisted Death," *Journal of Law, Medicine & Ethics* 41, no. 2 (summer 2013): 484–500.

18. Bonnie Steinbock, "Physician-Assisted Death and Severe, Treatment-Resistant Depression," *Hastings Center Report* 47, no. 5 (2017): 30–42.

19. Timothy E. Quill, Paul T. Menzel, Thaddeus M. Pope, and Judith K. Schwarz, eds., *Voluntarily Stopping Eating and Drinking: A Widely Available, Compassionate Option for Hastening Death* (New York, NY: Oxford University Press, 2021). Even in The Netherlands where euthanasia is legal, VSED is used nearly as often as PAD—2.1% of deaths compared to 2.8%.

Chapter 7

1. Catholic Church, "Declaration on Procured Abortion," *Sacred Congregation for the Doctrine of the Faith* (The Vatican, 1974), https://www.vatican.va/roman_curia/congregations/cfaith/ documents/rc_con_cfaith_doc_19741118_declaration-abortion_ en.html, accessed Feb. 27, 2022.

2. Ronald M. Green, *The Human Embryo Research Debates: Bioethics in the Vortex of Controversy* (New York, NY: Oxford University Press, 2001).

3. Mary Anne Warren, "On the Moral and Legal Status of Abortion," *The Monist* 57, no. 1 (1973): 43–61. A view similar to Warren's is Michael Tooley, *Abortion and Infanticide* (Oxford, UK: Clarendon Press, 1983).

4. Michael Tooley, ibid.

5. Peter Singer and Helga Kuhse, *Should the Baby Live? The Problem of Handicapped Infants* (Oxford, UK: Oxford University Press, 1985).

6. Don Marquis, "Why Abortion Is Immoral," *Journal of Philosophy* 86, no. 4 (1989): 183–202.

7. Jeff McMahan, *The Ethics of Killing: Problems at the Margins of Life* (Oxford, UK: Oxford University Press (2002).

8. David DeGrazia, *Human Identity and Bioethics* (New York, NY: Cambridge University Press, 2005).

9. Bonnie Steinbock, *Life Before Birth: The Moral and Legal Status of Embryos and Fetuses*, 2nd ed. (New York, NY: Oxford University Press, 2011), especially Chapter 1, "The Interest View," and Chapter 2, "Abortion."

10. George J. Annas, "Pregnant Women as Fetal Containers," *Hastings Center Report* 16, no. 6 (1986): 3–4.

11. Judith J. Thomson, "A Defense of Abortion," *Philosophy & Public Affairs* 1, no. 1 (1971): 47–66.

12. See Donald Regan, "Rewriting Roe v. Wade," *Michigan Law Review* 77 (1979): 1569–1646.

Chapter 8

1. See, for example, Ben Colburn, "Disability-based Arguments Against Assisted Dying Laws," *Bioethics* 1–7, 2022. https://doi.org/10.1111/bioe.13036, first published April 7, 2022, accessed May 4, 2022.

2. See, for example, G. Thomas Couser, "A Disability Perspective on Advance Directives," *Bioethics Today*, June 7, 2022, https://bioethicstoday.org/blog/a-disability-perspective-on-advance-directives%EF%BF%BC/.

3. See, for example, Richard J. Arneson, "Disability, Discrimination and Priority," in *Americans with Disabilities: Exploring Implications of the Law for Individuals and Institutions*, eds. Leslie Pickering Francis and Anita Silvers (New York, NY: Routledge, 2000), 18–33.

4. Centers for Disease Control and Prevention (CDC), "Learn More about Birth Defects," 2020, https://www.cdc.gov/ncbddd/birthdefects/, accessed Mar. 21, 2022.

5. Clare Blakeley, Debbie M. Smith, Edward D. Johnstone, and Anja Wittkowski, "Parental decision-making following a prenatal diagnosis that is lethal, life-limiting, or has long term implications for the future child and family: a meta-synthesis of qualitative literature," *BMC Medical Ethics* 20, no. 56 (2019), https://doi.org/10.1186/s12910-019-0393-7, accessed Mar. 25, 2022.

6. Adrienne Asch, "Prenatal Diagnosis and Selective Abortion: A Challenge to Practice and Policy," *American Journal of Public Health* 89, no. 11 (1999): 1649–1657, at 1653.

7. Shane Frederick and George Loewenstein, "Hedonic Adaptation," in *Well-being: The Foundations of Hedonic Psychology*, ed. Ed Diener and Norbert Schwarz (New York, NY: Russell Sage Foundation, 1999), 302–309.

8. Asch, 1999 (note 6).

9. John D. Lantos, "Trisomy 13 and 18—Treatment Decisions in a Stable Gray Zone," *JAMA* 316, no. 4 (2016): 396–398, at 397.

10. Whether it is possible for anyone to be better off unborn is a knotty philosophical question. For a discussion of that issue, see Bonnie Steinbock and Ron McClamrock, "When Is Birth Unfair to the Child?" *Hastings Center Report* 24, no. 6 (1994): 15–21.

11. Chris Kaposy, "The Ethical Case for Having a Baby With Down Syndrome," 2018, https://www.nytimes.com/2018/04/16/opin

ion/down-syndrome-abortion.html?searchResultPosition=1, accessed Mar. 21, 2022.

12. Adrienne Asch and David T. Wassermann, "Where Is the Sin in Synecdoche? Prenatal Testing and the Parent-Child Relationship," in *Quality of Life and Human Difference: Genetic Testing, Health Care, and Disability*, ed. David T. Wassermann, Robert S. Wachbroit, and Jerome E. Bickenbach (New York, NY: Cambridge University Press, 2005), Chapter 7, at 195.

13. The importance of appropriate prenatal counselling, along with the right of women to make their own choices about their pregnancies, without being judged, is emphasized in Adeline Perot and Ruth Horn, "Preserving Women's Reproductive Autonomy while Promoting the Rights of People with Disabilities?: The Case of Heidi Crowter and Maire Lea-Wilson in the Light of NIPT debates in England, France and Germany," *Journal of Medical Ethics*, published online March 28, 2022, doi: 10.1136/medethics-2021–107912.

Chapter 9

1. Mark V. Sauer, "Reproduction at an Advanced Maternal Age and Maternal Health," *Fertility and Sterility* 103, no. 5 (2015): 1136–43, at 1136.

2. Annaleece Merrill, "Is Adoption Hard?" 2018, https://adoption.org/is-adoption-hard. Accessed Mar. 22, 2022.

3. Anne Brice, "Staffer's Search for Birth Mom Reveals Dark History of Guatemalan Adoption," 2019, https://news.berkeley.edu/2019/07/09/gemma-givens-next-generation-guatemala/. Accessed Feb. 14, 2022.

4. Susan Sherwin, *No Longer Patient: Feminist Ethics and Health Care* (Philadelphia, PA: Temple University Press, 1992).

5. R. Alta Charo, "And Baby Makes Three—Or Four or Five or Six: Redefining the Family After the Reprotech Revolution," *Wisconsin Women's Law Journal* 7, no. 1 (2000): 1–23, at 23, https://repository.law.wisc.edu/s/uwlaw/media/11933. Accessed Feb. 14, 2022.

6. Fulton et al. v. City of Philadelphia, Pennsylvania, et al. https://www.supremecourt.gov/opinions/20pdf/19-123_g3bi.pdf. Accessed May 3, 2022.

7. Daniel Callahan, "Bioethics and Fatherhood," *Utah Law Review* 3 (1992): 735–746.

8. Françoise Baylis and Alana Cattapan, "Paying Surrogates, Sperm and Egg Donors Goes Against Canadian Values," 2018, https://theconversation.com/paying-surrogates-sperm-and-egg-donors-goes-against-canadian-values-94197#:~:text=In%20Canada%2C%20it's%20illegal%20to,the%20Assisted%20Human%20Reproduction%20Act, accessed Mar. 23, 2022.

9. Debra Satz, *Why Some Things Should Not Be for Sale: The Moral Limits of Markets* (New York, NY: Oxford University Press, 2010).

10. Elizabeth M. Landes and Richard A. Posner, "The Economics of the Baby Shortage," *The Journal of Legal Studies* 7, no. 2 (1978): 323–348.

11. Shmuly Yanklowitz, "Give a Kidney, Get a Check," *The Atlantic*, October 27, 2015, https://www.theatlantic.com/business/archive/2015/10/give-a-kidney-get-a-check/412609/, accessed Mar. 23, 2022.

12. Mark V. Sauer, "Exploitation or a woman's right?" *British Medical Journal* 314, no. 7091 (May 10, 1997): 1403.

13. Debra L. Spar, *The Baby Business: How Money, Science and Politics Driver the Commerce of Conception* (Boston, MA: Harvard Business School Press, 2006).

14. Ethics Committee of the American Society for Reproductive Medicine, "Financial Compensation of Oocyte Donors: An Ethics Committee Opinion," 2016, https://www.fertstert.org/article/S0015-0282(16)62871-6/pdf, accessed Mar. 23, 2022.

15. Denise Grady, "Surrogate Mothers Report Few Regrets," *The New York Times*, October 20, 1998, https://www.nytimes.com/1998/10/20/science/surrogate-mothers-report-few-regrets.html, accessed Mar. 23, 2022.

16. ABC News, "Baby Gammy: Surrogacy Row Family Cleared of Abandoning Child with Down Syndrome in Thailand," April 13, 2016. https://www.abc.net.au/news/2016-04-14/baby-gammy-twin-must-remain-with-family-wa-court-rules/7326196, accessed Mar. 23, 2022.

17. John A. Robertson, *Children of Choice: Freedom and the New Reproductive Technologies* (Princeton, NJ: Princeton University Press, 1994).

18. American College of Obstetrics and Gynecology, "ACOG Committee Opinion No. 360: Sex Selection," *Obstetrics & Gynecology* 109, no. 2, Part 1 (February 2007): 475–478.

19. Amartya Sen, "More than 100 Million Women Are Missing," *New York Review of Books*, December 20, 1990, 61–66.

20. Frank Newport, "Slight Preference for Having Boy Children Persists in U.S.," *Gallup Social & Policy Issues*, July 5, 2018, https://news.gallup.com/poll/236513/slight-preference-having-boy-children-persists.aspx, accessed Mar. 23, 2022.

21. Ethics Committee of the American Society for Reproductive Medicine, "Use of Reproductive Technology for Sex Selection for Nonmedical Reasons: an Ethics Committee Opinion," *Fertility and Sterility*, Vol 117, no. 4 (April 2022): 720–725. https://www.asrm.org/globalassets/asrm/asrm-content/news-and-publications/ethics-committee-opinions/use_of_reproductive_technology_for_sex_selection.pdf. Accessed May 3, 2022.

22. This occurred in 1998 when Dr. Michael Obasaju, a New York embryologist, mistakenly mixed up embryos from two different families. Two embryos created by a Black couple, Deborah and Robert Rogers, were implanted in a white woman, Donna Fasano, who gave birth to twin boys, one white and one Black. The Fasanos sought to keep the brothers together, but ultimately the genetic parents won sole custody of their son. Dr. Obasaju has recently been accused of making the same mistake again: Katherine Boniello, "Couple Says Fertility Doc Mixed Up Embryos Again," *New York Post*, April 2, 2022, https://nypost.com/2022/04/02/couple-says-doc-mixed-up-embryos-again/

23. Practice Committee of the American Society for Reproductive Medicine and the Practice Committee of the Society for Assisted Reproductive Technology, "2006 Guidelines for Gamete and Embryo Donation," *Fertility and Sterility* 86, no. 5, Supplement (November 1, 2006): S38–50, DOI:10.1016/j.fertnstert.2006.06.001.

Chapter 10

1. T. R. Reid, *The Healing of America: A Global Quest for Better, Cheaper, and Fairer Health Care* (New York, NY: Penguin Books, 2009). Commonwealth Fund, "China" (healthcare in China), https://www.commonwealthfund.org/international-health-policy-center/countries/china, accessed March 28, 2022.

2. Richard Arneson, "Liberalism, Distributive Subjectivism, and Equal Opportunity for Welfare," *Philosophy and Public Affairs* 19, no. 2 (1990): 158–193. Arneson's view is sometimes referred to as "Equality Opportunity for Welfare [well-being]." The general

view with which it is affiliated is Luck Egalitarianism; see
Shlomi Segall, *Health, Luck, and Justice* (Princeton, NJ: Princeton
University Press, 2010), 9–57. The brief quotation in the next
paragraph is from Segall, p. 13.

3. Norman Daniels, "Fair Equality of Opportunity and Decent
Minimums: A Reply to Buchanan," *Philosophy and Public Affairs*
14, no. 1 (1985): 106–110, at 108. See also Norman Daniels,
Just Health Care (New York, NY: Cambridge University Press,
1985) and *Just Health: Meeting Health Needs Fairly* (New York,
NY: Cambridge University Press, 2008).

4. Heidi D. Nelson, Kari Tyne, Arcana Naik, and Christina
Bougatsos, "Screening for Breast Cancer: An Update for the U.S.
Preventive Services Task Force," *Annals of Internal Medicine* 151,
no. 10 (November 2009): 727–737.

5. The actions protected by liberty rights, of course, must never
violate another person's rights. My legitimate right to refuse
medical procedures (my right of "informed consent"), for
example, does not include any alleged right not to be vaccinated
if remaining unvaccinated risks endangering the most important
right of others, the right to life.

6. Considerable portions of the substance of this and the next
two sections are contained in Paul T. Menzel, "Justice and the
Basic Structure of Health-Care Systems," in *Medicine and Social
Justice: Essays on the Distribution of Health Care*, ed. Rosamond
Rhodes, Margaret P. Battin, and Anita Silvers (New York,
NY: Oxford University Press, 2002), 24–37.

7. Tiana Mayere Lee, "An EMTALA Primer: The Impact of Changes
in the Emergency Medicine Landscape on EMTALA Compliance
and Enforcement," *Annals of Health Law* 13 (2004): 145–178.

8. The principle is often referred to in philosophical literature as
the "Principle of Fairness" or the "Duty of Fair Play." See H.L.A.
Hart, "Are There Any Natural Rights?" *Philosophical Review*
64, no. 2 (1955): 175–191, at 185; John Morelli, "The Fairness
Principle," *Philosophy and Law Newsletter* (American Philosophical
Association), spring 1985, pp. 2–4; and Paul T. Menzel, *Strong
Medicine: The Ethical Rationing of Health Care* (New York: Oxford
University Press, 1990), 29–31.

9. For important detail on the full principle of preventing unfair
free-riding that clarifies its respect for individual preference, see
Menzel 2002 (note 6), 37–41.

10. Bradford L. Kirkman-Liff, "Health Insurance Values and Implementation in the Netherlands and the Federal Republic of Germany," *JAMA* 265, no. 19 (1991): 2496–2502.

11. Richard Wilkinson and Michael Marmot, *Social Determinants of Health*, 2nd ed. (New York, NY: Oxford University Press, 2005).

12. Steven Johnson, *Extra Life: A Short History of Living Longer* (New York, NY: Riverhead Books, 2021), Introduction.

13. Nancy S. Jecker and Zohar Lederman, "Three for Me and None for You? An Ethical Argument for Delaying COVID-19 Boosters," *Journal of Medical Ethics*, October 8, 2021 (online first), http:// dx.doi.org/10.1136/medethics-2021-107824.

14. Keith Collins and Josh Holder, "Gap in Use of Vaccines Grows Wider, Showing Effect of Supply and Demand," *New York Times*, December 15, 2021, A8.

Chapter 11

1. In the United States, organ distribution that uses a point system is run by the United Network for Organ Sharing (UNOS), contractually designated by the U.S. government: Organ Procurement and Transplantation Network (OPTN), "Ethical Principles in the Allocation of Human Organs," 2015, at https:// optn.transplant.hrsa.gov/resources/ethics/ethical-principles-in-the-allocation-of-human-organs/, and "Organ Procurement and Transplantation Network Policies and Reports," 2021, at https:// www.organdonor.gov/about-dot/laws/optn.html.

2. Peter A. Ubel and George Loewenstein, "Distributing Scarce Livers: The Moral Reasoning of the General Public," *Social Science and Medicine* 42, no. 7 (1996): 1049–1055. Julie Ratcliffe, "Public Preferences for the Allocation of Donor Liver Grafts for Transplantation," *Health Economics* 9, no. 2 (2000): 137–148.

3. In this brief treatment we do not address an important other dimension of transplantation ethics: how more cadaver organs could be procured in an ethically defensible way. Policies for procurement include Explicit Donation, in which organs will not be taken unless the person or survivors explicitly consent, and Opting Out, in which viable organs may be taken unless the person explicitly objects. These and other options are treated in detail in Robert Veatch and Lainie Friedman Ross, *Transplantation Ethics*, 2nd ed. (Washington, DC: Georgetown University Press, 2014), Part II, "Procuring Organs," pp. 131–269.

4. Norman Daniels, *Am I My Parents Keeper? An Essay on Justice Between the Young and the Old* (New York, NY: Oxford University Press,1988). Alan Williams, "Intergenerational Equity: An Exploration of the 'Fair Innings' Argument," *Health Economics* 6, no. 2 (1997): 117–132.

5. Larry R. Churchill, "On Being an Elder in a Pandemic," *Bioethics Forum*, The Hastings Center, April 13, 2020, https://www.thehastingscenter.org/on-being-an-elder-in-a-pandemic/.

6. Evan Dyer, "Public Outrage over the Unvaccinated Is driving a Crisis in Bioethics," CBC News, January 22, 2022, https://www.cbc.ca/news/politics/pandemic-covid-vaccine-triage-omicron-1.6319844. On the general practice of providers taking their patients "as they are," see Alexander W. Cappelen and Ole Frithjof Norheim, "Responsibility in Health Care: A Liberal Egalitarian Approach," *Journal of Medical Ethics* 31, no. 18 (2005): 476–480.

7. Centers for Disease Control and Prevention (CDC), "Racism and Health," 2022, https://www.cdc.gov/healthequity/racism-disparities/. Harald Schmidt, Lawrence O. Gostin, and Michelle A. Williams, "Is It Lawful and Ethical to Prioritize Racial Minorities for COVID-19 Vaccines?" *JAMA* 324, no. 20 (November 24, 2020): 2023–2024.

8. Benjamin Franklin, letter sent anonymously from "an old citizen," *The Pennsylvania Gazette*, February 4, 1735. See https://www.ushistory.org/franklin/philadelphia/fire.htm.

9. Louis Lasagna, *The Hippocratic Oath: Modern Version* (Boston, MA: Tufts University, 1964), https://doctors.practo.com/the-hippocratic-oath-the-original-and-revised-version/#The_Revised_Hippocratic_Oath.

10. Halley S. Faust and Paul T. Menzel, eds., *Prevention vs. Treatment: What's the Right Balance?* (New York, NY: Oxford University Press, 2012), 1–8. In the same volume: George Miller, Charles Roehrig, Paul Hughes-Cromwick, and Ani Turner, "What Is Currently Spent on Prevention as Compared to Treatment?" 37–55. For international data see World Health Organization (WHO), *Global Spending on Health: A World in Transition*, 2019, https://www.who.int/publications/i/item/WHO-HIS-HGF-HFWorkingPaper-19.4.

11. Quoted in Jan Abel Olsen, "Time Preferences for Health Gains: An Empirical Investigation," *Health Economics* 2 (1993): 257–265, at 263.

12. Geoffrey Rose, *The Strategy of Preventive Medicine* (Oxford, UK: Oxford University Press, 1992), 12.

13. Leana Wen and Hugh Delehanty, "Q&A: 'We Are All in This Together. We Should Take Comfort in That,'" *AARP Bulletin* [American Association of Retired Persons], June 2021, p. 38.

14. Johnson, Steven, *Extra Life: A Short History of Living Longer* (New York, NY: Riverhead Books, 2021).

15. Alan Williams, *Medical Ethics: Health Service Efficiency and Clinical Freedom*, Portfolio 2 (York, England: University of York, Center for Health Economics, 1985).

16. Milton C. Weinstein, George Torrance G, and Alastair McGuire, "QALYs: the Basics," *Value in Health*, No. 12, suppl. 1 (2009): S5–S9.

17. Alan Williams, "Economics of Coronary Artery Bypass Grafting," *British Medical Journal* 291 (August, 1985): 326–329.

18. Paul T. Menzel, "Utilities for Health States: Whom to Ask," in *Encyclopedia of Health Economics*, ed. Anthony J. Culyer (Amsterdam, The Netherlands: Elsevier Science, 2014), 417–424. On hedonic adaptation, also referred to as the "relativity of happiness," see Shane Frederick and George Loewenstein, "Hedonic Adaptation," in *Well-being: The Foundations of Hedonic Psychology*, ed. Ed Diener and Norbert Schwarz (New York, NY: Russell Sage Foundation, 1999), 302–309, and Philip Brickman, Dan Coates, and Ronnie Janoff-Bulman, "Lottery Winners and Accident Victims: Is Happiness Relative?" *Journal of Personality and Social Psychology* 36, no. 8 (1978): 917–927.

19. Paul T. Menzel, *Strong Medicine: The Ethical Rationing of Health Care* (New York, NY: Oxford University Press, 1990), p. 86.

20. Erik Nord, Norman Daniels, and Mark Kamlet, "QALYs: Some Challenges," *Value in Health* 12, suppl 1 (2009): S10–S15.

21. Paul T. Menzel, "Can Cost-Effectiveness Accommodate the Equal Value of Life?" *APA Newsletter* 13, no. 1 (2013): 23–26, www.apaonline.org/resource/resmgr/medicine_newsletter/medicinev13n1.pdf.

22. Erik Nord, "Beyond QALYs: Multi-criteria Based Estimation of Maximum Willingness to Pay for Health Technologies," *European Journal of Health Economics* 19, no. 2 (2018): 267–275.

23. National Institute for Health and Care Excellence (NICE), *Appraising Life-Extending, End-of-Life Treatments* (London, 2009), www.nice.org.uk/guidance/gid-tag387/resources/app

raising-life-extending-end-of-life-treatments-paper2. A more radical challenge to counting every year of life saved as having equal value was made two decades earlier by John Harris, "QALYfying the Value of Life," *Journal of Medical Ethics* 13, no. 3 (1987): 117–123.

Chapter 12

1. Elizabeth Seeley, Susan Chimonas, and Aaron S. Kesselheim, "Can Outcomes-Based Pharmaceutical Contracts Reduce Drug Prices in the US? A Mixed Methods Assessment," *Journal of Law, Medicine & Ethics* 46, no. 4 (2018): 952–963.

2. Carl Elliott, "The Purchased Patient Advocate" (review of Sharon Batt, *Health Advocacy, Inc.: How Pharmaceutical Funding Changed the Breast Cancer Movement*), *Hastings Center Report* 48, no. 2 (2018): 40–41.

3. Marcia Angell, *The Truth About the Drug Companies: How They Deceive Us and What to Do About It* (New York, NY: Random House, 2004), 40 and 271. Merrill Goozner, *The $800 Million Pill: The Truth Behind the Cost of New Drugs* (Berkeley, CA: University of California Press, 2004), 3. Investopedia, "What Are the Average Research and Development Costs for Pharmaceutical Companies?" (July 8, 2021), investopedia.com/ask/answers/060115/how-much-drug-companys-spending-allocated-research-and-development-average.asp.

4. Angell 2004, ibid., 16, 75. Donald W. Light and Joel Lexchin, "Foreign Free Riders and the High Price of U.S. Medicines," *British Medical Journal* 331 (2005): 958–960. On the role of R&D costs for me-too drugs in the patent protected pricing of international contexts, see Paul T. Menzel, "Are Patents an Efficient and Internationally Fair Means of Funding Research and Development for New Medicines?" in *Ethics and the Business of Biomedicine*, ed. Denis Arnold (Cambridge, UK: Cambridge University Press, 2009), 62–82.

5. Peter J. Neumann, Joshua T. Cohen, and Daniel A. Ollendorf, *The Right Price: A Value-Based Prescription for Drug Costs* (New York, NY: Oxford University Press, 2021), 152–156, 161–163.

6. National Academies of Sciences, Engineering, and Medicine, *Making Medicines Affordable: A National Imperative* (Washington, DC: The National Academies Press, 2018), 170.

7. Fred D. Ledley, Sarah S. McCoy, Gregory Vaughan, and Ekaterina G. Cleary, "Profitability of Large Pharmaceutical Companies Compared with Other Large Public Companies," *JAMA* 323, no. 9 (2020): 834–843. Nancy S. Jecker and Caesar A. Atuire, "What's Yours Is Ours: Waiving Intellectual Property Protections for COVID-19 Vaccines," *Journal of Medical Ethics* 47, no. 9 (September 2021): 595–598.

8. Talal Hilal, Miguel Gonzalez-Velez, and Vinay Prasad, "Limitations in Clinical Trials Leading to Anticancer Drug Approvals by the US Food and Drug Administration," *JAMA Internal Medicine* 180, no. 8 (2020): 1108–1115, at 1111. Neumann, Cohen, and Ollendorf, 2021 (note 5), 124.

9. Ben Goldacre, *Bad Pharma: How Drug Companies Mislead Doctors and Harm Patients* (New York, NY: Faber and Faber, Inc., 2013), 131.

10. Goldacre, 2013, ibid., 225.

11. Neumann, Cohen, and Ollendort, 2021 (note 5), 124–125.

12. Neumann, Cohen, and Ollendorf, 2021 (note 5), 95–164, describe the basic process and historical emergence of HTA, including NICE and ICER, in the U.K. and U.S. They note important HTA activity as well in Canada, Australia, Scandinavia, Germany, France, Thailand (which advises also Singapore and Malaysia), and South Korea, along with emerging efforts in China. See also Yingyao Chen, Yao He, Xunyouzhi Chi, Yan Wei, and Lizheng Shi, "Development of Health Technology Assessment in China: New Challenges," *BioScience Trends* 12, no. 2 (2018): 102–108, at 105.

13. Neumann, Cohen, and Ollendorf, 2021 (note 5), 113–117, 175–179. Their commendably detailed and comprehensive treatise on value-based pricing considers numerous dimensions of drug cost besides $/QALY that may need to be considered, including affordability within a society's budget, at 113–117 and 175–179.

14. Paul T. Menzel, "The Value of Life at the End of Life: A Critical Assessment of Hope and Other Factors," *Journal of Law, Medicine & Ethics* 39, no. 2 (Summer 2011): 215–223.

15. Donald W. Light and Antonio F. Maturo, *Good Pharma: The Public Health Model of the Mario Negri Institute* (New York, NY: Palgrave Macmillan, 2015).

16. Light and Maturo, ibid. On the last point see Jonathan Kimmelman and Alex John London, "The Structure of Clinical

Translation: Efficiency, Information, and Ethics." *Hastings Center Report* 45, no. 2 (March-April, 2015): 27–39.

17. Anna L. Davis, James Dabney Miller, Joshua M. Sharfstein, and Aaron S. Kesselheim, eds., "Blueprint for Transparency at the U.S. Food and Drug Administration" (supplement issue), *Journal of Law, Medicine & Ethics* 45, S2 (winter 2017): 3–49.

18. Catherine Olivier and Bryn Williams-Jones, "Global Pharmacogenomics: Where Is the Research Taking Us?" *Global Public Health* 9, no. 3 (2014): 312–324.

19. Significant attempts at such funding are the Health Impact Fund and differential pricing across different countries: Aidan Hollis and Thomas Pogge, *The Health Impact Fund: Making New Medicines Accessible for All* (New Haven, CT: Incentives for Global Health, 2008), https://healthimpactfund.org/en/about/ . Jonathan D. Campbell and Zoltan Kalo, "Fair Global Drug Pricing," *Expert Review of Pharmacoeconomics & Outcomes Research* 18, no. 6 (2018): 581–583.

20. Josh Holder, "Tracking Coronavirus Vaccinations Around the World," New York Times, February 10, 2022, https://www. nytimes.com/interactive/2021/world/covid-vaccinations-trac ker.html. Nancy S. Jecker and Zohar Lederman, "Three for Me and None for You? An Ethical Argument for Delaying COVID-19 Boosters," *Journal of Medical Ethics*, Epub October 2021, doi:10.1136/medethics-2021-107824.

21. Stephanie Nolen and Rebecca Robbins, "Pfizer to Allow Cheaper Covid Pill in Poor Countries." *New York Times*, Nov. 17, 2021, A15. Jamie Smyth, Hannah Kuckler, and Andres Schipani, "Moderna Vows Never To Enforce Covid Jab Patents in Policy U-turn." *Financial Times*, March 7, 2022, https://www.ft.com/cont ent/425ec5ad-1ae0-4460-a588-6aadfe5d52d6?sharetype=blocked.

22. Jecker and Atuire, 2021 (note 7).

Chapter 13

1. Most notably, the case of Jesse Gelsinger. See Meir Rinde, "The Death of Jesse Gelsinger, 20 Years Later," Science History Institute, June 4, 2019, https://www.sciencehistory.org/distillati ons/the-death-of-jesse-gelsinger-20-years-later, accessed March 19, 2022.

2. Miguel Sena-Esteves, "First gene therapy for Tay-Sachs disease successfully given to two children," *The Conversation*, February

14, 2022, https://theconversation.com/first-gene-therapy-for-tay-sachs-disease-successfully-given-to-two-children-176870, accessed Mar. 23, 2022.

3. Sean Philpott-Jones, "Playing God," *Wordpress* (blog), August 10, 2017, https://seanphilpott.wordpress.com/2017/08/10/playing-god/.

4. National Academies of Sciences, Engineering, and Medicine, "With Stringent Oversight, Heritable Human Genome Editing Could be Allowed for Serious Conditions," 2017, https://www.nationalacademies.org/news/2017/02/with-stringent-oversight-heritable-human-genome-editing-could-be-allowed-for-serious-conditions, accessed March 10, 2022.

5. National Academics of Sciences, Engineering, and Medicine, ibid.

6. Ronald M. Green, *Babies by Design: The Ethics of Genetic Choice* (New Haven, CT: Yale University Press, 2007), 62.

7. David Cyranoski, "CRISPR Baby Scientist Fired by University," *Nature*, January 22, 2019, https://www.nature.com/articles/d41586-019-00246-2, accessed March 12, 2022.

8. Robert Klitzman, "Preparing for the Next Generation of Ethical Challenges Concerning Heritable Human Genome Editing," *American Journal of Bioethics* 21, no. 6 (June, 2021): 1–4.

9. For an excellent discussion of the absence of structural constraints in China that enabled He Jiankui to violate national and international norms, as well as the swift response of China to address the problem, see Henry T. Greely, *CRISPR People: The Science and Ethics of Editing Humans* (Cambridge, MA: MIT Press, 2021).

10. Preetika Rana, "How a Chinese Scientist Broke the Rules to Create the First Gene-Edited Babies; Dr. He Jiankui, Seeking Glory for His Nation and Justice for HIV-positive Parents, Kept His Experiment Secret, Ignored Peers' Warnings, and Faked a Test," *Wall Street Journal* (online), March 10, 2019, https://www.wsj.com/articles/how-a-chinese-scientist-broke-the-rules-to-create-the-first-gene-edited-babies-11557506697, accessed March 12, 2022.

11. Francoise Baylis, *Altered Inheritance: CRISPR and the Ethics of Human Genome Editing* (Cambridge, MA: Harvard University Press, 2019), 33.

12. Michael J. Sandel, *The Case Against Perfection: Ethics in the Age of Genetic Engineering* (Cambridge, MA: Belknap Press, 2009).

13. Baylis, 2019 (note 13), 26.
14. Chris Bailey, "Gene Therapies Offer Breakthrough Results but Extraordinary Costs," Massachusetts Municipal Association, March 18, 2020, https://www.mma.org/gene-therapies-offer-breakthrough-results-but-extraordinary-costs/#:~:text= Gene%20therapies%20are%20extremely%20expensive,in%20. the%20price%2Dsetting%20strategy, accessed March 12, 2022.
15. Allen Buchanan, *Better Than Human: The Promise and Perils of Biomedical Enhancement* (New York, NY: Oxford University Press, 2017).
16. Natalie de Souza, "Editing Humanity's Future," *The New York Review of Books*, April 29, 2021, https://www.nybooks.com/ articles/2021/04/29/crispr-editing-humanity-future/, accessed March 12, 2022.
17. UNESCO, "Universal Declaration on Human Genome and Human Rights," 1997, https://en.unesco.org/themes/ethics-science-and-technology/human-genome-and-human-rights, accessed March 12, 2022.
18. Nadia Primc, "Do We Have a Right to an Unmanipulated Genome? The Human Genome as the Common Heritage of Mankind," *Bioethics* 34, no. 1 (January, 2020): 41–48, at 42.
19. Quoted in Patrick Skerrett, "Experts Debate: Are We Playing with Fire When We Edit Human Genes?" *Stat*, November 17, 2015, https://www.statnews.com/2015/11/17/gene-editing-embryo-crispr/, accessed March 19, 2022.
20. Greely, 2021 (note 11), 209.
21. De Souza, 2021 (note 18).
22. Primc, 2020 (note 20), 46.
23. Jonathan Glover, *What Sort of Children Should There Be?* (London, UK: Penguin Random House, 1984).

FURTHER READING

Many sources in the notes for each chapter will be useful to readers who wish to explore a topic in greater depth. In addition, the further readings below will be helpful.

Chapter 1. The Philosophical Foundations of Bioethics

Blumenthal-Barby, Jennifer, Sean Aas, Dan Brudney, Jessica Flanigan, Matthew Liao, Alex London, Wayne Sumner, and Julian Savulescu. "The Place of Philosophy in Bioethics Today." *American Journal of Bioethics*, June 30, 2021, https://doi.org/10.1080/15265 161.2021.1940355.

Jonsen, Albert R., Mark Siegler, and William Winslade. *Clinical Ethics: A Practical Approach to Ethical Decisions in Clinical Medicine*, 7th ed. New York, NY: McGraw-Hill Education, 2010.

Rachels, James. *The Elements of Moral Philosophy*, 8th ed. New York, NY: McGraw Hill, 2014.

Steinbock, Bonnie, Alex John London, and John D. Arras, eds. Introduction: "Moral Reasoning in Medical Context," in their *Ethical Issues in Modern Medicine: Contemporary Readings in Bioethics*, 8th ed. New York, NY: McGraw Hill, 2012, pp. 10–40.

Timmons, Mark. *Moral Theory: An Introduction*. Lanham, MD: Rowman and Littlefield Publishers, 2013.

Chapter 2. The Shift from Paternalism to Autonomy

Blumenthal-Barby, Jennifer S. *Good Ethics and Bad Choices: The Relevance of Behavioral Economics for Medical Ethics*. Cambridge, MA: MIT Press, 2021.

Jonsen, Albert R. *The Birth of Bioethics*. New York, NY: Oxford University Press, 1998.

Meyers, Christopher. "Deception and the Clinical Ethicist." *American Journal of Bioethics* 21, no. 5 (May 2021): 4–12 and commentaries 13–45.

Millum, Joseph, and Danielle Bromwich. "Informed Consent: What Must Be Disclosed and What Must Be Understood?" *American Journal of Bioethics* 21, no. 5 (May 2021): 46–58 and commentaries 59–78.

Chapter 3. Advance Directives

Buchanan, Allen E., and Dan W. Brock. *Deciding for Others: The Ethics of Surrogate Decision Making*. Cambridge, UK: Cambridge University Press, 1990.

Cantor, Norman L. *Advance Directives and the Pursuit of Death with Dignity*. Bloomington, IN: Indiana University Press, 1993.

Steinbock, Bonnie, Alex John London, and John D. Arras, eds. *Ethical Issues in Modern Medicine: Contemporary Readings in Bioethics*, 8th ed. New York, NY: McGraw Hill, 2012, pp. 355–416.

Chapter 4. Research Ethics

Eyal, Nir. "Research Ethics and Public Trust in Vaccines: The Case of COVID-19 Challenge Trials." *Journal of Medical Ethics*, May 20, 2022, https://doi:10.1136/medethics-2021-108086.

Faden, Ruth R., and Tom L. Beauchamp. *A History and Theory of Informed Consent*. New York, NY: Oxford University Press, 1986.

Jones, James H. *Bad Blood: The Tuskegee Syphilis Experiment*. New York, NY: The Free Press, 1993.

Katz, Jay, Alexander Morgan Capron, and Eleanor Swift Glass, eds. *Experimentation with Human Beings*. New York, NY: Russell Sage Foundation, 2008.

London, Alex John. *For the Common Good: Philosophical Foundations of Research Ethics*. New York: Oxford University Press, 2022.

Miller, Franklin G. "Ethics of Placebo Controls in Coronavirus Vaccine Trials." *Hastings Bioethics Forum*, October 27, 2020, https://www.thehastingscenter.org/ethics-of-placebo-controls-in-coronavirus-vaccine-trials/.

Rothman, David J., and Sheila M. Rothman. *The Willowbrook Wars*. New York, NY: Harper and Row, 1984, and Routledge, 2004.

Chapter 5. Definition of Death

DeGrazia, David. "The Definition of Death." In *Stanford Encyclopedia of Philosophy*, ed. Edward N. Zalta, 2017, https://plato.stanford.edu/archives/spr2017/entries/death-definition/.

Lewis, Ariane, Richard J. Bonnie, and Thaddeus Pope. "It's Time to Revise the Uniform Determination of Death Act." *Annals of Internal Medicine* 172, no. 2 (January 21, 2020): 143–144, https://doi.org/10.7326/M19-2731.

McMahan, Jeff. *The Ethics of Killing: Problems at the Margins of Life.* Oxford, UK: Oxford University Press, 2002.

Truog, Robert D., and Franklin G. Miller. *Death, Dying, and Organ Transplantation: Reconstructing Medical Ethics at the End of Life.* New York, NY: Oxford University Press, 2012.

Youngner, Stuart J., Robert M. Arnold, and Renie Schapiro, eds. *The Definition of Death: Contemporary Controversies.* Baltimore, MD: Johns Hopkins University Press, 2002.

Chapter 6. Physician-Assisted Death

Battin, Margaret Pabst. *The Least Worst Death: Essays in Bioethics on the End of Life.* New York, NY: Oxford University Press, 1994.

Keown, John. *Euthanasia, Ethics and Public Policy: An Argument Against Legalization,* 2nd ed. Cambridge, UK: Cambridge University Press, 2018.

Sumner, L. W. *Physician-Assisted Death: What Everyone Needs to Know.* New York, NY: Oxford University Press, 2017.

Chapter 7. Abortion

Boonin, David. *A Defense of Abortion.* New York, NY: Cambridge University Press, 2002.

Callahan, Sidney, and Daniel Callahan, eds. *Abortion: Understanding Differences.* New York, NY: Plenum, 1984.

Dwyer, Susan, and Joel Feinberg, eds. *The Problem of Abortion.* Belmont, CA: Wadsworth Publishing Co., 1996.

Luker, Kristin. *Abortion and the Politics of Motherhood.* Berkeley, CA: University of California Press, 1984.

Steinbock, Bonnie. "Abortion." *Hastings Center Bioethics Briefings,* June 27, 2022, https://www.thehastingscenter.org/briefingbook/abortion/.

Warren, Mary Anne. *Moral Status: Obligations to Persons and Other Living Things.* New York, NY: Oxford University Press, 2000.

Chapter 8. The Disability Critique

Cureton, Adam, and David Wasserman. *The Oxford Handbook of Philosophy and Disability.* New York, NY: Oxford University Press, 2020.

Reynolds, John Michael. *The Life Worth Living: Disability, Pain, and Morality*. Minneapolis, MN: University of Minnesota Press, 2022.

Shakespeare, Tom. *Disability: The Basics*, 1st ed. New York, NY: Routledge, 2017. https://doi.org/10.4324/9781315624839.

Chapter 9. What Ethical Issues Are Raised by Assisted Reproductive Technology?

Anderson, Elizabeth S. "Is Women's Labor a Commodity?" *Philosophy & Public Affairs* 19, no. 1 (1990): 71–92.

Francis, Leslie, ed. *Oxford Handbook of Reproductive Ethics*. New York, NY: Oxford University Press, 2017.

Robertson, John A. *Children of Choice: Freedom and the New Reproductive Technologies*. Princeton, NJ: Princeton University Press, 1994.

Satz, Debra. *Why Some Things Should Not Be for Sale: The Moral Limits of Markets*. New York, NY: Oxford University Press, 2010.

Steinbock, Bonnie. "Sex Selection: Not Obviously Wrong." *Hastings Center Report* 32, no. 1 (January 2002): 23–28.

Chapter 10. Justice and Healthcare Systems

Barrett, Drue H., Leonard W. Ortmann, Angus Dawson, Carla Seanz, Andreas Reis, and Gail Bolan, eds. *Public Health Ethics: Spanning the Globe* (Public Health Ethics Analysis, Book 3). New York: Springer Publishing, 2016.

Brennan, Jason. *Libertarianism: What Everyone Needs to Know*. New York: Oxford University Press, 2012.

Culyer, Anthony J., Alan Maynard, and Alan Williams. "Alternative Systems of Health Care Provision: An Essay on Motes and Beams." In *A New Approach to the Economics of Health Care*, ed. Mancur Olson. Washington, DC: American Enterprise Institute, 1981, pp. 131–150.

Emanuel, Ezekiel J. *Which Country Has the World's Best Health Care?* New York, NY: Public Affairs, 2020.

Eyal, Nir, Samia A. Hurst, Ole F. Norheim, and Dan Wikler, eds. *Inequalities in Health: Concepts, Measures, and Ethics*. New York, NY: Oxford University Press, 2013.

Jecker, Nancy S., and Derrick K. S. Au. "Does Zero-COVID Neglect Health Disparities?" *Journal of Medical Ethics* 48, no. 3 (March 2022): 169–172, https://doi:10.1136/medethics-2021-107763.

Pauly, Mark V., Patricia Danzon, Paul J. Feldstein, and John Hoff. *Responsible National Health Insurance*. Washington, DC: The American Enterprise Institute Press, 1992.

Michael J. Sandel. *Justice: What's the Right Thing to Do?* New York, NY: Farrar, Straus and Giroux, 2009. (Especially chapters on utilitarianism, libertarianism, Immanuel Kant, and John Rawls.)

Villarosa, Linda. *Under the Skin: The Hidden Toll of Racism on American Lives and on the Health of Our Nation.* New York, NY: Doubleday, 2022.

Chapter 11. Allocation of Scarce Resources

Cato, Susumu, and Akira Inoue. "Libertarian Approaches to the COVID-19 Pandemic." *Bioethics* 36, no. 4 (May 2022): 445–452, https://doi.org/10.1111/bioe.13007 (first published February 7, 2022).

Gostin, Lawrence O., and Sarah Wetter. "Risk Trade-Offs and Equitable Decision-Making in the Covid-19 Pandemic." *Hastings Center Report* 52, no. 1 (January-February, 2022): 15–20.

Mastroianni, Anna C., Jeffrey P. Kahn, and Nancy E. Kass, eds. *The Oxford Handbook of Public Health Ethics.* New York, NY: Oxford University Press, 2019. (Especially Smith, Maxwell J. and Ross Upshur, "Pandemic Disease, Public Health, and Ethics," pp. 796–811.)

Ray, Keisha. "Racism and Health Equity." *Bioethics Briefings* (The Hastings Center), August 10, 2022, https://www.thehastingscenter.org/briefingbook/racism-and-health-equity/.

Schwartz, Meredith Celene, ed. *The Ethics of Pandemics.* Peterborough, ONT: Broadview Press, 2021.

White, Douglas B., and Bernard Lo. "Mitigating Inequities and Saving Lives with ICU Triage during the COVID-19 Pandemic." *American Journal of Respiratory and Critical Care Medicine* 203, no. 3 (February 1, 2021): 287–294.

Chapter 12. Justified Pharmaceutical Prices

Brody, Baruch A. *Ethical Issues in Drug Testing, Approval, and Pricing: The Clot-Dissolving Drugs.* New York, NY: Oxford University Press, 1995.

Kolchinsky, Peter. *The Great American Drug Deal: A New Prescription for Innovative and Affordable Medicines.* Boston, MA: Evelexa Press, 2019.

Light, Donald W., and Antonio F. Maturo. *Good Pharma: The Public Health Model of the Mario Negri Institute.* New York, NY: Palgrave Macmillan, 2015.

Light, Donald W., and Joel Lexchin. "The Costs of Coronavirus Vaccines and Their Pricing." *Journal of the Royal Society of Medicine* 114, no. 11 (November 2021): 502–504, https://doi:10.1170/0141076821 1053006.

Neumann, Peter J., Joshua T. Cohen, and Daniel A. Ollendorf. *The Right Price: A Value-Based Prescription for Drug Costs*. New York, NY: Oxford University Press, 2021.

Venkatapuram, Sridhar. "Global Health Justice: Now Is the Time." *Bioethics Forum* (The Hastings Center), February 23, 2022, https://www.thehastingscenter.org/global-health-justice/.

Chapter 13. Genetic Modification of Human Beings

Buchanan, Allen. *Beyond Humanity?: The Ethics of Biomedical Enhancement*. New York, NY: Oxford University Press, 2011.

Greely, Henry T. *CRISPR People: The Science and Ethics of Editing Humans*. Cambridge, MA: MIT Press, 2021.

Isaacson, Walter. *The Code Breaker: Jennifer Doudna, Gene Editing, and the Future of the Human Race*. New York, NY: Simon and Schuster, 2021.

Pediatric ethics and organ transplantation ethics could each easily comprise full chapters of such a *What Everyone Needs to Know* volume were it not for space limitations. Here we provide a few suggested readings for each of these two topics.

Pediatric Ethics

Fleischman, Alan R. *Pediatric Ethics: Protecting the Interests of Children*. New York, NY: Oxford University Press, 2016.

Johnston, Josephine, John C. Lantos, Aaron Goldenberg, Flavia Chen, Erik Parens, Barbara A. Koenig, and the NSIGHT Ethics and Policy Advisory Board. "Sequencing Newborns: A Call for Nuanced Use of Genomic Technologies." *Hastings Center Report* 48: 4 (2018): S2–S51. doi:10.1002/hast.874.

Miller-Smith, Laura, Asdis Finnsdottir Wagner, and John D. Lantos. *Bioethics in the Pediatric ICU: Ethical Dilemmas Encountered in the Care of Critically Ill Children*, 1st ed. New York, NY: Springer Publishing Co., 2019.

Will, Jonathan F. "Covid-19: Medical Decisions, Mandates, and High-Risk Minors." *Hastings Center Report* 52: 3 (2022): 4–5. doi:10.1002/hast.1389.

Note: The Treuman Katz Center for PediatricBioethics at Seattle Children's Research Institute holds a highly regarded and accessible annual Pediatrics Bioethics Conference each summer: https://www.seattlechildrens.org/research/centers-programs/bioethics/.

Organ Transplantation Ethics

Greenberg, Rebecca A., Aviva M. Goldberg, and David Rodrigue-Arias, eds. *Ethical Issues in Pediatric Organ Transplantation*. New York, NY: Springer Publishing Co., 2016.

Munson, Ronald. *Raising the Dead: Organ Transplants, Ethics, and Society*. New York, NY: Oxford University Press, 2002.

Veatch, Robert, and Lainie Friedman Ross. *Transplantation Ethics*, 2nd ed. Washington, DC: Georgetown University Press, 2014.

INDEX

For the benefit of digital users, indexed terms that span two pages (e.g., 52–53) may, on occasion, appear on only one of those pages.